SCOTT.

2003 U.S. POCKET STAMP CATALOGUE

EDITOR ....James E. Kloetzel
ASSOCIATE EDITOR...William A. Jones
ASSISTANT EDITOR/NEW ISSUES & VALUING.....................................Martin J. Frankevicz
VALUING ANALYSTS ....Leonard J. Gellman, Rich Wolff
EDITORIAL ASSISTANT ....Beth Brown
DESIGN MANAGER ....Teresa M. Wenrick
GRAPHIC DESIGNER ....Cinda McAlexander
IMAGE COORDINATOR..Nancy S. Martin
ELECTRONIC MEDIA MANAGER...Mark Kaufman
SALES/MARKETING DIRECTOR ....Bill Fay
ADVERTISING ....Renee Davis
CIRCULATION/PRODUCT PROMOTION MANAGER...Tim Wagner
EDITORIAL DIRECTOR/AMOS PRESS INC..Michael Laurence

CONTENTS

4A

F-VF Centering

VF Centering

XF Centering

Croton Stamp Company
PO Box 242, Goshen, NY 10924
Fax: 845-294-0552
Email: croton@warwick.net
WWW.CROTONSTAMP.COM

Name _____ Phone _____

Address _____

_____

Email _____

Stamp references (if any) _____

Monthly stamp budget (if any) _____

Mint Stamp Condition Preferences

Centering: F-VF ____ VF ____ XF ____

Hinging: Never Hinged ____ or Lightly Hinged ____

Stamp Want List (use catalogue #'s below #893 from this book):

_____

_____

_____

_____

_____

12A

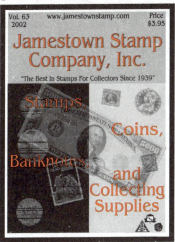
17A

AN OVERVIEW
OF THE WORLD'S
MOST POPULAR HOBBY

A fascinating hobby, an engrossing avocation and a universal pastime, stamp collecting is pursued by millions. Young and old, and from all walks of life, stamp collectors are involved in the indoor sport known as "the paper chase."

It was more than 160 years ago that Rowland Hill's far-reaching postal reforms became a reality and the world's first adhesive postage stamp, the Penny Black, was placed on sale at post offices in Great Britain. Not long after, a hobby was born that has continued to grow since.

Although there were only four stamps issued in England from 1840-47, the Penny Black, two types of the 2-penny blue and the 1-penny red, there were people who saved them. One story relates that a woman covered a wall in a room of her home with copies of the Penny Black.

As country after country began to issue postage stamps, the fraternity of stamp collectors flourished. Today, collectors number in the millions, while the number of stamp-issuing entities has exceeded 650.

The hobby of stamp collecting may take many forms. There are those people who collect the stamps of a single country. Others collect a single issue, such as the U.S. Transportation coils. Others specialize in but a single stamp, with all its nuances and variations. Some collectors save one type of postage stamp, such as airmails, commemoratives or other types. Another type of collection would consist only of covers (envelopes) bearing a stamp with a postmark from the first day of that stamp's issue.

Most popular, however, is collecting by country, especially one's own country. This catalogue is designed to aid in forming just such a collection. It lists the postage stamps of the United States and is a simplified edition of information found in Volume I of the *Scott Standard Postage Stamp Catalogue.*

AN OVERVIEW
OF THE WORLD'S
MOST POPULAR HOBBY

A fascinating hobby, an engrossing avocation and a universal pastime, stamp collecting is pursued by millions. Young and old, and from all walks of life, stamp collectors are involved in the indoor sport known as "the paper chase."

It was more than 160 years ago that Rowland Hill's far-reaching postal reforms became a reality and the world's first adhesive postage stamp, the Penny Black, was placed on sale at post offices in Great Britain. Not long after, a hobby was born that has continued to grow since.

Although there were only four stamps issued in England from 1840-47, the Penny Black, two types of the 2-penny blue and the 1-penny red, there were people who saved them. One story relates that a woman covered a wall in a room of her home with copies of the Penny Black.

As country after country began to issue postage stamps, the fraternity of stamp collectors flourished. Today, collectors number in the millions, while the number of stamp-issuing entities has exceeded 650.

The hobby of stamp collecting may take many forms. There are those people who collect the stamps of a single country. Others collect a single issue, such as the U.S. Transportation coils. Others specialize in but a single stamp, with all its nuances and variations. Some collectors save one type of postage stamp, such as airmails, commemoratives or other types. Another type of collection would consist only of covers (envelopes) bearing a stamp with a postmark from the first day of that stamp's issue.

Most popular, however, is collecting by country, especially one's own country. This catalogue is designed to aid in forming just such a collection. It lists the postage stamps of the United States and is a simplified edition of information found in Volume I of the *Scott Standard Postage Stamp Catalogue.*

Catalogue Information

The number (1616) in the first column of the example below is the stamp's identifying Scott number. Each stamp issued by the United States has a unique Scott number. Each illustration shows the Scott number beneath. In cases where two or more Scott numbers share a common design, the illustration will show the first Scott number that shows that design. Notes in the text will guide the user to find the correct design of subsequent Scott numbers showing the same design. This will be done by information in the header notes for the stamp or set, or by showing the design type by Scott number in parenthesis after its description (e.g., (1590) following the Scott 1616 listing.) Following in the same line are the denomination of the stamp, its color or other description along with the color of the paper (in italic type) if other than white, and the catalogue value both unused and used.

Scott Number	Denomination	Descrip.	Design, Type	Color	Color of the Stamp Paper	Unused Value	Used Value
1616	9c	Capitol	(1590)	slate grn	*gray*	.20	.20

Catalogue value

Scott Catalogue value is a retail price; what you could expect to pay for a sound stamp in a grade of Very Fine. The value listed is a reference that reflects recent actual dealer selling prices.

Dealer retail price lists, public auction results, published prices in advertising and individual solicitation of retail prices from dealers, collectors and specialty organizations have been used in establishing the values found in this catalogue.

Use this catalogue as a guide in your own buying and selling. The actual price you pay for a stamp may be higher or lower than the catalogue value because of one or more of the following factors: the grade and condition of the actual stamp; the amount of personal service a dealer offers; increased interest in the country or topic represented by the stamp or set; whether an item is a "loss leader," part of a special sale, or is otherwise being sold for a short period of time at a lower price; or if at a public auction you are able to obtain an item inexpensively because of little interest in the item at that time.

The Scott Catalogue values stamps on the basis of the cost of purchasing them individually. You will find packets, mixtures and collections where the unit cost of the material will be substantially less than the total catalogue value of the component stamps.

Values for pre-1890 unused issues are for stamps with approximately half or more of their original gum. Later issues are assumed to have full original gum.

Unused stamps are valued never-hinged beginning with Nos. 772, C19, E17, FA1, J88, O127 and RW1. No. 485 is also valued never-hinged.

Grade

A stamp's grade and condition are crucial to its value. Values quoted in this catalogue are for stamps graded at Very Fine, and with no faults. The accom-panying illustrations show an example of a Very Fine grade between the grades immediately below and above it: Fine to Very Fine and Extremely Fine.

FINE to VERY FINE stamps may be somewhat off center on one side, or slightly off center on two sides. Imperforate stamps will have two margins at least normal size and the design will not touch the edge. *Early issues may be printed in such a way that the design is naturally very close to the edges.* Used stamps will not have a cancellation that detracts from the design.

VERY FINE stamps may be slightly off center on one side, but the design will be well clear of the edge. The stamp will present a nice, balanced appearance. Imperforate stamps will have three normal-sized margins. *However, early perforated issues may be printed in such a way that the perforations may touch the design on one or more sides.* Used stamps will have light or otherwise neat cancellations. This is the grade used to establish Scott Catalgoue values.

EXTREMELY FINE stamps are close to being perfectly centered. Imperforate stamps will have even margins that are larger than normal. Even the earliest perforated issues will have perforations clear of the design on all sides.

Scott Publishing Co. recognizes that there is no formal, enforced grading scheme for postage stamps, and that the final price you pay for a stamp or obtain for a stamp you are selling will be determined by individual agreement at the time of the transaction.

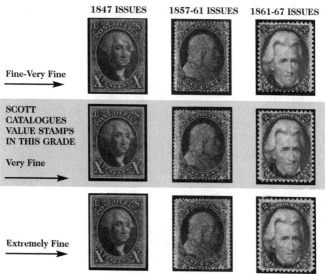

22A

Condition

The definitions given with the illustrations describe *grade,* which is centering and, for used stamps, cancellation. *Condition* refers to the soundness of the stamp; that is, faults, repairs and other factors influencing price.

Copies of a stamp that are of a lesser grade or condition trade at lower prices. Those of exceptional quality often command higher than catalogue prices.

Factors that can increase the value of a stamp include exceptionally wide margins, particularly fresh color, the presence of selvage (sheet margin), and plate or die varieties. Unusual cancels on used stamps (particularly those of the 19th century) can greatly enhance their value as well.

Factors other than faults that decrease the value of a stamp include loss of original gum or regumming, hinge remnants, foreign objects adhering to gum, natural inclusions, straight edges, or notations applied by collectors or dealers.

Faults include a missing piece, tear, clipped perforation, pin or other hole, surface scuff, thin spot, crease, toning, oxidation or other form of color changeling, short or pulled perforation, stains or such man-made changes as reperforations or the chemical removal or lightening of a cancellation.

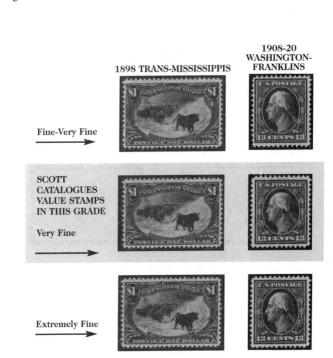

23A

Forming a collection

Methods of collecting stamps are many and varied. A person may begin by attempting to gather a single specimen of every face-different stamp issued by a country. An extension of that approach is to include the different types of each stamp, such as perforation varieties, watermark varieties, different printings and color changes. The stamps may be collected on cover (envelope) complete with postal markings, thus showing postal rates, types of cancellations and other postal information.

Collections also may be limited to types of stamps. The stamps issued by most countries are divided into such categories as regular postage (made up of definitives and commemoratives), airmail stamps, special delivery stamps, postage due stamps and others. Any of those groups may provide the basis for a good collection.

Definitive stamps are those regular issues used on most mail sent out on a daily basis. They are normally issued in extended sets, sometimes over a period of years. The sets feature a rising series of face values that allows a mailer to meet any current postal rate. Definitive stamps may be printed in huge quantities and are often kept in service by the Postal Service for long periods of time.

Commemorative stamps meet another need. They are primarily issued to celebrate an important event, honor a famous person or promote a special project or cause. Such stamps are issued on a limited basis for a limited time. They are usually more colorful and are often of a larger size than definitives.

Although few airmail stamps are currently issued by the United States, they continue to remain very popular among collectors. Just as with regular issues, airmail stamps are subject to several types of collecting. In addition to amassing the actual stamps, airmail enthusiasts pursue first-flight covers, airport dedication covers and even crash covers.

Not as popular, but still collected as units, are special delivery and postage due stamps. Special delivery stamps ensured speedier delivery of a letter once it reached its destination post office through normal postal means. Postage due stamps were used when a letter or parcel did not carry enough postage to pay for its delivery, subjecting the recipient to a fee to make up the difference. The United States no longer issues postage due stamps.

The resurrection in 1983 of Official Mail stamps-those used only by departments and offices of the federal government-has also brought about a resurgence of interest in them by stamp collectors. Originally issued between 1873 and 1911, Official Mail stamps were obsolete until recently. To be legally used, they must be on cards, envelopes or parcels that bear the return address of a federal office or facility.

"Topical" collecting is becoming more and more popular. Here the paramount attraction to the collector is the subject depicted on the stamp. The topics or themes from which to choose are virtually unlimited, other than by your own imagination. Animals, flowers, music, ships, birds and famous people on stamps make interesting collections. The degree of specializations is limitless, leading to such topics as graduates of a specific college or university, types of aircraft or the work of a specific artist.

There are several ways to obtain topical information, one of which is through the "By Topic" section of the *Scott Stamp Monthly.* "By Topic" is a regular feature of the magazine that divides the stamps of the world into more than 100 topical areas.

The album

To be displayed at their best, stamps should be properly housed. A quality album not only achieves this, but gives protection from dirt, loss and damage. When choosing an album, consider these three points: Is it within your means, does it meet your special interests and is it the best you can afford?

The Scott *Pony Express* and *Minuteman* albums are ideal companions to this Catalogue. Scott also publishes the National Album series for United States stamps, for a more complete collection.

Looseleaf albums are recommended for all collectors beyond the novice level. Not only do looseleaf albums allow for expansion of a collection, but the pages may be removed for mounting stamps as well as for display. A special advantage of a looseleaf album is that in many cases it may be kept current with supplements published annually on matching pages. All Scott albums noted are looseleaf and are supplemented annually.

Mounts and hinges

Mounts and hinges specially manufactured for collectors are used to affix stamps to album pages. Most stamp mounts are pre-gummed, clear plastic containers that hold a stamp safely and may be affixed to an album page with minimum effort. They are available in sizes to fit any stamp, block or even complete envelopes. Mounts are particularly important with unused stamps when there is a desire to not disturb the gum.

Although the mount is important, so is the venerable hinge. Innumerable stamps have been ruined beyond redemption by being glued to an album page. Hinges are inexpensive and effective. Use only peelable hinges. These may be removed from a stamp or album page without leaving an unsightly mark or causing damage to either.

Hinges are perfect for less-expensive stamps, used stamps and stamps that previously have been hinged. The use of stamp hinges is simple. Merely fold back, adhesive side out, about a quarter of the hinge (if it is not pre-folded). Lightly moisten the shorter side and affix it near the top of the back of the stamp. Then, holding the stamp with a pair of tongs, moisten the longer side of the hinge and place it (with stamp attached) in its proper place on the album page.

Stamp tongs

As previously noted, stamp tongs are a simple but important accessory and should always be used when handling a stamp. Fingers can easily damage or soil a stamp. Tongs cost little and will quickly pay for themselves. They come in a variety of styles. Beginners should start with tongs having a blunt or rounded tip. Those with sharp ends may inadvertently cause damage to a stamp. With just a little practice you will find tongs easier to work with than using your fingers...and your stamps will be better for it.

Benjamin
Franklin
1
3

George
Washington
2
4

Reproductions. The letters R.W.H. & E. at the bottom of each stamp are less distinct on the reproductions than on the originals.

5c. On the originals the left side of the white shift frill touches the oval on a level with the top of the "F" of "Five." On the reproductions it touches the oval about on a level with the top of the figure "5."

10c. On the reproductions, line of coat at left points to right tip of "X" and line of coat at right points to center of "S" of CENTS. On the originals, line of coat points to "T" of TEN and between "T" and "S" of CENTS. On the reproductions the eyes have a sleepy look, the line of the mouth is straighter, and in the curl of hair near the left cheek is a strong black dot, while the originals have only a faint one.

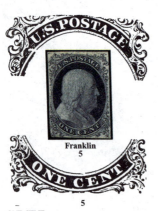

Franklin
5

5

ONE CENT.
Type I. Has complete curved lines outside the labels with "U.S. Postage" and "One Cent." The scrolls below the lower label are turned under, forming little balls. The ornaments at top are substantially complete.
Type Ib. Same as I but balls below the bottom label are not so clear. The plume-like scrolls at bottom are not complete.

6

Type Ia. Same as I at bottom but top ornaments and outer line at top are partly cut away.
Type Ic. Same as Ia, but bottom right plume and ball ornament incomplete. Bottom left plume complete or nearly complete.

7

Type II. Same as type I at top, but the little balls of the bottom scrolls and the bottoms of the lower plume ornaments are missing. The side ornaments are substantially complete.

8

Type III. The top and bottom curved lines outside the labels are broken in the middle. The side ornaments are complete.
Type IIIa. Similar to type III with the outer line broken at top or bottom but not both.

9

Type IV Similar to type II, but with the curved lines outside the labels recut at top or bottom or both.
Prices for types I and III are for stamps showing the marked characteristics plainly. Copies of type I showing the balls indistinctly and of type III with the lines only slightly broken, sell for much lower prices.

UNITED STATES

Scott No.	Description	Unused Value	Used Value	//////
1847, Imperf.				
1	5c Benjamin Franklin, red brown........	6,250.	575.00	
	Pen cancel....................................		290.00	
a.	5c dark brown.................................	7,000.	625.00	
b.	5c orange brown.............................	8,000.	850.00	
c.	5c red orange.................................	*12,500.*	*6,000.*	
d.	Double impression		—	
2	10c George Washington, black..............	*27,500.*	*1,400.*	
	Pen cancel....................................		700.00	
a.	Diagonal half used as 5c on cover..................................		*13,000.*	
b.	Vert. half used as 5c on cover........		*35,000.*	
c.	Horiz. half used as 5c on cover		—	
1875, Reproductions, Bluish Paper Without Gum, Imperf.				
3	5c Franklin (1), red brown..................	750.00		
4	10c Washington (2), black....................	950.00		
1851-57, Imperf.				
5	1c Franklin, blue, type I.....................	*200,000.*	*45,000.*	
5A	1c Franklin (5), blue, type Ib..............	16,000.	*6,250.*	
6	1c Franklin (5), blue, type Ia	*37,500.*	*10,000.*	
b.	Type Ic...	*6,250.*	*1,500.*	
7	1c Franklin (5), blue, type II...............	1,200.	160.00	
8	1c Franklin (5), blue, type III	*12,500.*	*3,000.*	
8A	1c Franklin (5), blue, type IIIa	4,500.	*1,100.*	
9	1c Franklin (5), blue, IV	750.00	125.00	
a.	Printed on both sides, reverse inverted............................		—	
10	3c Washington, orange brown, type I .	3,250.	100.00	
a.	Printed on both sides		*12,000.*	

3

Washington
10

Thomas Jefferson
12

10

THREE CENTS.
Type I. There is an outer frame line at top and bottom.

12

FIVE CENTS.
Type I. There are projections on all four sides.

13

13

TEN CENTS.
Type I. The "shells" at the lower corners are practically complete. The outer line below the label is very nearly complete. The outer lines are broken above the middle of the top label and the "X" in each upper corner.

14

Type II. The design is complete at the top. The outer line at the bottom is broken in the middle. The shells are partly cut away.

15

Type III. The outer lines are broken above the top label and the "X" numerals. The outer line at the bottom and the shells are partly cut away, as in Type II.

16

Type IV. The outer lines have been recut at top or bottom or both.
Types I, II, III, and IV have complete ornaments at the sides of the stamps and three pearls at each outer edge of the bottom panel.

17

4

Franklin
24

ONE CENT.
  Type V. Similar to type III of 1851-56 but with side ornaments partly cut away.

26

THREE CENTS.
  Type II. There are no outer frame lines at top and bottom. The side frame lines were recut so as to be continuous from the top to the bottom of the plate.
  Type IIa. The side frame lines extend only to the top and bottom of the stamp design.

30

30

FIVE CENTS.
  Type II. The projections at top and bottom are partly cut away.

35
(Two typical examples).

TEN CENTS.
  Type V. The side ornaments are slightly cut away. Usually only one pearl remains at each end of the lower label but some copies show two or three pearls at the right side. At the bottom the outer line is complete and the shells nearly so. The outer lines at top are complete except over the right "X."

37   **38**

39

TWELVE CENTS.
  Plate I. Outer frame lines complete.
  Plate III. Outer frame lines noticeably uneven or broken, sometimes partly missing.

5

63

63

1c. A dash has been added under the tip of the ornament at right of the numeral in upper left corner.

67

67

5c. A leaflet has been added to the foliated ornaments at each corner.

64

64

3c. Ornaments at corners have been enlarged and end in a small ball.

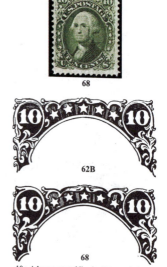

68

62B

68

10c. A heavy curved line has been cut below the stars and an outer line added to the ornaments above them.

HOW TO USE THIS BOOK

In cases where two or more Scott numbers share a common design, the illustration shows the first Scott number that bears that design. Subsequent Scott numbers showing the same design will have the first Scott number in parentheses following the description to guide the user to the correct design.

Scott No.	Description	Unused Value	Used Value	/////
11	3c Washington (10), dull red, type I....	240.00	11.00	
c.	Vert. half used as 1c on cover......................		5,000.	
d.	Diagonal half used as 1c on cover..................		5,000.	
e.	Double impression........................		5,000.	
12	5c Thomas Jefferson, red brown, type I	19,000.	1,000.	
13	10c Washington, green, type I...............	15,000.	800.00	
14	10c Washington (13), green, type II......	4,500.	210.00	
15	10c Washington (13), green, type III	4,500.	210.00	
16	10c Washington (13), green, type IV	27,500.	1,600.	
17	12c Washington, black.......................	5,250.	325.00	
a.	Diagonal half used as 6c on cover......................		2,500.	
b.	Vert. half used as 6c on cover.........		8,500.	
c.	Printed on both sides		10,000.	
1857-61, Perf. 15½				
18	1c Franklin (5), blue, type I................	2,000.	600.00	
19	1c Franklin (5), blue, type Ia	22,500.	6,500.	
b.	Type Ic.......................................	2,900.	1,400.	
20	1c Franklin (5), blue, type II...............	1,100.	250.00	
21	1c Franklin (5), blue, type III.............	12,500.	2,200.	
22	1c Franklin (5), blue, type IIIa	2,000.	500.00	
b.	Horiz. pair, imperf. btwn.		5,000.	
23	1c Franklin (5), blue, type IV	8,500.	700.00	
24	1c Franklin (5), blue, type V	175.00	40.00	
b.	Laid paper		—	
25	3c Washington (10), rose, type I	2,500.	90.00	
b.	Vert. pair, imperf. horiz.		10,000.	
26	3c Washington (10), dull red, type II ..	75.00	7.50	
a.	3c dull red, type IIa............................	225.00	60.00	
b.	Horiz. pair, imperf. vert., type II	4,000.	—	
c.	Vert. pair, imperf. horiz., type II..		10,000.	
d.	Horiz. pair, imperf. btwn., type II..		—	
e.	Double impression, type II		2,500.	
f.	As "a," horiz. strip of 3, imperf. vert., on cover		14,500	
27	5c Jefferson (12), brick red, type I	27,500.	1,400.	
28	5c Jefferson (12), red brown, type I....	5,000.	800.00	
b.	bright red brown............................	5,500.	1,000.	
28A	5c Jefferson (12), Indian red, type I	32,500.	3,000.	
29	5c Jefferson (12), brown, type I	2,500.	350.00	
30	5c Jefferson, orange brown, type II.....	1,200.	1,100.	
30A	5c Jefferson (30), brown, type II.........	2,000.	300.00	
b.	Printed on both sides	4,500.	4,750.	

Scott No.	Description	Unused Value	Used Value	/ / / / /
31	10c Washington (13), green, type I......	*17,500.*	900.00	
32	10c green, type II................................	5,250.	275.00	
33	10c green, type III...............................	5,250.	275.00	
34	10c green, type IV	*32,500.*	2,250.	
35	10c green, type V	275.00	65.00	
36	12c black, plate I................................	1,400.	260.00	
a.	Diagonal half used as 6c on cover (I)................................		*17,500.*	
b.	12c black, plate III.............................	750.00	180.00	
c.	Horiz. pair, imperf. between (I)......		*12,500.*	
37	24c gray lilac.....................................	1,600.	350.00	
a.	24c gray...	1,600.	350.00	
38	30c orange..	1,900.	450.00	
39	90c blue..	2,900.	*7,000.*	

1875, Reprints, Without Gum, Perf. 12

Scott No.	Description	Unused Value	Used Value	/ / / / /
40	1c bright blue (5)	*625.00*		
41	3c scarlet (10)....................................	*3,250.*		
42	5c orange brown (30)..........................	*1,250.*		
43	10c blue green (13).............................	*3,000.*		
44	12c greenish black (17)	*3,500.*		
45	24c black violet (37)...........................	*3,500.*		
46	30c yellow orange (38)........................	*3,500.*		
47	90c deep blue (39)..............................	*4,500.*		

1861

Scott No.	Description	Unused Value	Used Value	/ / / / /
62B	10c Washington, dark green (68)..........	*7,000.*	1,000.	

1861-62

Scott No.	Description	Unused Value	Used Value	/ / / / /
63	1c blue...	325.00	32.50	
a.	1c ultramarine	750.00	275.00	
b.	1c dark blue.......................................	650.00	90.00	
c.	Laid paper	—	—	
d.	Vert. pair, imperf. horiz.	—	—	
e.	Printed on both sides	—	2,500.	
64	3c pink...	8,000.	800.00	
a.	3c pigeon blood pink	*19,000.*	*3,500.*	
b.	3c rose pink	575.00	150.00	
65	3c rose	130.00	2.50	
b.	Laid paper	—	—	
d.	Vert. pair, imperf. horiz.	*3,500.*	750.00	
e.	Printed on both sides	*10,000.*	*2,750.*	
f.	Double impression		*6,000.*	
67	5c buff	*21,000.*	800.00	
a.	5c brown yellow.................................	*21,000.*	850.00	
b.	5c olive yellow	*9,000*	1,100.	
68	10c Washington, yellow green	850.00	50.00	
a.	10c dark green....................................	900.00	62.50	
b.	Vert. pair, imperf. horiz.		*3,500.*	

8

Scott No.	Description	Unused Value	Used Value	//////
69	12c Washington, black......................	1,400.	100.00	
70	24c Washington, red lilac	2,250.	190.00	
a.	24c brown lilac.............................	1,750.	140.00	
b.	24c steel blue...............................	9,000.	725.00	
c.	24c violet, thin paper	10,000.	1,300.	
d.	24c pale gray violet, thin paper..........	3,750.	1,500.	
71	30c Franklin, orange	1,750.	160.00	
a.	Printed on both sides		—	
72	90c Washington, blue..........................	3,000.	425.00	
a.	90c pale blue.................................	2,750.	400.00	
b.	90c dark blue.................................	3,250.	500.00	

1861-66

Scott No.	Description	Unused Value	Used Value	//////
73	2c Andrew Jackson, black	375 .00	50.00	
a.	Diagonal half used as 1c as part of 3c rate on cover.		1,750.	
b.	Diagonal half used alone as 1c on cover....................................		3,000.	
c.	Horiz. half used as 1c as part of 3c rate on cover		3,500	
d.	Vert. half used as 1c as part of 3c rate on cover		1,800.	
e.	Vert. half used alone as 1c on cover		—	
f.	Printed on both sides		10,000.	
g.	Laid paper	—	5,000.	
75	5c Jefferson (67), red brown...............	4,750.	475.00	
76	5c Jefferson (67), brown	1,300.	120.00	
a.	5c dark brown	1,450.	175.00	
b.	Laid paper		—	
77	15c Abraham Lincoln, black	2,250.	160.00	
78	24c Washington (70), lilac...................	1,350.	110.00	
a.	24c grayish lilac	1,350.	110.00	
b.	24c gray..	1,350.	110.00	
c.	24c blackish violet	30,000.	2,500.	
d.	Printed on both sides		3,500.	

1867, Perf. 12, Grill With Points Up
A. Grill Covering The Entire Stamp

Scott No.	Description	Unused Value	Used Value	//////
79	3c Washington (64), rose....................	5,250.	1,200.	
b.	Printed on both sides		—	
80	5c Jefferson (67), brown		—130,000.	
a.	5c dark brown		130,000.	
81	30c Franklin (71), orange		60,000.	

B. Grill About 18x15mm (22 by 18 points)

Scott No.	Description	Unused Value	Used Value	//////
82	3c Washington (64), rose.....................		175,000.	

Grill With Points Down
C. Grill About 13x16mm (16 to 17 by 18 to 21 points)

Scott No.	Description	Unused Value	Used Value	//////
83	3c Washington (64), rose....................	5,250.	1,000.	

69

12c. Ovals and scrolls have been added to the corners.

70   **71**

72   **Grill**

72

90c. Parallel lines form an angle above the ribbon with "U.S. Postage;" between these lines a row of dashes has been added and a point of color to the apex of the lower pair.

73   **77**

112   **113**

114   **115**

116   **117**

118   **120**

121   **122**

118

FIFTEEN CENTS. Type I. Picture unframed.

Type II. Picture framed.
Type III. Same as type I but without fringe of brown shading lines around central vignette.

Scott No.	Description	Unused Value	Used Value	/ / / / / /
D. Grill About 12x14mm (15 by 17 to 18 points)				
84	2c Jackson (73)	*15,000.*	3,500.	
85	3c Washington (64), rose	6,500.	1,000.	
Z. Grill About 11x14mm (13 to 14 by 17 to 18 points)				
85A	1c Franklin (63), blue		*935,000.*	
85B	2c Jackson (73)	7,500.	1,200.	
85C	3c Washington (64), rose	12,500.	3,250.	
85D	10c Washington (68), green		*90,000.*	
85E	12c Washington (69)	*11,000.*	1,600.	
85F	15c Lincoln (77)		*220,000.*	
E. Grill About 11x13mm (14 by 15 to 17 points)				
86	1c Franklin (63), blue	3,000.	450.00	
a.	1c dull blue	3,000.	425.00	
87	2c Jackson (73)	1,500.	150.00	
a.	Half used as 1c on cover, diagonal or vert.		*2,000.*	
88	3c Washington (64), rose	850.00	22.50	
a.	3c lake red	925.00	25.00	
89	10c Washington (68), green	5,000.	300.00	
90	12c Washington (69)	4,750.	350.00	
91	15c Lincoln (77)	9,500.	625.00	
F. Grill About 9x13mm (11 to 12 by 15 to 17 points)				
92	1c Franklin (63), blue	1,000.	200.00	
a.	1c pale blue	1,000.	200.00	
93	2c Jackson (73)	475.00	50.00	
a.	Vert. half used as 1c as part of 3c rate on cover		*1,250.*	
b.	Diagonal half used as 1c as part of 3c rate on cover		*1,250.*	
c.	Horiz. half used alone as 1c on cover		*2,500.*	
d.	Diagonal half used alone as 1c on cover		*2,500.*	
94	3c Washington (64), red	375.00	7.50	
a.	3c rose	375.00	7.50	
c.	Vert. pair, imperf. horiz.	*1,100.*		
d.	Printed on both sides	*2,250.*		
95	5c Jefferson (67), brown	3,250.	750.00	
a.	5c dark brown	3,500.	950.00	
96	10c Washington (68), yellow green.......	2,750.	200.00	
a.	10c dark green....................................	2,750.	200.00	
97	12c Washington (69)	2,900.	225.00	
98	15c Lincoln (77)	3,250.	300.00	
99	24c Washington (70), gray lilac	6,000.	900.00	
100	30c Franklin (71), orange	6,000.	750.00	
101	90c Washington (72), blue....................	11,000.	1,500.	

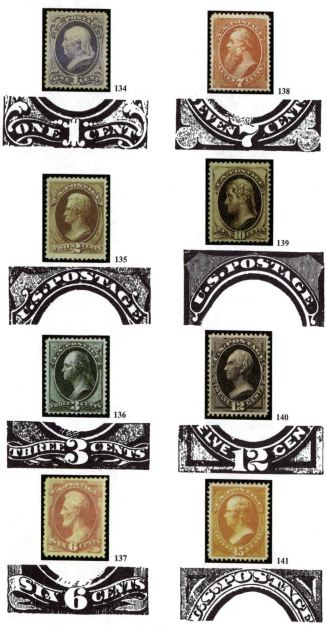

134

138

135

139

136

140

137

141

Scott No.	Description	Unused Value	Used Value	/ / / / / /

1875, Reprints, Without Grill, White Crackly Gum, Hard White Paper, Perf. 12

Scott No.	Description	Unused Value	Used Value	
102	1c Franklin (63), blue	800.00	1,100.	
103	2c Jackson (73)	3,500.	5,000.	
104	3c Washington (64), brown red	3,750.	6,250.	
105	5c Jefferson (67), brown	3,000.	2,900.	
106	10c Washington (68), green	3,250.	12,500.	
107	12c Washington (69)...........................	4,500.	6,500.	
108	15c Lincoln (77)	4,500.	9,000.	
109	24c Washington (70), deep violet.........	5,500.	10,000.	
110	30c Franklin (71), brownish orange	5,500.	12,500.	
111	90c Washington (72), blue...................	6,500.	50,000.	

1869, Perf. 12

G. Grill Measuring 9½ x 9mm

Scott No.	Description	Unused Value	Used Value	
112	1c Franklin, buff.............................	800.00	160.00	
b.	Without grill...................................	6,000.		
113	2c Pony Express, brown	750.00	75.00	
b.	Without grill...................................	2,750.		
c.	Half used as 1c on cover, diagonal, vert. or horiz.		4,000.	
d.	Printed on both sides		9,000.	
114	3c Locomotive, ultramarine.................	300.00	18.00	
a.	Without grill...................................	1,250.		
b.	Vert. one third used as 1c on cover...................................		—	
c.	Vert. two thirds used as 2c on cover...................................		4,000.	
e.	Printed on both sides		—	
115	6c Washington, ultramarine...............	3,000.	210.00	
b.	Vert. half used as 3c on cover.........		—	
116	10c Shield & Eagle, yellow	2,250.	140.00	
117	12c Ship, green	2,500.	150.00	
118	15c Landing of Columbus, brown & blue, Type I..	8,000.	650.00	
a.	Without grill...................................	11,000.		
119	15c Landing of Columbus (118), type II	3,500.	250.00	
b.	Center inverted..............................	275,000.	17,000.	
c.	Center double, one inverted............		35,000.	
120	24c Declaration of Independence, grn & vio	7,500.	750.00	
a.	Without grill...................................	10,000.		
b.	Center inverted..............................	275,000.	18,000.	
121	30c Shield, Eagle & Flags, blue & car..	7,500.	550.00	
a.	Without grill...................................	11,000.		
b.	Flags inverted................................	210,000.	70,000.	
122	90c Lincoln, carmine & black..............	9,750.	2,500.	
a.	Without grill...................................	16,000.		

156

1c. In pearl at left of numeral "1" is a small crescent.

159

6c. The first four vertical lines of the shading in the lower part of the left ribbon have been strengthened.

157

2c. Under the scroll at the left of "U.S." there is a small diagonal line. This mark seldom shows clearly. The stamp, No. 157, can be distinguished by its color.

160

7c. Two small semi-circles are drawn around the ends of the lines which outline the ball in the lower right hand corner.

158

3c. The under part of the upper tail of the left ribbon is heavily shaded.

A49a

161

10c. There is a small semi-circle in the scroll at the right end of the upper label.

| **142** | **143** | **144** |

14

Scott No.	Description	Unused Value	Used Value	//////

1875, Re-issues, Without Grill, Hard White Paper

Scott No.	Description	Unused Value	Used Value	
123	1c Franklin (112), buff......................	500.00	325.00	
124	2c Pony Express (113).......................	700.00	475.00	
125	3c Locomotive (114), blue	5,500.	20,000.	
126	6c Washington (115), blue	1,900.	2,100.	
127	10c Shield & Eagle (116)	2,100.	1,750.	
128	12c Ship (117)......................................	2,750.	2,750.	
129	15c Landing of Columbus (118), type III	2,000.	1,150	
a.	Imperf. horiz., single......................	4,000.	7,000.	
130	24c Declaration of Independence (120)	2,250.	1,600.	
131	30c Shield, Eagle & Flags (121)	3,000.	2,500.	
132	90c Lincoln (122), carmine and black ..	5,000.	5,500.	

1880, Soft Porous Paper

Scott No.	Description	Unused Value	Used Value	
133	1c Franklin (112), buff, with gum......	325.00	200.00	
a.	1c brown orange, without gum...........	240.00	175.00	

1870-71, Perf. 12, With Grill

Scott No.	Description	Unused Value	Used Value	
134	1c Franklin, ultramarine	2,100.	140.00	
135	1c Jackson, red brown	1,200.	70.00	
a.	Diagonal half used as 1c on cover..		—	
b.	Vert. half used as 1c on cover.........		—	
136	3c Washington, green	725.00	20.00	
137	6c Lincoln, carmine	4,500.	525.00	
138	7c Edwin M. Stanton, vermilion	3,250.	425.00	
139	10c Jefferson, brown............................	5,000.	650.00	
140	12c Henry Clay, dull violet...................	22,500.	3,000.	
141	15c Daniel Webster, orange..................	5,750.	1,200.	
142	24c Gen. Winfield Scott, purple............	—	6,250.	
143	30c Alexander Hamilton, black.............	15,000.	2,500.	
144	90c Commodore O. H. Perry, carmine..	14,000.	1,700.	

1870-71, Perf. 12, Without Grill

Scott No.	Description	Unused Value	Used Value	
145	1c Franklin (134), ultramarine.............	500.00	15.00	
146	2c Jackson (135), red brown	325.00	9.00	
a.	Diagonal half used as 1c on cover..		650.00	
b.	Vert. half used as 1c on cover.........		750.00	
c.	Horiz. half used as 1c on cover		750.00	
d.	Double impression		—	
147	3c Washington (136), green	300.00	1.50	
a.	Printed on both sides		1,750.	
b.	Double impression		1,250.	
148	6c Lincoln (137), carmine	725.00	25.00	
a.	Vert. half used as 3c on cover.........		—	
b.	Double impression		1,500.	
149	7c Stanton (138), vermilion.................	900.00	90.00	
150	10c Jefferson (139), brown....................	825.00	20.00	
151	12c Clay (140), dull violet.....................	1,900.	160.00	
152	15c Webster (141), bright orange..........	2,100.	160.00	
a.	Double impression		1,400.	

173

12c. The balls of the figure "2" are crescent shaped.

174

15c. In the lower part of the triangle in the upper left corner two lines have been made heavier forming a "V". This mark can be found on some of the Continental and American (1879) printings, but not all stamps show it.

Secret marks were added to the dies of the 24c, 30c and 90c but new plates were not made from them. The various printings of these stamps can be distinguished only by the shades and paper.

179   **205**

206

1c. The vertical lines in the upper part of the stamp have been so deepened that the background often appears to be solid. Lines of shading have been added to the upper arabesques.

207

3c. The shading at the sides of the central oval appears only about one-half the previous width. A short horizontal dash has been cut about 1 mm below the "TS" of "CENTS."

208

6c. On the original stamps four vertical lines can be counted from the edge of the panel to the outside of the stamp. On the re-engraved stamps there are but three lines in the same place.

209

10c. On the original stamps there are five vertical lines between the left side of the oval and the edge of the shield. There are only four lines on the re-engraved stamps. In the lower part of the latter, also, the horizontal lines of the background have been strengthened.

210

211

212

Scott No.	Description	Unused Value	Used Value	/ / / / / /
153	24c Scott (142), purple	1,600.	140.00	
154	30c Hamilton (143), black	5,500.	190.00	
155	90c Perry (144), carmine	4,250.	300.00	

1873, Perf. 12

Scott No.	Description	Unused Value	Used Value	/ / / / / /
156	1c Franklin (134), ultramarine	250.00	3.75	
e.	With grill	2,000.		
f.	Imperf., pair	—	550.00	
157	2c Jackson (135), brown	375.00	17.50	
c.	With grill	1,850.	750.00	
d.	Double impression	—	—	
e.	Vert. half used as 1c on cover		—	
158	3c Washington (136), green	130.00	.60	
e.	With grill	500.00		
h.	Horiz. pair, imperf. vert.		—	
i.	Horiz. pair, imperf. btwn.		1,300.	
j.	Double impression		2,500.	
k.	Printed on both sides		—	
159	6c Lincoln (137), dull pink	425.00	17.50	
b.	With grill	1,800.		
160	7c Stanton (138), orange vermilion	1,250.	80.00	
a.	With grill	3,500.		
161	10c Jefferson (139), brown	700.00	18.00	
c.	With grill	3,500.		
d.	Horiz. pair, imperf. btwn.		2,500.	
162	12c Clay (140), blackish violet	2,000.	95.00	
a.	With grill	5,500.		
163	15c Webster (141), yellow orange	2,100.	110.00	
a.	With grill	5,250.		
164	24c Scott (142), purple, vertically ribbed paper	—		
165	30c Hamilton (143), gray blk	2,750.	100.00	
c.	With grill	22,500.		
166	90c Perry(144), rose car	2,750.	250.00	

1875, Re-issues, Without Gum, Hard White Paper, Perf. 12

Scott No.	Description	Unused Value	Used Value	/ / / / / /
167	1c Franklin (134), ultramarine	12,500.		
168	2c Jackson (135), dark brown	5,750.		
169	3c Washington (136), blue green	15,000.	—	
170	6c Lincoln (137), dull rose	14,500.		
171	7c Stanton (138), reddish vermilion	3,250.		
172	10c Jefferson (139), pale brown	14,500.		
173	12c Clay (140), dark violet	4,750.		
174	15c Webster (141), bright orange	14,500.		
175	24c Scott (142), dull purple	3,250.	5,000.	
176	30c Hamilton (143), greenish black	12,000.		
177	90c Perry (144), violet carmine	14,000.		

219   219D   221   222

223   224   225   226

227   228   229

230   231   232

233   234   235

236   237   238

Scott No.	Description	Unused Value	Used Value	/ / / / / /

Yellowish Wove Paper, Perf. 12

Scott No.	Description	Unused Value	Used Value	
178	2c Jackson (135), vermilion	400.00	10.00	
b.	Half used as 1c on cover................		—	
c.	With grill	750.00		
179	5c Zachary Taylor, blue	575.00	20.00	
c.	With grill	3,000.		

Re-issues, Without Gum, Hard White Paper, Perf. 12

180	2c Jackson (135), carmine vermilion ..	*35,000.*		
181	2c Taylor (179), bright blue................	*75,000.*		

1879, Perf. 12, Soft Paper

182	1c Franklin (134), dark ultramarine	300.00	3.50	
183	2c Jackson (135), vermilion	130.00	3.00	
a.	Double impression	—	—	
184	3c Washington (136), green	100.00	.60	
b.	Double impression	—	—	
185	5c Taylor (179), blue	500.00	12.00	
186	6c Lincoln (137), pink	1,000.	20.00	
187	10c Jefferson (138), brown	2,750.	25.00	
188	10c Jefferson (138), brown w/secret mk.	1,900.	25.00	
189	15c Webster (141), red orange	350.00	22.50	
190	30c Hamilton (143), full black	1,100.	55.00	
191	90c Perry (144), carmine......................	2,250.	275.00	

1880, Special Printing, Without Gum, Soft Porous Paper, Perf. 12

192	1c Franklin (134), dark ultramarine ...	*27,500.*		
193	2c Jackson (135), black brown	*15,000.*		
194	3c Washington (136), blue green	*50,000.*		
195	6c Lincoln (137), dull rose	*25,000.*		
196	7c Stanton (138), scarlet vermilion	*4,500.*		
197	10c Jefferson (139), deep brown	*30,000.*		
198	12c Clay (140), blackish purple	*8,000.*		
199	15c Webster (141), orange	*27,500.*		
200	24c Scott (142), dark violet	*7,500.*		
201	30c Hamilton (143), greenish black	*18,000.*		
202	90c Perry (144), dull carmine	*25,000.*		
203	30c Jackson (135), scarlet vermilion ...	*55,000.*		
204	90c Taylor (179), deep blue	*85,000.*		

1882, Perf. 12

205	5c James Garfield, yellow brown........	300.00	9.00	

Special Printing, Soft Porous Paper, Without Gum

205C	5c Garfield (205), gray brown	*40,000.*		

1881-82, Perf. 12

206	1c Franklin (134), gray blue................	85.00	.90	

239   240   241

242   243   244

245   246   247   248

253   254   255   256

257   258   259   260

261   262   263

Scott No.	Description	Unused Value	Used Value	/ / / / / /
207	3c Washington (136), blue green	85.00	.55	
c.	Double impression		—	
208	6c Lincoln (137), rose......................	550.00	80.00	
a.	6c brown red	525.00	110.00	
209	10c Jefferson (139), brown..................	160.00	6.00	
b.	10c black brown	1,000.	150.00	
c.	Double impression		—	

1883, Perf. 12

210	2c Washington, red brown..................	50.00	.60	
211	4c Jackson, blue green........................	300.00	17.50	

Special Printing, Soft Porous Paper, Without Gum

211B	2c Washington (210), pale red brown, with gum	450.00	—	
c.	Horiz. pair, imperf. btwn.	1,900.	—	
211D	4c Jackson (211), dp blue grn, w/o gum	35,000.		

1887, Perf. 12

212	1c Franklin, ultramarine	110.00	1.75	
213	2c Washington (210), green	50.00	.40	
b.	Printed on both sides		—	
214	3c Washington (136), vermilion..........	80.00	60.00	

1888, Perf. 12

215	4c Jackson (211), carmine....................	225.00	20.00	
216	5c Garfield (205), indigo....................	250.00	14.00	
217	30c Hamilton (143), orange brown	450.00	110.00	
218	90c Perry (144), purple........................	1,300.	250.00	

1890-93, Perf. 12

219	1c Franklin, dull blue..........................	27.50	.60	
219D	2c Washington, lake............................	250.00	1.10	
220	2c Washington (219D), carmine	22.50	.55	
a.	Cap on left "2"...............................	125.00	2.50	
c.	Cap on both "2s"............................	550.00	20.00	
221	3c Jackson, purple	80.00	7.50	
222	4c Lincoln, dark brown......................	90.00	2.75	
223	5c U. S. Grant, chocolate	80.00	2.75	
224	6c Garfield, brown red........................	85.00	20.00	
225	8c William T. Sherman, lilac	60.00	13.00	
226	10c Webster, green................................	190.00	3.50	
227	15c Clay, indigo...................................	250.00	20.00	
228	30c Jefferson, black	400.00	30.00	
229	90c Perry, orange	600.00	125.00	

1893, Perf. 12

230	1c Columbian Exposition, deep blue ..	22.50	.40	
231	2c Columbian Exposition, brown violet	21.00	.30	
232	3c Columbian Exposition, green.........	60.00	15.00	

**Wmk. 190-"USPS"
in Single-lined
Capitals**

**Wmk. 191-Double-
lined "USPS" in
Capitals**

Triangle A (Type I)   Triangle B (Type II)

TWO CENTS.

Type I. The horizontal lines of the ground work run across the triangle and are of the same thickness within it as without.

Type II. The horizontal lines cross the triangle but are thinner within it than without.

**Triangle C   Type IV design
(Type III & IV**

Type III. The horizontal lines do not cross the double frame lines of the triangle. The lines within the triangle are thin, as in type II.

Type IV. Same triangle C as type III, but other design differences including, (1) re-cutting and lengthening of hairline, (2) shaded toga button, (3) strengthening of lines on sleeve, (4) additional dots on ear, (5) "T" of "TWO" straight at right, (6) background lines extend into white oval opposite "U" of "UNITED".

ONE DOLLAR

Type I

Type I. The circles enclosing "$1" are broken where they meet the curved line below "One Dollar." The fifteen left vertical rows of impressions from plate 76 are Type I, the balance being Type II.

Type II

Type II. The circles are complete.

TEN CENTS

Type I

Type I. Tips of foliate ornaments do not impinge on white curved line below "TEN CENTS."

Type II

Type II. Tips of ornaments break curved line below "E" of "TEN" and "T" of "CENTS."

Scott No.	Description	Unused Value	Used Value	/ / / / / /
233	4c Columbian Exposition, ultra..........	87.50	7.50	
a.	4c Columbian Exposition, blue (error)	*19,000.*	*15,000.*	
234	5c Columbian Exposition, chocolate ..	95.00	8.00	
235	6c Columbian Exposition, purple	85.00	22.50	
a.	6c Columbian Exposition, red violet ..	85.00	22.50	
236	8c Columbian Exposition, magenta	75.00	11.00	
237	10c Columbian Exposition, black brown	140.00	8.00	
238	15c Columbian Exposition, dark green.	240.00	65.00	
239	30c Columbian Exposition, orange brown	300.00	85.00	
240	50c Columbian Exposition, slate blue...	600.00	160.00	
241	$1 Columbian Exposition, salmon	1,300.	650.00	
242	$2 Columbian Exposition, brown red .	1,400.	600.00	
243	$3 Columbian Exposition, yellow green	2,100.	1,100.	
a.	$3 Columbian Exposition, olive green	2,100.	1,100.	
244	$4 Columbian Exposition, crimson lake	2,900.	1,350.	
a.	$4 Columbian Exposition, rose carmine	2,900.	1,350.	
245	$5 Columbian Exposition, black	3,250.	1,700.	

1894, Perf. 12, Unwatermarked

Scott No.	Description	Unused Value	Used Value	/ / / / / /
246	1c Franklin (247), ultramarine............	32.50	4.50	
247	1c Franklin, blue	67.50	2.25	
248	2c Washington, pink, type I................	27.50	3.25	
249	2c Washington (248), carmine lake, type I	150.00	3.00	
250	2c Washington (248), carmine, type I.	30.00	1.20	
a.	2c rose, type I..............................	30.00	2.25	
b.	2c scarlet, type I..........................	30.00	.45	
c.	Vert. pair, imperf. horiz.	*4,500.*		
d.	Horiz, pair, imperf. btwn.	*2,000.*		
251	2c Washington (248), carmine, type II	300.00	6.00	
a.	2c scarlet, type II...........................	300.00	4.00	
252	2c Washington (248), carmine, type III	120.00	6.00	
a.	2c scarlet, type III.........................	120.00	6.00	
b.	Horiz. pair, imperf. vert.	*1,500.*		
c.	Horiz. pair, imperf. btwn.	*1,750.*		
253	3c Jackson, purple	110.00	9.00	
254	4c Lincoln, dark brown......................	150.00	4.25	
255	5c Grant, chocolate	110.00	6.00	
c.	Vert. pair, imperf. horiz.	*2,750.*		
256	6c Garfield, dull brown......................	175.00	22.50	
a.	Vert. pair, imperf. horiz.	*1,600.*		
257	8c Sherman, violet brown...................	140.00	16.00	
258	10c Webster, dark green	275.00	11.00	
259	15c Clay, dark blue	300.00	55.00	
260	50c Jefferson, orange...........................	550.00	120.00	
261	$1 Perry, black, type I........................	1,000.	350.00	
261A	$1 Perry (261), type II	2,300.	700.00	
262	$2 James Madison, bright blue............	3,100.	1,100.	
263	$5 John Marshall, dark green	5,000.	2,250.	

ScottMounts

Protect your stamps from the harmful effects of dust and moisture. Available in clear or black backs.

Pre-Cut Single Mounts

Size	Description	# Mounts	Item	Price
40 x 25	U.S. Stand. Com.-Hor.	40	901	$2.99
25 x 40	U.S. Stand. Com.-Vert.	40	902	2.99
25 x 22	U.S. Reg Issue-Hor.	40	903	2.99
22 x 25	U.S. Reg. Issue-Vert.	40	904	2.99
41 x 31	U.S. Semi-Jumbo-Hor.	40	905	2.99
31 x 41	U.S. Semi-Jumbo-Vert.	40	906	2.99
50 x 31	U.S. Jumbo-Hor.	40	907	2.99
31 x 50	U.S. Jumbo-Vert.	40	908	2.99
25 x 27	U.S. Famous Americans	40	909	2.99
33 x 27	United Nations	40	910	2.99
40 x 27	United Nations	40	911	2.99
67 x 25	PNC, Strips of Three	40	976	5.29
67 x 34	Pacific '97 Triangle	10	984	2.99
111 x 25	PNC, Strips of Five	25	985	5.29
51 x 36	U.S. Hunting Permit/ Express Mail	40	986	5.29

Pre-Cut Plate Block, FDC & Postal Card Mounts

Size	Description	# Mounts	Item	Price
57 x 55	Reg Issue Plate Block	25	912	$5.29
73 x 63	Champions of Liberty	25	913	5.29
106 x 55	Rotary Press Stand. Com.	20	914	5.29
105 x 57	Giori Press Stand. Com.	20	915	5.29
165 x 94	First Day Cover	10	917	5.29
140 x 90	Postal Card Size	10	918	5.29

Strips 215mm Long

Size	Description	# Mounts	Item	Price
20	U.S. 19th Century/Hor. Coil	22	919	$6.99
22	U.S. Early Air Mail	22	920	6.99
24	U.S., Canada, Great Britain	22	921	6.99
25	U.S. Comm. and Regular	22	922	6.99
27	U.S. Famous Americans	22	923	6.99
28	U.S. 19th Century	22	924	6.99
30	U.S. 19th Century	22	925	6.99
31	U.S. Jumbo and Semi-Jumbo	22	926	6.99
33	United Nations	22	927	6.99
36	U.S. Hunting Permit, Canada	15	928	6.99
39	U.S. Early 20th Century	15	929	6.99
41	U.S. Semi-Jumbo	15	930	6.99
	Multiple Assortment: one strip of each size 22-41 (Two 25mm strips)	12	931	6.99
44	U.S. Vertical Coil Pair	15	932	6.99
48	U.S. Farley, Cutter Pair	15	933	6.99
50	U.S. Jumbo	15	934	6.99
52	U.S. Standard Comm. Block	15	935	6.99
55	U.S. Century of Progress	15	936	6.99
57	U.S. Famous Americans Block	15	937	6.99
61	U.S. Blocks, Israel Tab	15	938	6.99

Strips 240mm Long

Size	Description	# Mounts	Item	Price
63	U.S. Jumbo Com.-Hor.Block	10	939	$7.99
66	Israel Tab Block	10	940	7.99
68	U.S. Farley, Gutter Pair			

Available from your favorite stamp dealer or direct from:

SCOTT
1-800-572-6885

	& Souvenir Sheets	10	941	6.75
74	U.S. TIPEX Souvenir Sheet	10	942	6.75
80	U.S. Stand. Com.-Vert. Block	10	943	6.75
82	U.S. Blocks of 4	10	944	6.75
84	Israel Tab Block	10	945	6.75
89	U.S. Postal Card Size	10	946	6.75
100	U.N. Margin Inscribed Block	7	947	6.75
120	Souvenir Sheets and Blocks	7	948	6.75

Strips 265mm Long

40	Standard Comm. Vertical	10	949	$7.99
55	U.S. Reg. Plate Block Strip 20	10	950	7.99
59	U.S. Double Issue Strip	10	951	7.99
70	U.S. Jumbo Com. Plate Block	10	952	10.99
91	Great Britain Souvenir Sheet	10	953	10.99
105	U.S. Stand. Plate No. Strip	10	954	10.99
107	Same as above-Wide Margin	10	955	10.99
111	U.S. Gravure-Intaglio Plate No. Strip	10	956	12.99
127	U.S. Jumbo Comm. Plate No. Strip	10	957	14.99
137	Great Britain Coronation	10	958	14.99
158	U.S. Apollo-Soyuz Plate No. Strip	10	959	15.99
231	U.S. Full Post Office Pane Regular and Comm.	5	961	15.99

Souvenir Sheets/Small Panes

111 x 25	PNC, Strips of Five	25	985	$5.29
204 x 153	U.S. Bicent. New Year 2000	4	962	7.99
187 x 144	U.N. Flag Sheet	10	963	13.49
160 x 200	New U.N., Israel Sheet	10	964	13.49
120 x 207	AMERIPEX President Sht.	4	965	5.29
229 x 131	World War II Com. Sheet	5	968	7.49
111 x 91	Columbian Souv. Sheet	6	970	3.99
148 x 196	Apollo Moon Landing	4	972	6.99
129 x 122	U.S. Definitive Mini-Sheet	9	989	8.99
189 x 151	Chinese New Year	5	990	8.99
150 x 185	Dr. Davis/World Cup	5	991	8.99
198 x 151	Cherokee	5	992	8.99
198 x 187	Postal Museum	4	994	8.99
156 x 187	Sign Lang., Statehood	5	995	8.99
188 x 197	Country-Western	5	996	8.99
151 x 192	Olympic	5	997	8.99
174 x 185	Buffalo Soldiers	5	998	8.99
130 x 198	Silent Screen Stars	5	999	8.99
190 x 199	Leg. West, Civil, Comic	4	1000	8.99
178 x 181	Cranes	4	1001	8.99
183 x 212	Wonders of the Sea	3	1002	8.99
156 x 264	$14 Eagle	4	1003	8.99
159 x 270	$9.95 Moon Landing	4	1004	8.99
159 x 259	Priority/Express Mail	4	1005	8.99
223 x 187	Marilyn Monroe	3	1006	8.99
185 x 181	Challenger Shuttle	4	1007	8.99
152 x 228	Indian Dances/Antique Autos	5	1008	8.99
165 x 150	River Boat/Hanukkah	6	1009	8.99
275 x 200	Large Gutter Blocks	2	1010	8.99
161 x 160	Pacific '97 Sheet	6	1011	8.99
174 x 130	Bugs Bunny	6	1012	8.99
196 x 158	Football Coaches	4	1013	8.99
184 x 184	American Dolls	4	1014	8.99
186 x 230	Classic Movie Monsters	3	1015	8.99
187 x 160	Trans-Mississippi Sheet	4	1016	8.99
192 x 230	Celebrate The Century	3	1017	8.99
156 x 204	Space Discovery	4	1018	8.99
182 x 209	American Ballet	5	1019	8.99
139 x 151	Christmas Wreaths	5	1020	8.99
129 x 126	Justin Morrill, Henry Luce	8	1021	8.99
184 x 165	Bright Eyes	4	1022	8.99
185 x 172	Shuttle Landing	4	1023	8.99
172 x 233	Sonoran Desert	5	1024	8.99
150 x 166	Prostate Cancer	5	1025	8.99
201 x 176	Famous Trains	4	1026	8.99
176 x 124	Canada Historic Vehicles	5	1027	8.99
245 x 114	Canada Provincial Leaders	5	1028	8.99
177 x 133	Canada Year of Family	5	1029	8.99
181 x 213	Arctic Animals	3	1034	8.99
179 x 242	Louise Nevelson	3	1037	8.99
179 x 217	Library Of Congress	3	1038	8.99
182 x 232	Youth Team Sports	3	1039	8.99

Scott No.	Description	Unused Value	Used Value	/ / / / / /
1895, Watermark 191, Perf. 12				
264	1c Franklin (247), blue	6.50	.50	
265	2c Washington (248), carmine, type I.	30.00	1.75	
266	2c Washington (248), carmine, type II	30.00	3.50	
267	2c Washington (248), carmine, type III	5.50	.25	
a.	2c pink, type III.	6.00	.60	
b.	2c vermilion, type III.	*27.50*		
c.	2c rose carmine, type III.	—		
268	3c Jackson (253), purple	37.50	1.40	
269	4c Lincoln (254), dark brown	40.00	2.00	
270	5c Grant (255), chocolate	37.50	2.25	
271	6c Garfield (256), dull brown	95.00	5.00	
a.	Wmkd. USIR	*10,000.*	*7,500.*	
272	8c Sherman (257), violet brown	65.00	1.60	
a.	Wmkd. USIR	*5,000.*	750.00	
273	10c Webster (258), dark green	95.00	1.60	
274	15c Clay (259), dark blue	225.00	10.00	
275	50c Jefferson (260), orange	300.00	22.50	
a.	50c Jefferson (260), red orange	325.00	27.50	
276	$1 Perry (261), black, type I	650.00	80.00	
276A	$1 Perry (261), black, type II	1,300.	175.00	
277	$2 Madison (262), bright blue	1,100.	350.00	
a.	$2 dark blue	1,100.	400.00	
278	$5 Marshall (263), dark green	2,400.	500.00	
1897-1903, Watermark 191, Perf. 12				
279	1c Franklin (247), deep green	9.00	.40	
279B	2c Washington (248), red, type IV	9.00	.40	
c.	2c rose carmine, type IV	250.00	75.00	
d.	2c orange red, type IV	10.00	.35	
e.	Booklet pane of 6	425.00	*900.00*	
f.	2c carmine, type IV	10.00	.30	
g.	2c pink, type IV	11.00	.45	
h.	2c vermilion, type IV	10.00	.30	
i.	2c brown orange, type IV	*100.00*	*6.00*	
280	4c Lincoln (254), rose brown	30.00	1.10	
a.	4c lilac brown	30.00	1.10	
b.	4c orange brown	30.00	1.10	
281	5c Grant (255), dark blue	35.00	1.00	
282	6c Garfield (256), lake	45.00	2.75	
a.	6c purple lake	60.00	4.00	
282C	10c Webster (258), brown, type I	180.00	2.75	
283	10c Webster (258), orange brown, type II	125.00	2.50	
284	15c Clay (259), olive green	160.00	8.75	
285	1c Trans-Mississippi Expo	30.00	6.50	
286	2c Trans-Mississippi Expo	27.50	1.75	
287	4c Trans-Mississippi Expo	150.00	24.00	
288	5c Trans-Mississippi Expo	140.00	21.00	
289	8c Trans-Mississippi Expo	180.00	42.50	
a.	Vert. pair, imperf. horiz.	*22,500.*		

285   286   287

288   289   290

291   292   293

294   295   296

297   298   299

Scott No.	Description	Unused Value	Used Value	/ / / / / /
290	10c Trans-Mississippi Expo	180.00	27.50	
291	50c Trans-Mississippi Expo	700.00	190.00	
292	$1 Trans-Mississippi Expo	1,250.	550.00	
293	$2 Trans-Mississippi Expo	2,100.	1,000.	
1901, Watermark 191, Perf. 12				
294	1c Pan-American Exposition	18.00	3.00	
a.	Center inverted	*10,000.*	*8,500.*	
295	2c Pan-American Exposition	17.50	1.00	
a.	Center inverted	*42,500.*	*17,500.*	
296	4c Pan-American Exposition	82.50	15.00	
a.	Center inverted	*22,500.*		
297	5c Pan-American Exposition	95.00	14.00	
298	8c Pan-American Exposition	120.00	50.00	
299	10c Pan-American Exposition	170.00	30.00	
1902-03, Watermark 191, Perf. 12				
300	1c Franklin	12.00	.25	
b.	Booklet pane of 6	600.00	*2,750.*	
301	2c Washington	16.00	.25	
c.	Booklet pane of 6	500.00	*2,250.*	
302	3c Jackson	55.00	2.75	
303	4c Grant	60.00	1.40	
304	5c Lincoln	60.00	1.60	
305	6c Garfield	72.50	2.75	
306	8c Martha Washington	45.00	2.00	
307	10c Webster	70.00	1.60	
308	13c Benjamin Harrison	50.00	7.50	
309	15c Clay	170.00	5.00	
310	50c Jefferson	475.00	22.50	
311	$1 David G. Farragut	775.00	55.00	
312	$2 Madison	1,250.	190.00	
313	$5 Marshall, dark green	3,000.	750.00	
1906-08, Imperf.				
314	1c Franklin (300)	18.00	15.00	
314A	4c Grant (303), brown	*45,000.*	*40,000.*	
315	5c Lincoln (304), blue	250.00	*600.00*	
1908, Coil Stamps, Perf. 12 Horizontally				
316	1c Franklin (300)	*45,000.*	—	
317	5c Lincoln (304)	*6,000.*	—	
Perf. 12 Vertically				
318	1c Franklin (300)	*5,750.*	—	
1903, Watermark 191, Perf. 12				
319	2c Washington, carmine, type I	6.00	.25	
a.	2c lake, type I	—	—	
b.	2c carmine rose, type I	8.00	.40	
c.	2c scarlet, type I	6.00	.30	
d.	Vert. pair, imperf. horiz.	*6,000.*		
e.	Vert. pair, imperf. btwn.	*1,750.*		

300 301 302 303 304

305 306 307 308 309

310 311 312 313 319

Type I   **Type II**

Type I. Leaf next to left "2" penetrates the border.
Type II. Strong line forming border left of leaf.

323

324

325

326

327

28

Scott No.	Description	Unused Value	Used Value	/ / / / /
f.	2c lake, type II	8.00	.25	
g.	Booklet pane of 6, carmine, type I.	120.00	250.00	
h.	As "g," type II	350.00		
i.	2c carmine, type II	75.00	50.00	
j.	2c carmine rose, type II	50.00	.75	
k.	2c scarlet, type II	50.00	.45	
m.	As "g," lake, type I	—		
n.	As "g," carmine rose, type I	200.00	290.00	
p.	As "g," scarlet, type I	180.00	275.00	
q.	As "g," lake, type II	225.00	450.00	

1906, Imperf.

320	2c Washington (319), carmine, type I.	17.50	14.00	
a.	2c lake, type II	47.50	40.00	
b.	2c scarlet, type I	18.00	12.50	
c.	2c carmine rose, type I	55.00	40.00	
d.	2c carmine, type II	300.00		

1908, Coil Stamps, Perf. 12 Horizontally

321	2c Washington (319), car., type I, pair	125,000.	—	

Perf. 12 Vertically

322	2c Washington (319), car., type II	5,500.	—	

1904, Watermark 191, Perf. 12

323	1c Louisiana Purchase	30.00	4.00	
324	2c Louisiana Purchase	27.50	1.75	
a.	Vert. pair, imperf. horiz.	10,000.		
325	3c Louisiana Purchase	90.00	30.00	
326	5c Louisiana Purchase	95.00	25.00	
327	10c Louisiana Purchase	180.00	30.00	

1907, Watermark 191, Perf. 12

328	1c Jamestown Exposition	30.00	4.00	
329	2c Jamestown Exposition	35.00	3.50	
330	5c Jamestown Exposition	135.00	27.50	

1908-09, Watermark 191, Perf. 12

331	1c Franklin, green	7.25	.25	
a.	Booklet pane of 6	160.00	140.00	
332	2c Washington, carmine	6.75	.25	
a.	Booklet pane of 6	135.00	130.00	
333	3c Washington, deep violet, type I	35.00	2.50	
334	4c Washington (333), orange brown	42.50	1.00	
335	5c Washington (333), blue	52.50	2.00	
336	6c Washington (333), red orange	65.00	5.00	
337	8c Washington (333), olive green	50.00	2.50	
338	10c Washington (333), yellow	70.00	1.40	
339	13c Washington (333), blue green	42.50	19.00	
340	15c Washington (333), pale ultramarine	70.00	5.50	

328　　　329　　　330

Franklin
331

Washington
332

Washington
333

Franklin
414

367　　　370　　　372

397　　　398　　　399

400

TYPE I

THREE CENTS.
　Type I. The top line of the toga rope is weak and the rope shading lines are thin. The fifth line from the left is missing.
　The line between the lips is thin.
　Used on both flat plate and rotary press printings.

Scott No.	Description	Unused Value	Used Value	/ / / / /
341	50c Washington (333), violet	350.00	20.00	
342	$1 Washington (333), violet brown	525.00	90.00	

Imperf.

343	1c Franklin (331)	5.00	4.50	
344	2c Washington (332)...........................	6.00	3.00	
345	3c Washington (333), deep violet, type I	11.50	20.00	
346	4c Washington (333), orange brown ...	19.00	22.50	
347	5c Washington (333), blue...................	36.00	35.00	

1908-10, Coil Stamps, Perf. 12 Horizontally

348	1c Franklin (331)	37.50	22.50	
349	2c Washington (332)...........................	80.00	12.50	
350	4c Washington (333), orange brown ...	170.00	125.00	
351	5c Washington (333), blue...................	180.00	160.00	

Coil Stamps, Perf. 12 Vertically

352	1c Franklin (331)	95.00	47.50	
353	2c Washington (332)...........................	95.00	12.00	
354	4c Washington (333), orange brown ...	220.00	85.00	
355	5c Washington (333), blue...................	230.00	120.00	
356	10c Washington (333), yellow..............	2,750.	1,250.	

1909, Bluish paper, Perf. 12

357	1c Franklin (331)	90.00	100.00	
358	2c Washington (332)...........................	85.00	100.00	
359	3c Washington (333), deep violet, type I	2,000.	2,500.	
360	4c Washington (333), orange brown ...	24,000.		
361	5c Washington (333), blue...................	5,000.	12,500.	
362	6c Washington (333), red orange	1,500.	5,000.	
363	8c Washington (333), olive green	26,000.		
364	10c Washington (333), yellow..............	1,800.	5,500.	
365	13c Washington (333), blue green	3,000.	2,250.	
366	15c Washington (333), pale ultra	1,450.	11,000.	

1909, Watermark 191, Perf. 12

367	2c Lincoln Memorial	5.50	1.75	

Imperf.

368	2c Lincoln Memorial (367)	21.00	20.00	

Bluish paper

369	2c Lincoln Memorial (367)	210.00	260.00	

Perf. 12

370	2c Alaska-Yukon-Pacific Exposition ..	8.75	2.00	

Imperf.

371	2c Alaska-Yukon-Pacific Exposition (370)	24.00	22.50	

Perf. 12

372	2c Hudson-Fulton	12.50	4.50	

Imperf.

373	2c Hudson-Fulton (372)	27.50	25.00	

TYPE I

TWO CENTS.

Type I. There is one shading line in the first curve of the ribbon above the left "2" and one in the second curve of the ribbon above the right "2."

The button of the toga has a faint outline.

The top line of the toga rope, from the button to the front of the throat, is also very faint.

The shading lines at the face terminate in front of the ear with little or no joining, to form a lock of hair.

Used on both flat and rotary press printings.

TYPE Ia

TWO CENTS.

Type Ia. Design characteristics similar to type I except that all lines of design are stronger.

The toga button, toga rope and rope shading lines are heavy. The latter characteristics are those of type II, which, however, occur only on impressions from rotary plates.

Used only on flat plates 10208 and 10209.

TYPE II

TWO CENTS.

Type II. Shading lines in ribbons as on type I. The toga button, rope, and shading lines are heavy.

The shading lines of the face at the lock of hair end in a strong vertical curved line.

Used on rotary press printings only.

TYPE III

TWO CENTS.

Type III. Two lines of shading in the curves of the ribbons.

Other characteristics similar to type II.

Used on rotary press printings only.

Scott No.	Description	Unused Value	Used Value	/ / / / /
1910-11, Watermark 190, Perf. 12				
374	1c Franklin (331)	6.75	.25	
a.	Booklet pane of 6........................	175.00	*125.00*	
375	2c Washington (332)...........................	6.75	.25	
a.	Booklet pane of 6........................	95.00	95.00	
b.	2c lake..	*425.00*		
c.	Double impression	*500.00*		
376	3c Washington (333), deep violet, type I	20.00	1.75	
377	4c Washington (333), brown	32.50	.75	
378	5c Washington (333), blue..................	32.50	.50	
379	6c Washington (333), red orange	37.50	.70	
380	8c Washington (333), olive green	115.00	12.50	
381	10c Washington (333), yellow..............	105.00	4.50	
382	15c Washington (333), pale ultra	275.00	15.00	
1910, Imperf.				
383	1c Franklin (331)	2.25	2.00	
384	2c Washington (332)...........................	3.75	2.50	
1910, Coil Stamps, Perf. 12 Horizontally				
385	1c Franklin (331)	40.00	17.50	
386	2c Washington (332)...........................	70.00	22.50	
1910-11, Coil Stamps, Perf. 12 Vertically				
387	1c Franklin (331)	200.00	65.00	
388	2c Washington (332)...........................	1,000.	400.00	
389	3c Washington (333), deep violet, type I	*65,000.*	*12,000.*	
1910, Perf. 8½ Horizontally				
390	1c Franklin (331)	5.00	*6.50*	
391	2c Washington (332)...........................	40.00	14.00	
1910-13, Perf. 8½ Vertically				
392	1c Franklin (331)	25.00	22.50	
393	2c Washington (332)...........................	47.50	8.50	
394	3c Washington (333), deep violet, type I	57.50	52.50	
395	4c Washington (333), brown	57.50	47.50	
396	5c Washington (333), blue..................	57.50	47.50	
1913, Watermark 190, Perf. 12				
397	1c Panama-Pacific Exposition............	17.50	1.50	
398	2c Panama-Pacific Exposition............	21.00	.50	
a.	2c carmine lake.................................	*1,000.*		
399	5c Panama-Pacific Exposition............	80.00	9.50	
400	10c Panama-Pacific Expo., orange yellow	135.00	20.00	
400A	10c Panama-Pacific Expo. (400), orange	220.00	16.00	
1914-15, Perf. 10				
401	1c Panama-Pacific Expo. (397)..........	25.00	5.50	
402	2c Panama-Pacific Expo. (398)..........	75.00	1.50	
403	5c Panama-Pacific Expo. (399)..........	175.00	15.00	
404	10c Panama-Pacific Expo. (400), orange	900.00	62.50	

TYPE II

TYPE IV

THREE CENTS.
 Type II. The top line of the toga rope is strong and the rope shading lines are heavy and complete.
 The line between the lips is heavy.
 Used on both flat plate and rotary press printings.

TWO CENTS.
 Type IV. Top line of the toga rope is broken. Shading lines in toga button are so arranged that the curving of the first and last form " ID."
 Line of color in left "2" is very thin and usually broken.
 Used on offset printings only.

TYPE V

TYPE Va

TWO CENTS.
 Type V. Top line of toga is complete.
 Five vertical shading lines in toga button.
 Line of color in left "2" is very thin and usually broken.
 Shading dots on the nose and lip are as indicated on the diagram.
 Used on offset printings only.

TWO CENTS.
 Type Va. Characteristics same as type V, except in shading dots of nose. Third row from bottom has 4 dots instead of 6. Overall height of type Va is 1/3 mm. less than type V.
 Used on offset printings only.

Scott No.	Description	Unused Value	Used Value	/ / / / / /
1912-14, Watermark 190, Perf. 12				
405	1c Washington (333), green	7.00	.20	☐☐☐☐☐
a.	Vert. pair, imperf. horiz.	1,500.	—	☐☐☐☐☐
b.	Booklet pane of 6	60.00	50.00	☐☐☐☐☐
406	2c Washington (333), carmine, type I.	7.00	.20	☐☐☐☐☐
a.	Booklet pane of 6	60.00	65.00	☐☐☐☐☐
b.	Double impression	—		☐☐☐☐☐
c.	2c lake, type I	1,500.	—	☐☐☐☐☐
407	7c Washington (333), black	80.00	11.00	☐☐☐☐☐
1912, Imperf.				
408	1c Washington (333), green	1.10	.65	☐☐☐☐☐
409	2c Washington (333), carmine, type I.	1.30	.65	☐☐☐☐☐
Coil Stamps, Perf. 8½ Horizontally				
410	1c Washington (333), green	6.00	4.25	☐☐☐☐☐
411	2c Washington (333), carmine, type I.	10.00	3.75	☐☐☐☐☐
Coil Stamps, Perf. 8½ Vertically				
412	1c Washington (333), green	25.00	5.50	☐☐☐☐☐
413	2c Washington (333), carmine, type I.	50.00	1.25	☐☐☐☐☐
1912-14, Watermark 190, Perf. 12				
414	8c Franklin, pale olive green	45.00	1.25	☐☐☐☐☐
415	9c Franklin (414), salmon red	55.00	12.50	☐☐☐☐☐
416	10c Franklin (414), orange yellow	45.00	.40	☐☐☐☐☐
a.	10c brown yellow	850.00	—	☐☐☐☐☐
417	12c Franklin (414), claret brown	50.00	4.25	☐☐☐☐☐
418	15c Franklin (414), gray	85.00	3.50	☐☐☐☐☐
419	20c Franklin (414), ultra	200.00	15.00	☐☐☐☐☐
420	30c Franklin (414), orange red	125.00	15.00	☐☐☐☐☐
421	50c Franklin (414), violet	425.00	17.50	☐☐☐☐☐
1912, Watermark 191, Perf. 12				
422	50c Franklin (414), violet	250.00	15.00	☐☐☐☐☐
423	$1 Franklin (414), violet brown	525.00	60.00	☐☐☐☐☐
1914, Watermark 190, Perf. 12 x 10				
423A	1c Washington (333), green	4,500.	4,000.	☐☐☐☐☐
423B	2c Washington (333), rose red, type 1	25,000.	4,500.	☐☐☐☐☐
423C	5c Washington (333), blue		7,000.	☐☐☐☐☐
1914, Watermark 190, Perf. 10 x 12				
423D	1c Washington (333), green		4,250.	☐☐☐☐☐
423E	2c Washington (333), rose red, type 1.		-	☐☐☐☐☐
1914-15, Watermark 190, Perf. 10				
424	1c Washington (333), green	2.50	.20	☐☐☐☐☐
c.	Vert. pair, imperf. horiz.	1,750.	1,500.	☐☐☐☐☐
d.	Booklet pane of 6	5.25	3.25	☐☐☐☐☐
e.	As "d.," imperf.	1,600.		☐☐☐☐☐
f.	Vert. pair, imperf. between and with straight edge at top	9,000.		☐☐☐☐☐

TYPE VI

TYPE VII

TWO CENTS.
Type VI. General characteristics same as type V, except that line of color in left "2" is very heavy.
Used on offset printings only.

TWO CENTS.
Type VII. Line of color in left "2" is invariably continuous, clearly defined, and heavier than in type V or Va, but not as heavy as in type VI.
Additional vertical row of dots has been added to the upper lip.
Numerous additional dots have been added to hair on top of head.
Used on offset printings only.

TYPE III

TYPE IV

THREE CENTS.
Type III. The top line of the toga rope is strong but the fifth shading line is missing as in type I.
Center shading line of the toga button consists of two dashes with a central dot.
The "P" and "O" of "POSTAGE" are separated by a line of color.
The frame line at the bottom of the vignette is complete.
Used on offset printings only.

THREE CENTS.
Type IV. Shading lines of toga rope are complete.
Second and fourth shading lines in toga button are broken in the middle and the third line is continuous with a dot in the center.
"P" and "O" of "POSTAGE" are joined.
Frame line at bottom of vignette is broken.
Used on offset printings only.

Scott No.	Description	Unused Value	Used Value	/ / / / / /
425	2c Washington (333), rose red, type I.	2.30	.20	
e.	Booklet pane of 6............................	17.50	*17.50*	
426	3c Washington (333), deep violet, type I	15.00	1.25	
427	4c Washington (333), brown	35.00	.50	
428	5c Washington (333), blue..................	35.00	.50	
429	6c Washington (333), red orange	50.00	1.40	
430	7c Washington (333), black................	90.00	4.00	
431	8c Franklin (414), pale olive green	36.00	2.00	
432	9c Franklin (414), salmon red	50.00	7.50	
433	10c Franklin (414), orange yellow	47.50	.50	
434	11c Franklin (414), dark green.............	25.00	7.50	
435	12c Franklin (414), claret brown..........	27.50	4.00	
a.	12c Franklin (414), copper red.............	30.00	5.00	
437	15c Franklin (414), gray	135.00	7.25	
438	20c Franklin (414), ultramarine............	220.00	4.00	
439	30c Franklin (414), orange red.............	260.00	16.00	
440	50c Franklin (414), violet.....................	575.00	16.00	

1914, Coil Stamps, Perf. 10 Horizontally

441	1c Washington (333), green	1.00	1.00	
442	2c Washington (333), carmine, type I.	10.00	6.00	

Coil Stamps, Perf. 10 Vertically

443	1c Washington (333), green	25.00	5.00	
444	2c Washington (333), carmine, type I.	40.00	1.50	
a.	2c lake..		*1,250.*	
445	3c Washington (333), violet, type I.....	225.00	125.00	
446	4c Washington (333), brown	125.00	42.50	
447	5c Washington (333), blue..................	45.00	27.50	

1914-16, Coil Stamps, Perf. 10 Horizontally, Rotary Press Printing

448	1c Washington (333), green	6.00	3.25	
449	2c Washington (333), red, type I	2,600.	600.00	
450	2c Washington (333), carmine, type III	10.00	4.00	

1914-16, Coil Stamps, Perf. 10 Vertically, Rotary Press Printing

452	1c Washington (333), green	10.00	2.00	
453	2c Washington (333), car rose, type I.	150.00	5.00	
454	2c Washington (333), red, type II........	82.50	10.00	
455	2c Washington (333), carmine, type III	8.50	1.00	
456	3c Washington (333), violet, type I.....	240.00	90.00	
457	4c Washington (333), brown	25.00	17.50	
458	5c Washington (333), blue..................	30.00	17.50	

1914, Coil Stamp, Imperf., Rotary Press Printing

459	2c Washington (333), carmine, type I.	240.00	*950.00*	

1915, Watermark 191, Perf. 10

460	$1 Franklin (414), violet black	850.00	100.00	

1915, Watermark 190, Perf. 11

461	2c Washington (333), pale car red, type I	150.00	*275.00*	

Scott No.	Description	Unused Value	Used Value	/ / / / / /

1916-17, Perf. 10, Unwatermarked

Scott No.	Description	Unused Value	Used Value
462	1c Washington (333), green	7.00	.35
a.	Booklet pane of 6	9.50	8.00
463	2c Washington (333), carmine, type I.	4.50	.25
a.	Booklet pane of 6	95.00	65.00
464	3c Washington (333), violet, type I.....	75.00	14.00
465	4c Washington (333), orange brown ...	45.00	1.80
466	5c Washington (333), blue	75.00	1.80
467	5c Washington (333), car (error in plate of 2c)	550.00	750.00
468	6c Washington (333), red orange	95.00	7.50
469	7c Washington (333), black	130.00	12.50
470	8c Franklin (414), olive green	60.00	7.00
471	9c Franklin (414), salmon red	60.00	16.00
472	10c Franklin (414), orange yellow	110.00	1.75
473	11c Franklin (414), dark green	40.00	18.00
474	12c Franklin (414), claret brown	55.00	6.50
475	15c Franklin (414), gray	200.00	14.00
476	20c Franklin (414), light ultramarine	250.00	15.00
476A	30c Franklin (414), orange red	3,750.	—
477	50c Franklin (414), light violet	1,100.	70.00
478	$1 Franklin (414), violet black	800.00	20.00
479	$2 Madison (312), dark blue	275.00	40.00
480	$5 Marshall (313), light green	225.00	40.00

Imperf.

Scott No.	Description	Unused Value	Used Value
481	1c Washington (333), green	1.00	.65
482	2c Washington (333), carmine, type I.	1.40	1.25
482A	2c Washington (333), deep rose, type Ia		37,500.
483	3c Washington (333), violet, type I.....	13.00	7.50
484	3c Washington (333), violet, type II ...	10.00	5.00
485	5c Washington (333), carmine (error in plate of 2c), in block of 9	20,000.	

1916-22, Coil Stamps, Perf. 10 Horizontally, Rotary Press Printing

Scott No.	Description	Unused Value	Used Value
486	1c Washington (333), green	.90	.40
487	2c Washington (333), carmine, type II	13.50	4.00
488	2c Washington (333), carmine, type III	2.50	1.75
489	3c Washington (333), violet, type I.....	5.00	1.50

1916-22, Coil Stamps, Perf.10 Vertically

Scott No.	Description	Unused Value	Used Value
490	1c Washington (333), green	.55	.25
491	2c Washington (333), carmine, type II	2,200.	750.00
492	2c Washington (333), carmine, type III	9.50	.35
493	3c Washington (333), violet, type I.....	16.00	3.00
494	3c Washington (333), violet, type II ...	10.00	1.10
495	4c Washington (333), orange brown ...	10.00	4.00
496	5c Washington (333), blue	3.50	1.00
497	10c Franklin (414), orange yellow	20.00	11.00

Scott No.	Description	Unused Value	Used Value	/ / / / /
Types of 1912-14 Issue				
1917-19, Perf. 11				
498	1c Washington (333), green	.35	.25	
a.	Vert. pair, imperf. horiz.	600.00		
b.	Horiz. pair, imperf. btwn.	325.00		
c.	Vert. pair, imperf. btwn.................	450.00	—	
d.	Double impression	250.00	750.00	
e.	Booklet pane of 6...........................	2.50	1.25	
f.	Booklet pane of 30.........................	1,000.		
499	2c Washington (333), rose, type I	.35	.25	
a.	Vert. pair, imperf. horiz.	175.00		
b.	Horiz. pair, imperf. vert.	300.00	225.00	
c.	Vert. pair, imperf. btwn.................	850.00	225.00	
e.	Booklet pane of 6...........................	4.00	1.75	
f.	Booklet pane of 30.........................	28,000.		
g.	Double impression	175.00	—	
500	2c Washington (333), deep rose, type Ia	275.00	225.00	
501	3c Washington (333), light violet, type I	11.00	.25	
b.	Booklet pane of 6...........................	75.00	50.00	
c.	Vert. pair, imperf. horiz.	750.00		
d.	Double impression	2,750.	2,750.	
502	3c Washington (333), dark violet, type II	14.00	.75	
b.	Booklet pane of 6...........................	60.00	50.00	
c.	Vert. pair, imperf. horiz.	500.00	—	
d.	Double impression	500.00	300.00	
503	4c Washington (333), brown	10.00	.30	
b.	Double impression	—		
504	5c Washington (333), blue..................	9.00	.25	
a.	Horiz. pair, imperf. btwn.	2,500.	—	
505	5c Washington (333), rose (error in plate of 2c)	350.00	525.00	
506	6c Washington (333), red orange	12.50	.30	
507	7c Washington (333), black...............	27.50	1.25	
508	8c Franklin (414), olive bister	12.00	.50	
b.	Vert. pair, imperf. btwn..................	—	—	
509	9c Franklin (414), salmon red	14.00	1.75	
510	10c Franklin (414), orange yellow	17.00	.20	
a.	10c brown yellow..........................	600.00		
511	11c Franklin (414), light green..............	9.00	2.50	
512	12c Franklin (414), claret brown..........	9.00	.35	
a.	12c brown carmine	9.50	.40	
513	13c Franklin (414), apple green	11.00	6.00	
514	15c Franklin (414), gray	37.50	1.00	
515	20c Franklin (414), light ultramarine	47.50	.40	
b.	Vert. pair, imperf. btwn..................	1,500.		
c.	Double impression	1,250.		
516	30c Franklin (414), orange red..............	37.50	1.00	
b.	Double impression	—		

Scott No.	Description	Unused Value	Used Value	/ / / / /
517	50c Franklin (414), red violet...............	67.50	.60	
b.	Vert. pair, imperf. btwn. & at bottom	—	6,000.	
518	$1 Franklin (414), violet brown...........	52.50	1.50	
b.	$1 deep brown.....................................	1,800.	1,050.	

1917-19, Watermark 191

519	2c Washington (332)	450.00	1,100.	

1918, Perf. 11, Unwatermarked

523	$2 Franklin, orange red & black..........	600.00	230.00	
524	$5 Franklin (523), deep green & black	200.00	35.00	

1918-20, Perf. 11, Offset Printing

525	1c Washington (333), gray green	2.50	.90	
a.	1c dark green..	5.00	1.75	
c.	Horiz. pair, imperf. btwn.	100.00		
d.	Double impression	40.00	30.00	
526	2c Washington (333), carmine, type IV	27.50	4.00	
527	2c Washington (333), carmine, type V	20.00	1.25	
a.	Double impression	65.00	12.50	
b.	Vert. pair, imperf. horiz.	600.00		
c.	Horiz. pair, imperf. vert.	1,000.	—	
528	2c Washington (333), carmine, type Va	9.50	.40	
c.	Double impression	27.50		
g.	Vert. pair, imperf. btwn..................	3,500.		
528A	2c Washington (333), carmine, type VI	52.50	1.75	
d.	Double impression	160.00	—	
f.	Vert. pair, imperf. horiz.	—		
h.	Vert. pair, imperf. btwn..................	1,000.		
528B	2c Washington (333), carmine, type VII	22.50	.75	
e.	Double impression	70.00		
529	3c Washington (333), violet, type III ..	3.25	.40	
a.	Double impression	40.00	—	
b.	Printed on both sides	1,500.		
530	3c Washington (333), purple, type IV.	1.80	.30	
a.	Double impression	30.00	7.00	
b.	Printed on both sides	350.00		

Imperf.

531	1c Washington (333), green	9.50	8.00	
532	2c Washington (333), car rose, type IV	40.00	27.50	
533	2c Washington (333), carmine, type V	110.00	80.00	
534	2c Washington (333), carmine, type Va	11.00	7.00	
534A	2c Washington (333), carmine, type VI	45.00	25.00	
534B	2c Washington (333), carmine, type VII	2,100.	1,250.	
535	3c Washington (333), violet, type IV..	9.00	5.00	
a.	Double impression	90.00	—	

Perf. 12½

536	1c Washington (333), gray green	22.50	20.00	
a.	Horiz. pair, imperf. vert.	900.00		

Scott No.	Description	Unused Value	Used Value	/ / / / / /

1919, Perf. 11, Flat Plate Printing

Scott No.	Description	Unused Value	Used Value	
537	3c Victory, violet....................	9.00	3.25	
a.	3c deep red violet............................	*1,400.*	*2,000.*	
b.	3c light reddish violet......................	9.00	3.00	
c.	3c red violet	50.00	12.00	

1919, Perf. 11x10, Rotary Press Printings,
Size: 19½ to 20mm wide by 22 to 22¼ mm high

Scott No.	Description	Unused Value	Used Value	
538	1c Washington (333), green	11.00	8.50	
a.	Vert. pair, imperf. horiz.	50.00	*100.00*	
539	2c Washington (333), car rose, type II	*2,750.*	*4,750.*	
540	2c Washington (333), car rose, type III	13.00	8.50	
a.	Vert. pair, imperf. horiz.	50.00	*100.00*	
b.	Horiz. pair, imperf. vert.	*1,250.*		
541	3c Washington (333), violet, type II ...	45.00	30.00	

1920, Perf. 10x11, Size: 19x22½-22¾ mm

Scott No.	Description	Unused Value	Used Value	
542	1c Washington (333), green	14.00	1.10	

1921, Perf. 10, Size: 19x22½ mm

Scott No.	Description	Unused Value	Used Value	
543	1c Washington (333), green	.50	.30	
a.	Horiz. pair, imperf. btwn.	*1,750.*		

1922, Perf. 11, Size: 19x22½ mm

Scott No.	Description	Unused Value	Used Value	
544	1c Washington (333), green	*18,000.*	*3,500.*	

1921, Perf. 11, Size: 19½-20x22mm

Scott No.	Description	Unused Value	Used Value	
545	1c Washington (333), green	190.00	175.00	
546	2c Washington (333), car rose, type III	125.00	*160.00*	

1920, Perf. 11

Scott No.	Description	Unused Value	Used Value	
547	$2 Franklin (523), carmine & black....	175.00	40.00	
a.	$2 lake & black	220.00	40.00	
548	1c Pilgrim Tercentenary......................	4.50	2.25	
549	2c Pilgrim Tercentenary......................	6.50	1.60	
550	5c Pilgrim Tercentenary......................	45.00	12.50	

1922-25, Perf. 11

Scott No.	Description	Unused Value	Used Value	
551	½c Nathan Hale, olive brown..............	.20	.20	
552	1c Franklin, deep green	1.50	.20	
a.	Booklet pane of 6......................	6.00	*2.00*	
553	1½c Warren G. Harding, yellow brown .	2.50	.20	
554	2c Washington, carmine	1.30	.20	
a.	Horiz. pair, imperf. vert.	300.00		
b.	Vert. pair, imperf. horiz.	*4,000.*		
c.	Booklet pane of 6..........................	6.75	*2.00*	
555	3c Lincoln, violet..............................	17.50	1.25	
556	4c Martha Washington, yellow brown	19.00	.35	
a.	Vert. pair, imperf. horiz.	*10,500.*		
557	5c Theodore Roosevelt, dark blue.......	19.00	.25	

41

523   537

548   549   550

551   552   553   554

555   556   557   558

559   560   561   562

563   564   565   566

Scott No.	Description	Unused Value	Used Value	/ / / / /
a.	Imperf., pair	*1,400.*		
b.	Horiz. pair, imperf. vert.	—		
558	6c Garfield, red orange......................	35.00	.85	
559	7c William McKinley, black...............	9.00	.65	
560	8c Grant, olive green	50.00	.75	
561	9c Jefferson, rose	14.00	1.10	
562	10c James Monroe, orange....................	17.50	.30	
a.	Vert. pair, imperf. horiz.	*2,250.*		
b.	Imperf., pair	*1,500.*		
563	11c Rutherford B. Hayes, light blue......	1.40	.50	
a.	11c light bluish green	1.40	.50	
d.	Imperf., pair		*17,500.*	
564	12c Grover Cleveland, brown violet......	6.00	.30	
a.	Horiz. pair, imperf. vert.	*1,750.*		
565	14c American Indian, blue	4.00	.85	
566	15c Statue of Liberty, gray	21.00	.25	
567	20c Golden Gate, carmine rose.............	20.00	.25	
a.	Horiz. pair, imperf. vert.	*1,500.*		
568	25c Niagara Falls, yellow green	18.00	.60	
b.	Vert. pair, imperf. horiz.	*2,000.*		
569	30c American Buffalo, olive brown......	32.50	.50	
570	50c Arlington Amphitheater, lilac........	52.50	.30	
571	$1 Lincoln Memorial, violet black......	42.50	.55	
572	$2 U.S. Capitol, deep blue	85.00	9.00	
573	$5 "America," carmine & blue	140.00	15.00	
a.	$5 carmine lake & dark blue	200.00	17.50	

1923-25, Imperf.

575	1c Franklin (552), green	7.00	5.00	
576	1½c Harding (553), yellow brown	1.40	1.50	
577	2c Washington (554), carmine	1.50	1.25	

Rotary Press Printings, Perf. 11x10, Size: 19¾ x 22¼ mm

578	1c Franklin (552), green	95.00	*160.00*	
579	2c Washington (554), carmine	85.00	*140.00*	

Perf. 10

581	1c Franklin (552), green	11.00	.65	
582	1½c Harding (553), brown	5.50	.60	
583	2c Washington (554), carmine	3.00	.25	
a.	Booklet pane of 6..........................	90.00	*50.00*	
584	3c Lincoln (555), violet	32.50	2.75	
585	4c Martha Washington (556)	19.00	.55	
586	5c Theodore Roosevelt (557), blue	19.00	.30	
a.	Horiz. pair, imperf. vertically..........		*10,000.*	
587	6c Garfield (558), red orange..............	9.25	.50	
588	7c McKinley (559)...............................	13.50	6.25	
589	8c Grant (560).....................................	30.00	4.00	
590	9c Jefferson (561), rose	6.00	2.25	

567 568 569

570 571 572

573 610

Type I.

Type I. Type II.

Type II.

Type I–No heavy hair lines at top center of head. Outline of left acanthus scroll generally faint at top and toward base at left side.

Type II–The heavy hair lines at top center of head; two being outstanding in the white area. Outline of left acanthus scroll very strong and clearly defined at top (under left edge of lettered panel) and at lower curve (above and to the left of numeral oval). Type II is found only on Nos. 599a and 634A.

614 615 616

Scott No.	Description	Unused Value	Used Value	//////
591	10c Monroe (562), orange	72.50	.40	☐☐☐☐☐

Perf. 11

594	1c Franklin (552), green	*19,000.*	6,500.	☐☐☐☐☐
595	2c Washington (554), carmine	300.00	*325.00*	☐☐☐☐☐
596	1c Franklin (552), green		70,000.	☐☐☐☐☐

Nos. 578-579, 594-595 were made from coil waste of Nos. 597 and 599 and measure approx. 19 3/4 x 22 1/4 mm. No 596 was made from rotary press sheet waste and measures approx. 19 1/4 x 22 1/2 mm.

1923-29, Coil Stamps, Perf. 10 Vertically, Rotary Press Printing

597	1c Franklin (552), green	.30	.20	☐☐☐☐☐
598	1 1/2c Harding (553), brown	1.00	.20	☐☐☐☐☐
599	2c Washington (554), carmine, type I.	.40	.20	☐☐☐☐☐
599A	2c Washington (554), carmine, type II	125.00	11.00	☐☐☐☐☐
600	3c Lincoln (555), violet	7.25	.20	☐☐☐☐☐
601	4c Martha Washington (556)	4.50	.35	☐☐☐☐☐
602	5c Theodore Roosevelt (557), dark blue	1.75	.20	☐☐☐☐☐
603	10c Monroe (562), orange	4.00	.20	☐☐☐☐☐

Perf. 10 Horizontally

604	1c Franklin (552), green	.35	.20	☐☐☐☐☐
605	1 1/2c Harding (553), yellow brown	.35	.20	☐☐☐☐☐
606	2c Washington (554), carmine	.35	.20	☐☐☐☐☐

1923, Perf. 11, Flat Plate Printing, Size: 19 1/4 x22 1/4 mm

610	2c Harding Memorial, black	.65	.25	☐☐☐☐☐
a.	Horiz. pair, imperf. vert.	*2,000.*		☐☐☐☐☐

Imperf.

611	2c Harding Memorial (610)	6.25	4.00	☐☐☐☐☐

1923, Perf. 10, Rotary Press Printing, Size: 19 1/4 x 22 1/2 mm

612	2c Harding Memorial (610)	17.50	1.75	☐☐☐☐☐

1923, Perf. 11

613	2c Harding Memorial (610)		37,500.	☐☐☐☐☐

1924-26, Perf. 11

614	1c Huguenot-Walloon Tercentenary	2.75	3.25	☐☐☐☐☐
615	2c Huguenot-Walloon Tercentenary	5.50	2.25	☐☐☐☐☐
616	5c Huguenot-Walloon Tercentenary	22.50	13.00	☐☐☐☐☐
617	1c Lexington-Concord	2.50	2.50	☐☐☐☐☐
618	2c Lexington-Concord	5.00	4.00	☐☐☐☐☐
619	5c Lexington-Concord	20.00	13.00	☐☐☐☐☐
620	2c Norse-American	4.00	3.00	☐☐☐☐☐
621	5c Norse-American	15.00	11.00	☐☐☐☐☐
622	13c Benjamin Harrison, green	13.50	.55	☐☐☐☐☐
623	17c Woodrow Wilson, black	15.00	.25	☐☐☐☐☐

1926, Perf. 11

627	2c Sesquicentennial Exposition	3.25	.50	☐☐☐☐☐
628	5c Ericsson Memorial	6.50	3.25	☐☐☐☐☐

617

618

619

620

621

622

623

627

628

629

643

644

645

Scott No.	Description	Unused Value	Used Value	/ / / / /
629	2c Battle of White Plains....................	2.25	1.70	☐☐☐☐☐
a.	Vert. pair, imperf. btwn.................	—		☐☐☐☐☐
630	2c Battle of White Plains (629), sht of 25	375.00	450.00	

1926, Imperf., Rotary Press Printings
631	1½c Harding (553), yellow brown	1.90	1.70	☐☐☐☐☐

1926-34, Perf. 11x10½
632	1c Franklin (552), green	.20	.20	☐☐☐☐☐
a.	Booklet pane of 6...........................	5.50	3.00	☐☐☐☐☐
b.	Vert. pair, imperf. btwn..................	3,500.	125.00	☐☐☐☐☐
c.	Horiz. pair, imperf btwn.	7,500.		☐☐☐☐☐
633	1½c Harding (553), yellow brown	2.00	.20	☐☐☐☐☐
634	2c Washington (554), carmine, type I.	.20	.20	☐☐☐☐☐
b.	2c carmine lake	—	—	☐☐☐☐☐
c.	Horiz. pair, imperf. btwn.	7,000.		☐☐☐☐☐
d.	Booklet pane of 6...........................	1.75	1.25	☐☐☐☐☐
634A	2c Washington (554), carmine, type II	350.00	13.50	☐☐☐☐☐
635	3c Lincoln (555), violet	.40	.20	☐☐☐☐☐
a.	3c bright violet...............................	.20	.20	☐☐☐☐☐
636	4c Martha Washington (556)..............	2.10	.20	☐☐☐☐☐
637	5c Theodore Roosevelt (557), dark blue	2.10	.20	☐☐☐☐☐
638	6c Garfield (558), red orange..............	2.10	.20	☐☐☐☐☐
639	7c McKinley (559)..............................	2.10	.20	☐☐☐☐☐
a.	Vert. pair, imperf. btwn..................	300.00	100.00	☐☐☐☐☐
640	8c Grant (560)...................................	2.10	.20	☐☐☐☐☐
641	9c Jefferson (561), orange red............	2.10	.20	☐☐☐☐☐
642	10c Monroe (562), orange	3.50	.20	☐☐☐☐☐

1927, Perf. 11
643	2c Vermont Sesquicentennial	1.40	.80	☐☐☐☐☐
644	2c Burgoyne Campaign	3.75	2.10	☐☐☐☐☐

1928, Perf. 11
645	2c Valley Forge	1.05	.50	☐☐☐☐☐
a.	2c lake	—		☐☐☐☐☐

1928, Perf. 11x10½, Rotary Press Printing
646	2c Battle of Monmouth (Molly Pitcher), ovptd. on Washington	1.10	1.10	☐☐☐☐☐
a.	"Pitcher" only.................................	500.00		☐☐☐☐☐
647	2c Hawaii Sesquicentennial, ovptd. on Washington, carmine..............	5.00	4.50	☐☐☐☐☐
648	5c Hawaii Sesquicentennial, ovptd. on T. Roosevelt, dark blue	14.50	13.50	☐☐☐☐☐

1928, Perf. 11
649	2c Aeronautics Conference	1.25	.80	☐☐☐☐☐
650	5c Aeronautics Conference	5.25	3.25	☐☐☐☐☐

No. 634
Overprinted

MOLLY PITCHER

Scott 646

No. 634 and 637
Overprinted

HAWAII 1778 · 1928

Scott 647-648

649

650

Nos. 632-634,
635-642
Overprinted

Kans.

Scott 658-668

651

Nos. 632-634,
635-642
Overprinted

Nebr.

Scott 669-679

654

657

680

681

682

683

684

685

688

Scott No.	Description	Unused Value	Used Value	//////
1929, Perf. 11				
651	2c George Rogers Clark	.65	.50	☐☐☐☐☐
1929, Perf. 11x10½, Rotary Press Printing				
653	½c Hale (551), olive brown..................	.20	.20	☐☐☐☐☐
1929, Perf. 11				
654	2c Electric Light	.70	.70	☐☐☐☐☐
Perf. 11x10½, Rotary Press Printing				
655	2c Electric Light (654).........................	.65	.20	☐☐☐☐☐
Coil Stamp (Rotary Press), Perf. 10 Vertically				
656	2c Electric Light (654).........................	14.00	1.75	☐☐☐☐☐
1929, Perf. 11				
657	2c Sullivan Expedition.........................	.70	.60	☐☐☐☐☐
a.	2c lake	350.00	—	☐☐☐☐☐
1929, Perf. 11x10½, Rotary Press Printing, Overprinted				
658	1c Kans. ovpt., on Franklin, green	2.50	2.00	☐☐☐☐☐
a.	Vert. pair, one without ovpt.	325.00		☐☐☐☐☐
659	1½c Kans. ovpt., on Harding, brown	4.00	2.90	☐☐☐☐☐
a.	Vert. pair, one without ovpt.	350.00		☐☐☐☐☐
660	2c Kans. ovpt., on Washington, carmine	4.50	1.00	☐☐☐☐☐
661	3c Kans. ovpt., on Lincoln, violet	22.50	15.00	☐☐☐☐☐
a.	Vert. pair, one without ovpt.	450.00		☐☐☐☐☐
662	4c Kans. ovpt., on Martha Washington	22.50	9.00	☐☐☐☐☐
a.	Vert. pair, one without ovpt.	425.00		☐☐☐☐☐
663	5c Kans. ovpt., on T. Roosevelt, dp blue	14.00	9.75	☐☐☐☐☐
664	6c Kans. ovpt., on Garfield, red orange	32.50	18.00	☐☐☐☐☐
665	7c Kans. ovpt., on McKinley	30.00	27.50	☐☐☐☐☐
a.	Vert. pair, one without ovpt.	—		☐☐☐☐☐
666	8c Kans. ovpt., on Grant	110.00	70.00	☐☐☐☐☐
667	9c Kans. ovpt., on Jefferson, light rose	16.00	11.25	☐☐☐☐☐
668	10c Kans. ovpt., on Monroe, orange yel	25.00	12.00	☐☐☐☐☐
669	1c Nebr. ovpt., on Franklin, green.......	4.00	2.25	☐☐☐☐☐
a.	Vert. pair, one without ovpt.	—		☐☐☐☐☐
670	1½c Nebr. ovpt., on Harding, brown......	3.75	2.50	☐☐☐☐☐
671	2c Nebr. ovpt., on Washington, carmine	3.75	1.30	☐☐☐☐☐
672	3c Nebr. ovpt., on Lincoln, violet........	15.00	12.00	☐☐☐☐☐
a.	Vert. pair, one without ovpt.	425.00		☐☐☐☐☐
673	4c Nebr. ovpt., on Martha Washington	22.50	15.00	☐☐☐☐☐
674	5c Nebr. ovpt., on T. Roosevelt, dp blue	20.00	15.00	☐☐☐☐☐
675	6c Nebr. ovpt., on Garfield, red orange	47.50	24.00	☐☐☐☐☐
676	7c Nebr. ovpt., on McKinley	27.50	18.00	☐☐☐☐☐
677	8c Nebr. ovpt., on Grant	37.50	25.00	☐☐☐☐☐
678	9c Nebr. ovpt., on Jefferson, light rose	42.50	27.50	☐☐☐☐☐
a.	Vert. pair, one without ovpt.	650.00		☐☐☐☐☐
679	10c Nebr. ovpt., on Monroe, orange yel	135.00	22.50	☐☐☐☐☐

689   690   692   693

694   695   696   697

698   699   700   701

702   703   704   705

706   707   708   709

710   711   712   713

Scott No.	Description	Unused Value	Used Value	//////

1929, Perf. 11

680	2c Battle of Fallen Timbers................	.80	.80	☐☐☐☐☐
681	2c Ohio River Canalization................	.70	.65	☐☐☐☐☐

1930, Perf. 11

682	2c Massachusetts Bay Colony	.60	.50	☐☐☐☐☐
683	2c Carolina-Charleston	1.20	1.20	☐☐☐☐☐

1930, Perf. 11x10½, Rotary Press Printing

684	1½c Harding, brown............................	.35	.20	☐☐☐☐☐
685	4c William H. Taft, brown	.90	.20	☐☐☐☐☐

Coil Stamps, Perf. 10 Vertically

686	1½c Harding (684), brown....................	1.80	.20	☐☐☐☐☐
687	4c Taft (685), brown...........................	3.25	.45	☐☐☐☐☐

1930, Perf. 11

688	2c Battle of Braddock's Field.............	1.00	.85	☐☐☐☐☐
689	2c Von Steuben..................................	.55	.55	☐☐☐☐☐
a.	Imperf., pair....................................	2,750.		☐☐☐☐☐

1931, Perf. 11

690	2c Pulaski	.30	.25	☐☐☐☐☐

1931, Perf. 11x10½, Rotary Press Printing

692	11c Hayes (563).................................	2.60	.20	☐☐☐☐☐
693	12c Cleveland (564)	5.50	.20	☐☐☐☐☐
694	13c Benjamin Harrison (622), yellow green	2.00	.20	☐☐☐☐☐
695	14c American Indian (565), dark blue..	3.75	.25	☐☐☐☐☐
696	15c Statue of Liberty (566)..................	8.00	.20	☐☐☐☐☐

Perf. 10½ x11

697	17c Wilson (623).................................	4.50	.20	☐☐☐☐☐
698	20c Golden Gate (567).........................	8.25	.20	☐☐☐☐☐
699	25c Niagara Falls (568), blue green......	8.50	.20	☐☐☐☐☐
700	30c American Buffalo (569), brown.....	16.00	.20	☐☐☐☐☐
701	50c Arlington Amphitheater (570)	37.50	.20	☐☐☐☐☐

1931, Perf. 11, Flat Plate

702	2c Red Cross	.25	.20	☐☐☐☐☐
a.	Red cross omitted..........................	40,000.		☐☐☐☐☐
703	2c Yorktown, carmine rose & black ...	.40	.25	☐☐☐☐☐
a.	2c lake & black................................	4.50	.75	☐☐☐☐☐
b.	2c dark lake & black	450.00		☐☐☐☐☐
c.	Horiz. pair, imperf. vert...................	5,000.		☐☐☐☐☐

1932, Perf. 11x10½, Rotary Press Printings

704	½c Washington Bicentennial, olive brown	.20	.20	☐☐☐☐☐
705	1c Washington Bicentennial, green	.20	.20	☐☐☐☐☐
706	1½c Washington Bicentennial, brown...	.40	.20	☐☐☐☐☐
707	2c Washington Bicentennial, car rose	.20	.20	☐☐☐☐☐

714 715 716 717

718 719 720 723 724

725 726 727 728

729 732 733 734

736 737 739

740 741 742

Scott No.	Description	Unused Value	Used Value	/ / / / /
708	3c Washington Bicentennial, deep violet	.55	.20	☐☐☐☐☐
709	4c Washington Bicentennial, light brown	.25	.20	☐☐☐☐☐
710	5c Washington Bicentennial, blue	1.60	.20	☐☐☐☐☐
711	6c Washington Bicentennial, red orange	3.25	.20	☐☐☐☐☐
712	7c Washington Bicentennial, black.....	.25	.20	☐☐☐☐☐
713	8c Washington Bicentennial, olive bister	2.75	.50	☐☐☐☐☐
714	9c Washington Bicentennial, pale red.....	2.40	.20	☐☐☐☐☐
715	10c Washington Bicentennial, orange yel.	10.00	.20	☐☐☐☐☐

Perf. 11

716	2c Olympic Winter Games.................	.40	.20	☐☐☐☐☐

Perf. 11x10½, Rotary Press Printing

717	2c Arbor Day......................................	.20	.20	☐☐☐☐☐

Perf. 11x10½

718	3c Olympic Games............................	1.40	.20	☐☐☐☐☐
719	5c Olympic Games............................	2.20	.20	☐☐☐☐☐
720	3c Washington, deep violet.................	.20	.20	☐☐☐☐☐
b.	Booklet pane of 6	40.00	7.50	☐☐☐☐☐
c.	Vert. pair, imperf. btwn.	1,250.	1,250.	☐☐☐☐☐

Coil Stamps, Perf. 10 Vertically, Rotary Press Printing

721	3c Washington (720)	2.75	.20	☐☐☐☐☐

Perf. 10 Horizontally

722	3c Washington (720)	1.50	.35	☐☐☐☐☐

Perf. 10 Vertically

723	6c Garfield (558), deep orange...........	11.00	.30	☐☐☐☐☐

1932-33, Perf. 11

724	3c William Penn	.30	.20	☐☐☐☐☐
a.	Vert. pair, imperf. horiz.................	—		☐☐☐☐☐
725	3c Daniel Webster	.30	.25	☐☐☐☐☐
726	3c Georgia Bicentennial......................	.30	.20	☐☐☐☐☐

1933, Perf. 10½x11, Rotary Press Printing

727	3c Peace of 1783	.20	.20	☐☐☐☐☐
728	1c Century of Progress, yellow green	.20	.20	☐☐☐☐☐
729	3c Century of Progress, violet	.20	.20	☐☐☐☐☐

1933, Imperf., Flat Plate Printing

730	American Phil. Society, Sheet of 25	27.50	27.50	☐☐☐☐☐
a.	1c Single stamp, Century of Progress (728)	.75	.50	☐☐☐☐☐
731	American Phil. Society, Sheet of 25	25.00	25.00	☐☐☐☐☐
a.	3c Single stamp, Century of Progress (729)	.65	.50	☐☐☐☐☐

743

744

745

747

746

748

749

752

753

754

755

772

773

774

775

54

Scott No.	Description	Unused Value	Used Value	//////
732	3c National Recovery Act...................	.20	.20	
733	3c Byrd Antarctic	.50	.50	
734	5c Kosciuszko...................................	.55	.25	
a.	Horiz. pair, imperf. vert...............	2,250.		

1934, Imperf.

735	3c National Stamp Exhibition, Sheet of 6	12.50	10.00	
a.	Single stamp, Byrd Antarctic.........	2.00	1.65	
736	3c Maryland Tercentenary	.20	.20	

Perf. 11x10½

737	3c Mothers of America	.20	.20	

Perf. 11

738	3c Mothers of America (737).............	.20	.20	
739	3c Wisconsin Tercentenary	.20	.20	
a.	Vert. pair, imperf. horiz.	350.00		
b.	Horiz. pair, imperf. vert.................	525.00		
740	1c National Parks - Yosemite	.20	.20	
a.	Vert. pair, imperf. horiz., with gum	1,300.		
741	2c National Parks - Grand Canyon.....	.20	.20	
a.	Vert. pair, imperf. horiz., with gum	475.00		
b.	Horiz. pair, imperf. vert., with gum	600.00		
742	3c National Parks - Mt. Rainier..........	.20	.20	
a.	Vert. pair, imperf. horiz., with gum.....................................	700.00		
743	4c National Parks - Mesa Verde..........	.35	.40	
a.	Vert. pair, imperf. horiz., with gum.....................................	1,000.		
744	5c National Parks - Yellowstone	.70	.65	
a.	Horiz. pair, imperf. vert., with gum.....................................	600.00		
745	6c National Parks - Crater Lake	1.10	.85	
746	7c National Parks - Acadia	.60	.75	
a.	Horiz. pair, imperf. vert., with gum.....................................	725.00		
747	8c National Parks - Zion	1.60	1.50	
748	9c National Parks - Glacier.................	1.50	.65	
749	10c National Parks - Great Smoky Mtns., gray black............................	3.00	1.25	

Imperf.

750	American Philatelic Society, sheet of 6	30.00	27.50	
a.	3c Single stamp, National Parks (742)	3.50	3.25	
751	Trans-Mississippi Phil. Exhib, sheet of 6	12.50	12.50	
a.	1c Single stamp, National Parks (740)	1.40	1.60	

Scott No.	Description	Unused Value	Used Value	/ / / / / /

1935, Perf. 10½x11, Rotary Press Printing

| 752 | 3c Peace of 1783 Issue (727).............. | .20 | .20 | ☐☐☐☐☐ |

Perf. 11, Flat Plate Printing

| 753 | 3c Byrd Antarctic (733) .... | .50 | .45 | ☐☐☐☐☐ |

No. 753 is similar to No. 733. Positive identification is by blocks or pairs showing guide lines between stamps. These lines between stamps are found only on No. 753.

Imperf.

754	3c Mothers of America (737)..............	.60	.60	☐☐☐☐☐
755	3c Wisconsin Tercentenary (739)	.60	.60	☐☐☐☐☐
756	1c National Parks - Yosemite (740)	.20	.20	☐☐☐☐☐
757	2c National Parks - Grand Canyon (741)	.25	.25	☐☐☐☐☐
758	3c National Parks - Mt. Rainier (742)	.50	.45	☐☐☐☐☐
759	4c National Parks - Mesa Verde (743)	.95	.95	☐☐☐☐☐
760	5c National Parks - Yellowstone (744)	1.50	1.30	☐☐☐☐☐
761	6c National Parks - Crater Lake (745)	2.40	2.10	☐☐☐☐☐
762	7c National Parks - Acadia (746)........	1.50	1.40	☐☐☐☐☐
763	8c National Parks - Zion (747)	1.60	1.50	☐☐☐☐☐
764	9c National Parks - Glacier (748).......	1.90	1.65	☐☐☐☐☐
765	10c National Parks - Great Smoky Mountains (749), gray black........	3.75	3.25	☐☐☐☐☐
766	American Phil. Society, Pane of 25	25.00	25.00	☐☐☐☐☐
a.	1c Single stamp, Century of Progress (728)	.70	.50	☐☐☐☐☐
767	American Phil. Society, Pane of 25	23.50	23.50	☐☐☐☐☐
a.	3c Single stamp, Century of Progress (729)	.60	.50	☐☐☐☐☐
768	National Stamp Exhibition, Pane of 6	20.00	15.00	☐☐☐☐☐
a.	3c Single stamp, Byrd Antarctic (733)	2.80	2.40	☐☐☐☐☐
769	Trans-Mississippi Phil. Exhib, Pane of 6	12.50	11.00	☐☐☐☐☐
a.	1c Single stamp - Yosemite (740)	1.85	1.80	☐☐☐☐☐
770	American Phil. Society, Pane of 6 .	30.00	24.00	☐☐☐☐☐
a.	3c Single stamp, Mt. Rainier - (742)..	3.25	3.10	☐☐☐☐☐
771	16c Air Post Special Delivery (CE1)....	2.40	2.40	☐☐☐☐☐

Nos. 766-770 were issued in sheets of 9 panes of 25 stamps each. Single items from these sheets are identical with other varieties, 766 and 730, 766a and 730a, 767 and 731, 767a and 731a, 768 and 735, 768a and 735a, 769 and 756, 770 and 758. Positive identification is by blocks or pairs showing wide gutters between stamps. These wide gutters occurs only on Nos. 766-770 and measure, horizontally, 13mm on Nos. 766-767, 16mm on No. 768, and 23mm on Nos. 769-770.

1935, Perf. 11x10½ , 11

772	3c Connecticut Tercentenary...............	.20	.20	☐☐☐☐☐
773	3c California Pacific Exposition.........	.20	.20	☐☐☐☐☐
774	3c Boulder Dam	.20	.20	☐☐☐☐☐
775	3c Michigan Centenary.......................	.20	.20	☐☐☐☐☐

Scott No.	Description	Unused Value	Used Value	//////
1936				
776	3c Texas Centennial	.20	.20	
777	3c Rhode Island Tercentenary.............	.20	.20	
778	3rd Intl. Phil. Exhib., Sht. of 4, imperf.	1.75	1.75	
a.	3c Connecticut Tercentenary (772).....	.40	.35	
b.	3c California Pacific Exposition (773)	.40	.35	
c.	3c Michigan Centennial (775).............	.40	.35	
d.	3c Texas Centennial (776).................	.40	.35	
782	3c Arkansas Centennial......................	.20	.20	
783	3c Oregon Territory............................	.20	.20	
784	3c Susan B. Anthony...........................	.20	.20	
1936-37				
785	1c Army - Washington & Greene	.20	.20	
786	2c Army - A. Jackson & Scott............	.20	.20	
787	3c Army - Sherman, Grant & Sheridan	.20	.20	
788	4c Army - Lee & "Stonewall" Jackson	.30	.20	
789	5c Army - West Point	.60	.25	
790	1c Navy - Jones & Barry	.20	.20	
791	2c Navy - Decatur & MacDonough ...	.20	.20	
792	3c Navy - Farragut & Porter	.20	.20	
793	4c Navy - Sampson, Dewey & Schley	.30	.20	
794	5c Navy - Academy Seal & Cadets	.60	.25	
1937				
795	3c Ordinance of 1787........................	.20	.20	
796	5c Virginia Dare	.20	.20	
797	10c Society of Philatelic Americans, blue green, imperf......................	.60	.40	
798	3c Constitution Sesquicentennial........	.20	.20	
799	3c Hawaii...	.20	.20	
800	3c Alaska	.20	.20	
801	3c Puerto Rico....................................	.20	.20	
802	3c Virgin Islands	.20	.20	
1938-54, Perf. 11x10½, 11				
803	½c Benjamin Franklin.........................	.20	.20	
804	1c George Washington	.20	.20	
b.	Booklet pane of 6	2.00	.50	
805	1½c Martha Washington	.20	.20	
b.	Horiz. pair, imperf. btwn...............	160.00	25.00	
806	2c John Adams	.20	.20	
b.	Booklet pane of 6	4.75	.85	
807	3c Thomas Jefferson	.20	.20	
a.	Booklet pane of 6	8.50	*2.00*	
b.	Horiz. pair, imperf. btwn...............	*1,500.*	—	
c.	Imperf., pair.....................................	*2,500.*		
808	4c James Madison	.75	.20	
809	4½c White House	.20	.20	
810	5c James Monroe	.20	.20	

57

776

777

782

783

784

785

786

787

788

789

790

791

HOW TO USE THIS BOOK

The number in the first column is its Scott number or identifying number. Following that is the denomination of the stamp and its color. Finally, the value, unused and used is shown.

792

793

796

794

795

799

797

798

800

801

802

803

804

805

806

807   808   809   810

811   812   813   814

815   816   817   818

819   820   821   822

823   824   825   826

827   828   829   830

Scott No.	Description	Unused Value	Used Value	/ / / / / /
811	6c John Quincy Adams	.20	.20	
812	7c Andrew Jackson	.25	.20	
813	8c Martin Van Buren	.30	.20	
814	9c William Henry Harrison	.30	.20	
815	10c John Tyler	.25	.20	
816	11c James Knox Polk	.65	.20	
817	12c Zachary Taylor	.90	.20	
818	13c Millard Fillmore	1.25	.20	
819	14c Franklin Pierce	.90	.20	
820	15c James Buchanan	.40	.20	
821	16c Abraham Lincoln	.90	.25	
822	17c Andrew Johnson	.85	.20	
823	18c Ulysses S. Grant	1.75	.20	
824	19c Rutherford B. Hayes	1.25	.35	
825	20c James A. Garfield	.70	.20	
826	21c Chester Arthur	1.25	.20	
827	22c Grover Cleveland	1.00	.40	
828	24c Benjamin Harrison	3.50	.20	
829	25c William McKinley	.60	.20	
830	30c Theodore Roosevelt	3.50	.20	
831	50c William Howard Taft	5.00	.20	
832	$1 Woodrow Wilson, purple & black	6.75	.20	
a.	Vert. pair, imperf. horiz.	1,600.		
b.	Wmkd. USIR	220.00	65.00	
c.	$1 red violet & black	6.00	.20	
d.	As "c," vert. pair, imperf. horiz.	1,500.		
e.	Vert. pair, imperf. btwn.	2,750.		
f.	As "c," vert. pair, imperf. btwn.	8,500.		
833	$2 Warren G. Harding	20.00	3.75	
834	$5 Calvin Coolidge, carmine and black	95.00	3.00	
a.	$5 red brown & black	3,000.	7,000.	
1938				
835	3c Constitution Ratification	.25	.20	
836	3c Swedish-Finnish Tercentenary	.20	.20	
837	3c Northwest Territory Sesquicentennial	.20	.20	
838	3c Iowa Territory Centennial	.20	.20	
1939, Coil Stamps, Perf. 10 Vertically				
839	1c George Washington (804)	.30	.20	
840	1½c Martha Washington (805)	.30	.20	
841	2c John Adams (806)	.40	.20	
842	3c Thomas Jefferson (807)	.50	.20	
843	4c James Madison (808)	7.50	.40	
844	4½c White House (809)	.70	.40	
845	5c James Monroe (810)	5.00	.35	
846	6c John Quincy Adams (811)	1.10	.20	
847	10c John Tyler (815)	11.00	.50	

831

832

833

834

835

836

837

838

852

853

854

855

856

857

858

Scott No.	Description	Unused Value	Used Value	//////

Perf. 10 Horizontally

Scott No.	Description	Unused Value	Used Value	//////
848	1c George Washington (804)	.85	.20	
849	1½c Martha Washington (805)	1.25	.30	
850	2c John Adams (806)	2.50	.40	
851	3c Thomas Jefferson (807)	2.25	.35	

1939

Scott No.	Description	Unused Value	Used Value	//////
852	3c Golden Gate Intl. Exposition	.20	.20	
853	3c New York World's Fair	.20	.20	
854	3c Washington Inauguration	.40	.20	
855	3c Baseball Centennial	1.75	.20	
856	3c Panama Canal	.25	.20	
857	3c Printing Tercentenary	.20	.20	
858	3c 50th Anniversary of Statehood	.20	.20	

1940

Scott No.	Description	Unused Value	Used Value	//////
859	1c Washington Irving	.20	.20	
860	2c James Fenimore Cooper	.20	.20	
861	3c Ralph Waldo Emerson	.20	.20	
862	5c Louise May Alcott	.30	.20	
863	10c Samuel L. Clemens	1.65	1.20	
864	1c Henry Wadsworth Longfellow	.20	.20	
865	2c John Greenleaf Whittier	.20	.20	
866	3c James Russell Lowell	.20	.20	
867	5c Walt Whitman	.35	.20	
868	10c James Whitcomb Riley	1.75	1.25	
869	1c Horace Mann	.20	.20	
870	2c Mark Hopkins	.20	.20	
871	3c Charles W. Eliot	.20	.20	
872	5c Frances E. Willard	.40	.20	
873	10c Booker T. Washington	1.25	1.10	
874	1c John James Audubon	.20	.20	
875	2c Dr. Crawford W. Long	.20	.20	
876	3c Luther Burbank	.20	.20	
877	5c Dr. Walter Reed	.25	.20	
878	10c Jane Addams	1.10	.85	
879	1c Stephen Collins Foster	.20	.20	
880	2c John Philip Sousa	.20	.20	
881	3c Victor Herbert	.20	.20	
882	5c Edward A. MacDowell	.40	.20	
883	10c Ethelbert Nevin	3.75	1.35	
884	1c Gilbert Charles Stuart	.20	.20	
885	2c James A. McNeill Whistler	.20	.20	
886	3c Augustus Saint-Gaudens	.20	.20	
887	5c Daniel Chester French	.50	.20	
888	10c Frederic Remington	1.75	1.25	
889	1c Eli Whitney	.20	.20	
890	2c Samuel F.B. Morse	.20	.20	

859   860   861

862   863   864

865   866   867

868   869   870

871   872   873

Scott No.	Description	Unused Value	Used Value	/ / / / / /
891	3c Cyrus Hall McCormick..................	.25	.20	
892	5c Elias Howe......................................	1.10	.30	
893	10c Alexander Graham Bell	11.00	2.00	
894	3c Pony Express	.25	.20	
895	3c Pan American Union......................	.20	.20	
896	3c Idaho Statehood.............................	.20	.20	
897	3c Wyoming Statehood........................	.20	.20	
898	3c Coronado Expedition	.20	.20	
899	1c National Defense...........................	.20	.20	
a.	Vert. pair, imperf. btwn.	650.00	—	
b.	Horiz. pair, imperf. btwn..............	35.00	—	
900	2c National Defense...........................	.20	.20	
a.	Horiz. pair, imperf. btwn.	40.00	—	
901	3c National Defense...........................	.20	.20	
a.	Horiz. pair, imperf. btwn..............	27.50	—	
902	3c Thirteenth Amendment	.20	.20	

1941

903	3c Vermont Statehood.........................	.20	.20	

1942

904	3c Kentucky Statehood	.20	.20	
905	3c Win the War, violet........................	.20	.20	
b.	3c purple	—	—	
906	5c Chinese Resistance........................	.50	.20	

1943

907	2c Allied Nations...............................	.20	.20	
908	1c Four Freedoms..............................	.20	.20	

1943-44, Nos. 910-921 like No. 909

909	5c Poland	.20	.20	
910	5c Czechoslovakia..............................	.20	.20	
a.	Double impression of "Czecholovakia"	—		
911	5c Norway...	.20	.20	
a.	Double impression of "Norway" ...	—		
912	5c Luxembourg...................................	.20	.20	
a.	Double impression of "Luxembourg"	—		
913	5c Netherlands....................................	.20	.20	
914	5c Belgium	.20	.20	
a.	Double impression of "Belgium"..	—		
915	5c France	.20	.20	
916	5c Greece	.35	.25	
917	5c Yugoslavia.....................................	.25	.20	
a.	Reverse printing of flag colors (blue and dark rose over black) ...	—		
918	5c Albania..	.20	.20	
a.	Double impression of "Albania"....	—		
919	5c Austria	.20	.20	
a.	Double impression of "Austria".....	—		

65

874   875   876

877   878   879

880   881   882

883   884   885

886   887   888

Scott No.	Description	Unused Value	Used Value	/ / / / / /
920	5c Denmark	.20	.20	
921	5c Korea	.20	.20	
a.	Double impression of "Korea"	—		
1944				
922	3c Transcontinental Railroad	.20	.20	
923	3c Steamship	.20	.20	
924	3c Telegraph	.20	.20	
925	3c Philippines	.20	.20	
926	3c Motion Pictures	.20	.20	
1945				
927	3c Florida Statehood	.20	.20	
928	5c United Nations Conference	.20	.20	
929	3c Iwo Jima (Marines)	.20	.20	
1945-46				
930	1c Franklin D. Roosevelt	.20	.20	
931	2c Franklin D. Roosevelt	.20	.20	
932	3c Franklin D. Roosevelt	.20	.20	
933	5c Franklin D. Roosevelt	.20	.20	
1945				
934	3c Army	.20	.20	
935	3c Navy	.20	.20	
936	3c Coast Guard	.20	.20	
937	3c Alfred E. Smith	.20	.20	
938	3c Texas Statehood	.20	.20	
1946				
939	3c Merchant Marine	.20	.20	
940	3c Veterans of World War II	.20	.20	
941	3c Tennessee Statehood	.20	.20	
942	3c Iowa Statehood	.20	.20	
943	3c Smithsonian Institution	.20	.20	
944	3c Kearny Expedition	.20	.20	
1947				
945	3c Thomas A. Edison	.20	.20	
946	3c Joseph Pulitzer	.20	.20	
947	3c Postage Stamp Centenary	.20	.20	
948	CIPEX, Sheet of 2, imperf	.55	.45	
a.	5c Franklin (1), blue	.20	.20	
b.	10c Washington (2), brown orange	.25	.25	
949	3c Doctors	.20	.20	
950	3c Utah	.20	.20	
951	3c U.S. Frigate *Constitution*	.20	.20	
952	3c Everglades National Park	.20	.20	
1948				
953	3c George Washington Carver	.20	.20	

889

890

891

892

893

894

895

896

897

898

899

900

901

905

907

902

903

904

906

908

909

922

923

924

925

926

927

928

929

930

931

932

933

934

935

936

937   938   939

940   941   942

943   944   945

946   947   948

949

950

951

952

953

954

Scott No.	Description	Unused Value	Used Value	/ / / / / /
954	3c California Gold	.20	.20	
955	3c Mississippi Territory	.20	.20	
956	3c Four Chaplains	.20	.20	
957	3c Wisconsin Statehood	.20	.20	
958	5c Swedish Pioneers	.20	.20	
959	3c Progress of Women	.20	.20	
960	3c William Allen White	.20	.20	
961	3c U.S.-Canada Friendship	.20	.20	
962	3c Francis Scott Key	.20	.20	
963	3c Salute to Youth	.20	.20	
964	3c Oregon Territory	.20	.20	
965	3c Harlan F. Stone	.20	.20	
966	3c Palomar Mountain Observatory	.20	.20	
a.	Vert. pair, imperf. btwn.	550.00		
967	3c Clara Barton	.20	.20	
968	3c Poultry Industry	.20	.20	
969	3c Gold Star Mothers	.20	.20	
970	3c Fort Kearny	.20	.20	
971	3c Volunteer Firemen	.20	.20	
972	3c Indian Centennial	.20	.20	
973	3c Rough Riders	.20	.20	
974	3c Juliette Low	.20	.20	
975	3c Will Rogers	.20	.20	
976	3c Fort Bliss	.20	.20	
977	3c Moina Michael	.20	.20	
978	3c Gettysburg Address	.20	.20	
979	3c American Turners	.20	.20	
980	3c Joel Chandler Harris	.20	.20	

1949

Scott No.	Description	Unused Value	Used Value	/ / / / / /
981	3c Minnesota Territory	.20	.20	
982	3c Washington and Lee University	.20	.20	
983	3c Puerto Rico Election	.20	.20	
984	3c Annapolis Tercentenary	.20	.20	
985	3c Grand Army of the Republic	.20	.20	
986	3c Edgar Allan Poe	.20	.20	

1950

Scott No.	Description	Unused Value	Used Value	/ / / / / /
987	3c American Bankers Association	.20	.20	
988	3c Samuel Gompers	.20	.20	
989	3c Statue of Freedom	.20	.20	
990	3c White House	.20	.20	
991	3c Supreme Court	.20	.20	
992	3c U.S. Capitol	.20	.20	
993	3c Railroad Engineers	.20	.20	
994	3c Kansas City, Missouri	.20	.20	
995	3c Boy Scouts	.20	.20	
996	3c Indiana Territory	.20	.20	
997	3c California Statehood	.20	.20	

955

956

957

958

959

960

961

962

963

964

965

966

967

968

969

970

971

972

72

Scott No.	Description	Unused Value	Used Value	/ / / / / /
1951				
998	3c United Confederate Veterans	.20	.20	
999	3c Nevada Centennial	.20	.20	
1000	3c Landing of Cadillac......................	.20	.20	
1001	3c Colorado Statehood......................	.20	.20	
1002	3c American Chemical Society	.20	.20	
1003	3c Battle of Brooklyn........................	.20	.20	
1952				
1004	3c Betsy Ross	.20	.20	
1005	3c 4-H Clubs	.20	.20	
1006	3c B. & O. Railroad...........................	.20	.20	
1007	3c American Automobile Association	.20	.20	
1008	3c NATO..	.20	.20	
1009	3c Grand Coulee Dam........................	.20	.20	
1010	3c Lafayette	.20	.20	
1011	3c Mt. Rushmore................................	.20	.20	
1012	3c Engineering...................................	.20	.20	
1013	3c Service Women..............................	.20	.20	
1014	3c Gutenberg Bible	.20	.20	
1015	3c Newspaper Boys............................	.20	.20	
1016	3c Red Cross	.20	.20	
1953				
1017	3c National Guard	.20	.20	
1018	3c Ohio Statehood.............................	.20	.20	
1019	3c Washington Territory.....................	.20	.20	
1020	3c Louisiana Purchase........................	.20	.20	
1021	5c Opening of Japan..........................	.20	.20	
1022	3c American Bar Association	.20	.20	
1023	3c Sagamore Hill...............................	.20	.20	
1024	3c Future Farmers of America	.20	.20	
1025	3c Trucking Industry..........................	.20	.20	
1026	3c General George S. Patton, Jr.........	.20	.20	
1027	3c New York City	.20	.20	
1028	3c Gadsden Purchase	.20	.20	
1954				
1029	3c Columbia University	.20	.20	
1954-68, Perf. 11x10½, 10½ x11, 11				
1030	½c Benjamin Franklin........................	.20	.20	
1031	1c George Washington	.20	.20	
1031A	1¼c Palace of the Governors................	.20	.20	
1032	1½c Mount Vernon	.20	.20	
1033	2c Thomas Jefferson	.20	.20	
1034	2½c Bunker Hill Monument.................	.20	.20	

973

974

975

976

977

978

979

980

981

982

983

989

984

985

986

987

988

74

Scott No.	Description	Unused Value	Used Value	/ / / / / /
1035	3c Statue of Liberty, untagged............	.20	.20	
a.	Booklet pane of 6.......................	4.00	*1.25*	
b.	Tagged.......................................	.30	.25	
c.	Imperf. pair..............................	*2,000.*		
d.	Horiz. pair, imperf. btwn...........	—		
g.	As "a," vert. imperf. btwn.	*5,000.*		
1036	4c Abraham Lincoln, untagged	.20	.20	
a.	Booklet pane of 6.......................	2.75	1.25	
b.	Tagged.......................................	.60	.40	
d.	As "a," vert. imperf. horiz........	—		
1037	4½c Hermitage	.20	.20	
1038	5c James Monroe	.20	.20	
1039	6c Theodore Roosevelt......................	.25	.20	
b.	Imper., pair..............................	*11,000*		
1040	7c Woodrow Wilson	.20	.20	
a.	7c Dark rose carmine	.20	.20	
1041	8c Statue of Liberty, 22.7 mm high....	.25	.20	
a.	Double impression of carmine......	*650.00*		
1041B	8c Statue of Liberty(1041), 22.9 mm high	.40	.20	
1042	8c Statue of Liberty..........................	.20	.20	
1042A	8c General John J. Pershing.............	.20	.20	
1043	9c Alamo	.30	.20	
a.	9c Dark rose lilac	.30	.20	
1044	10c Independence Hall, untagged........	.30	.20	
b.	10c Dark rose lake.......................	.25	.20	
d.	Tagged.......................................	2.00	1.00	
1044A	11c Statue of Liberty, untagged........	.30	.20	
c.	Tagged.......................................	2.00	1.60	
1045	12c Benjamin Harrison, untagged	.35	.20	
a.	Tagged.......................................	.35	.20	
1046	15c John Jay, untagged......................	.60	.20	
a.	Tagged.......................................	1.10	.50	
1047	20c Monticello...................................	.40	.20	
a.	20c Deep bright ultramarine	.40	.20	
1048	25c Paul Revere.................................	1.10	.20	
1049	30c Robert E. Lee	.70	.20	
a.	30c Intense black.........................	1.10	.75	
1050	40c John Marshall..............................	1.50	.20	
1051	50c Susan B. Anthony........................	1.50	.20	
1052	$1 Patrick Henry..............................	4.50	.20	
1053	$5 Alexander Hamilton.....................	65.00	6.75	

1954-73, Perf. 10 Vertically, Horizontally (1¼c, 4½c)

Scott No.	Description	Unused Value	Used Value	/ / / / / /
1054	1c George Washington (1031)............	.20	.20	
b.	Imperf., pair..............................	*2,500.*	—–	
1054A	1¼c Palace of the Governors (1031A)...................................	.20	.20	
1055	2c Thomas Jefferson (1033), untagged	.35	.20	

75

990

991

992

993

994

995

996

997

998

999

1000

1001

1002

1003

1004

1005

1006

1007

1008

1009

1010

1011

1012

1013

1014

1015

1016

1017

1018

1019

1020

1021

1022

1023

1024

1025

1026

1027

1028

1029

1030

1031

1031A

1032

1033

1034

1035

1036

1037

1038

1039

1040

1041

1042

1042A

1043

1044

Scott No.	Description	Unused Value	Used Value	/ / / / / /
a.	Tagged...	.20	.20	
b.	Imperf. pair, untagged			
	(Bureau precanceled)		550.00	
c.	As "a," imperf. pair, tagged............	600.00		
1056	2½c Bunker Hill Monument (1034)......	.25	.25	
1057	3c Statue of Liberty (1035), untagged	.35	.20	
a.	Imperf., pair..................................	1,750.	—	
b.	Tagged...	1.00	.50	
1058	4c Abraham Lincoln (1036)...............	.50	.20	
a.	Imperf., pair..................................	120.00	120.00	
1059	4½c Hermitage (1037)	1.50	1.20	
1059A	25c Paul Revere (1048),			
	untagged	.50	.30	
b.	Tagged...	.80	.20	
c.	Imperf., pair..................................	55.00		
1954				
1060	3c Nebraska Territory......................	.20	.20	
1061	3c Kansas Territory	.20	.20	
1062	3c George Eastman	.20	.20	
1063	3c Lewis and Clark Expedition	.20	.20	
1955				
1064	3c Pennsylvania Academy			
	of the Fine Arts............................	.20	.20	
1065	3c Land Grant Colleges	.20	.20	
1066	8c Rotary International	.20	.20	
1067	3c Armed Forces Reserve	.20	.20	
1068	3c New Hampshire............................	.20	.20	
1069	3c Soo Locks	.20	.20	
1070	3c Atoms for Peace	.20	.20	
1071	3c Fort Ticonderoga..........................	.20	.20	
1072	3c Andrew W. Mellon	.20	.20	
1956				
1073	3c Benjamin Franklin........................	.20	.20	
1074	3c Booker T. Washington	.20	.20	
1075	FIPEX, Sheet of 2, imperf.	2.00	2.00	
a.	3c Statue of Liberty (1035)...............	.80	.80	
b.	8c Statue of Liberty (1041)................	1.00	1.00	
1076	3c FIPEX	.20	.20	
1077	3c Wildlife Conservation, Wild Turkey	.20	.20	
1078	3c Wildlife Conserv., Pronghorn Antelope	.20	.20	
1079	3c Wildlife Conservation,			
	King Salmon	.20	.20	
1080	3c Pure Food and Drug Laws	.20	.20	
1081	3c Wheatland.....................................	.20	.20	
1082	3c Labor Day.....................................	.20	.20	
1083	3c Nassau Hall...................................	.20	.20	
1084	3c Devils Tower.................................	.20	.20	
1085	3c Children	.20	.20	

1044A

1045

1046

1047

1048

1049

1050

1051

1052

1053

1060

1061

1062

1063

1064

1065

1066

1067

1068

1069

1070

1071

1072

1074

1073

1075

1076

1077

1078

1079

1080

1081

| 1082 | 1083 | 1084 | 1087 |

| 1085 | 1086 | 1088 |

| 1089 | 1090 | 1091 |

| 1092 | 1093 | 1094 |

| 1095 | 1096 | 1097 |

Scott No.	Description	Unused Value	Used Value	/ / / / / /
1957				
1086	3c Alexander Hamilton	.20	.20	
1087	3c Polio	.20	.20	
1088	3c Coast and Geodetic Survey	.20	.20	
1089	3c Architects	.20	.20	
1090	3c Steel Industry	.20	.20	
1091	3c International Naval Review	.20	.20	
1092	3c Oklahoma Statehood	.20	.20	
1093	3c School Teachers	.20	.20	
1094	4c 48-Star Flag	.20	.20	
1095	3c Shipbuilding	.20	.20	
1096	8c Ramon Magsaysay	.20	.20	
1097	3c Lafayette Bicentenary	.20	.20	
1098	3c Wildlife Conserv., Whooping Cranes	.20	.20	
1099	3c Religious Freedom	.20	.20	
1958				
1100	3c Gardening and Horticulture	.20	.20	
1104	3c Brussels Exhibition	.20	.20	
1105	3c James Monroe	.20	.20	
1106	3c Minnesota Statehood	.20	.20	
1107	3c Geophysical Year	.20	.20	
1108	3c Gunston Hall	.20	.20	
1109	3c Mackinac Bridge	.20	.20	
1110	4c Simon Bolivar, olive bister	.20	.20	
1111	8c Bolivar (1110), carmine, ultra & ocher	.20	.20	
1112	4c Atlantic Cable	.20	.20	
1958-59				
1113	1c Lincoln	.20	.20	
1114	3c Lincoln Bust	.20	.20	
1115	4c Lincoln-Douglas Debates	.20	.20	
1116	4c Lincoln Statue	.20	.20	
1958				
1117	4c Lajos Kossuth, green	.20	.20	
1118	8c Kossuth (1117), carmine, ultra & ocher	.20	.20	
1119	4c Freedom of Press	.20	.20	
1120	4c Overland Mail	.20	.20	
1121	4c Noah Webster	.20	.20	
1122	4c Forest Conservation	.20	.20	
1123	4c Fort Duquesne	.20	.20	
1959				
1124	4c Oregon Statehood	.20	.20	
1125	4c Jose de San Martin	.20	.20	
a.	Horiz. pair, imperf. btwn.	1,500.		

1098

1099

1100

1109

1104

1105

1106

1107

1108

1110

1112

1113

1115

1114

1116

1117

1119

Scott No.	Description	Unused Value	Used Value	//////
1126	8c San Martin (1125), car., ultra & ocher	.20	.20	
1127	4c NATO....................................	.20	.20	
1128	4c Arctic Explorations	.20	.20	
1129	8c World Peace through World Trade .	.20	.20	
1130	4c Silver Centennial	.20	.20	
1131	4c St. Lawrence Seaway.................	.20	.20	
1132	4c 49-Star Flag	.20	.20	
1133	4c Soil Conservation	.20	.20	
1134	4c Petroleum Industry	.20	.20	
1135	4c Dental Health..........................	.20	.20	
1136	4c Ernst Reuter, gray....................	.20	.20	
1137	8c Reuter (1136), carmine, ultra & ocher	.20	.20	
a.	Ocher omitted.............................	3,750.		
b.	Ultramarine omitted	3,750.		
c.	Ocher & ultramarine omitted........	4,000.		
d.	All colors omitted........................	2,500.		
1138	4c Dr. Ephraim McDowell..................	.20	.20	
a.	Vert. pair, imperf. btwn.	450.00		
b.	Vert. pair, imperf. horiz.	350.00		
1960-61				
1139	4c Credo - Washington...................	.20	.20	
1140	4c Credo - Franklin	.20	.20	
1141	4c Credo - Jefferson	.20	.20	
1142	4c Credo - Key	.20	.20	
1143	4c Credo - Lincoln	.20	.20	
1144	4c Credo - Henry...........................	.20	.20	
1960				
1145	4c Boy Scout Jubilee.....................	.20	.20	
1146	4c Olympic Winter Games..............	.20	.20	
1147	4c Thomas G. Masaryk, blue............	.20	.20	
a.	Vert. pair, imperf. btwn.	3,250.		
1148	8c Masaryk (1147), carmine, ultra & ocher	.20	.20	
a.	Horiz. pair, imperf. btwn..............	—		
1149	4c World Refugee Year..................	.20	.20	
1150	4c Water Conservation	.20	.20	
a.	Brown orange omitted....................	4,000	—	
1151	4c SEATO....................................	.20	.20	
a.	Vert. pair, imperf. btwn.	150.00		
1152	4c American Woman.......................	.20	.20	
1153	4c 50-Star Flag	.20	.20	
1154	4c Pony Express	.20	.20	
1155	4c Employ the Handicapped..............	.20	.20	
1156	4c World Forestry Congress..............	.20	.20	
1157	4c Mexican Independence	.20	.20	
1158	4c U.S.-Japan Treaty......................	.20	.20	

1120

1121

1122

1123

1124

1125

1127

1128

1129

1130

1131

1132

1133

1135

1134

1136

1138

Scott No.	Description	Unused Value	Used Value	//////
1159	4c Ignacy Jan Paderewski, blue	.20	.20	
1160	8c Paderewski (1159), car., ultra & ocher	.20	.20	
1161	4c Robert A. Taft................................	.20	.20	
1162	4c Wheels of Freedom	.20	.20	
1163	4c Boys' Clubs of America	.20	.20	
1164	4c First Automated Post Office...........	.20	.20	
1165	4c Gustaf Mannerheim, blue.............	.20	.20	
1166	8c Mannerheim (1165), car., ultra & ocher	.20	.20	
1167	4c Camp Fire Girls............................	.20	.20	
1168	4c Giuseppe Garibaldi, green	.20	.20	
1169	8c Garibaldi (1168), carmine, ultra & ocher	.20	.20	
1170	4c Senator Walter F. George	.20	.20	
1171	4c Andrew Carnegie...........................	.20	.20	
1172	4c John Foster Dulles.........................	.20	.20	
1173	4c Echo I...	.20	.20	
1961				
1174	4c Mahatma Gandhi, red orange	.20	.20	
1175	8c Gandhi (1174), carmine, ultra & ocher	.20	.20	
1176	4c Range Conservation	.20	.20	
1177	4c Horace Greeley..............................	.20	.20	
1961-65				
1178	4c Firing on Fort Sumter....................	.20	.20	
1179	4c Battle of Shiloh.............................	.20	.20	
1180	5c Battle of Gettysburg	.20	.20	
1181	5c Battle of the Wilderness................	.20	.20	
1182	5c Surrender at Appomattox	.25	.20	
a.	Horiz. pair, imperf. vert.................	4,500.		
1961				
1183	4c Kansas Statehood	.20	.20	
1184	4c Senator George W. Norris..............	.20	.20	
1185	4c Naval Aviation	.20	.20	
1186	4c Workmen's Compensation	.20	.20	
1187	4c Frederic Remington.......................	.20	.20	
1188	4c Republic of China	.20	.20	
1189	4c Naismith - Basketball....................	.20	.20	
1190	4c Nursing	.20	.20	
1962				
1191	4c New Mexico Statehood..................	.20	.20	
1192	4c Arizona Statehood.........................	.20	.20	
1193	4c Project Mercury.............................	.20	.20	
1194	4c Malaria Eradication.......................	.20	.20	
1195	4c Charles Evans Hughes	.20	.20	
1196	4c Seattle World's Fair.......................	.20	.20	
1197	4c Louisiana Statehood......................	.20	.20	
1198	4c Homestead Act	.20	.20	
1199	4c Girl Scouts....................................	.20	.20	

1139

1140

1141

1142

1143

1144

1145

1146

1147

1149

1150

1152

1151

1154

1153

1155

1156   1157   1158   1159

1161   1162   1163

1164   1165   1167

1168   1170   1171   1172

1173   1174   1176

1177

1178

1179

1180

1181

1183

1184

1185

1191

1182

1186

1187

1193

1188

1189

1190

1192

Scott No.	Description	Unused Value	Used Value	//////
1200	4c Senator Brien McMahon	.20	.20	
1201	4c Apprenticeship	.20	.20	
1202	4c Sam Rayburn	.20	.20	
1203	4c Dag Hammarskjold, blk, brn and yel	.20	..20	
1204	4c Hammarskjold (1203), (yel inverted)	.20	.20	
1205	4c Christmas	.20	.20	
1206	4c Higher Education	.20	.20	
1207	4c Winslow Homer	.20	.20	
a.	Horiz. pair, imperf. btwn. and at right	6,750.		

1963-66

Scott No.	Description	Unused Value	Used Value	//////
1208	5c Flag, untagged	.20	.20	
a.	Tagged	.20	.20	
b.	Horiz. pair, imperf. btwn.	1,500.		

1962-66, Perf. 11x10½

Scott No.	Description	Unused Value	Used Value	//////
1209	1c Andrew Jackson, untagged	.20	.20	
a.	Tagged	.20	.20	
1213	5c George Washington, untagged	.20	.20	
a.	Booklet pane 5 + label	3.00	2.00	
b.	Tagged	.50	.20	
c.	As "a," tagged	2.00	1.50	
d.	Horiz. pair, imperf. btwn	2,000.		

Coil Stamps, Perf. 10 Vertically

Scott No.	Description	Unused Value	Used Value	//////
1225	1c Jackson (1209), untagged	.20	.20	
a.	Tagged	.20	.20	
1229	5c Washington (1213), untagged	1.10	.20	
a.	Tagged	1.40	.20	
b.	Imperf., pair	400.00		

1963

Scott No.	Description	Unused Value	Used Value	//////
1230	5c Carolina Charter	.20	.20	
1231	5c Food for Peace	.20	.20	
1232	5c West Virginia Statehood	.20	.20	
1233	5c Emancipation Proclamation	.20	.20	
1234	5c Alliance for Progress	.20	.20	
1235	5c Cordell Hull	.20	.20	
1236	5c Eleanor Roosevelt	.20	.20	
1237	5c Science	.20	.20	
1238	5c City Mail Delivery	.20	.20	
1239	5c Red Cross Centenary	.20	.20	
1240	5c Christmas, untagged	.20	.20	
a.	Tagged	.65	.50	
1241	5c John James Audubon	.20	.20	

1964

Scott No.	Description	Unused Value	Used Value	//////
1242	5c Sam Houston	.20	.20	
1243	5c Charles M. Russell	.20	.20	
1244	5c New York World's Fair	.20	.20	
1245	5c John Muir	.20	.20	

1195

1196

1202

1194

1197

1198

1199

1200

1201

1203

1206

1207

1205

1208

1209

1213

1230

1232

1233

Scott No.	Description	Unused Value	Used Value	/ / / / / /
1246	5c John F. Kennedy	.20	.20	
1247	5c New Jersey Tercentenary	.20	.20	
1248	5c Nevada Statehood	.20	.20	
1249	5c Register and Vote	.20	.20	
1250	5c William Shakespeare	.20	.20	
1251	5c Doctors Mayo	.20	.20	
1252	5c American Music	.20	.20	
a.	Blue omitted	1,000.		
1253	5c Homemakers	.20	.20	
1254	5c Christmas - Holly, untagged	.25	.20	
a.	Tagged	.60	.50	
b.	Printed on gummed side	—		
1255	5c Christmas - Mistletoe, untagged	.25	.20	
a.	Tagged	.60	.50	
1256	5c Christmas - Poinsettia, untagged	.25	.20	
a.	Tagged	.60	.50	
1257	5c Christmas - Conifer, untagged	.25	.20	
a.	Tagged	.60	.50	
b.	Block of 4, #1254-1257	1.00	1.00	
c.	Block of 4, #1254a-1257a	2.50	2.25	
1258	5c Verrazano-Narrows Bridge	.20	.20	
1259	5c Fine Arts	.20	.20	
1260	5c Amateur Radio	.20	.20	
1965				
1261	5c Battle of New Orleans	.20	.20	
1262	5c Physical Fitness - Sokol	.20	.20	
1263	5c Crusade against Cancer	.20	.20	
1264	5c Winston Churchill	.20	.20	
1265	5c Magna Carta	.20	.20	
1266	5c International Cooperation Year	.20	.20	
1267	5c Salvation Army	.20	.20	
1268	5c Dante Alighieri	.20	.20	
1269	5c Herbert Hoover	.20	.20	
1270	5c Robert Fulton	.20	.20	
1271	5c Florida Settlement	.20	.20	
a.	Yellow omitted	350.00		
1272	5c Traffic Safety	.20	.20	
1273	5c John Singleton Copley	.20	.20	
1274	11c Intl. Telecommunication Union	.35	.20	
1275	5c Adlai Stevenson	.20	.20	
1276	5c Christmas, untagged	.20	.20	
a.	Tagged	.75	.25	
1965-78, Perf. 11x10½, 10½ x11				
1278	1c Thomas Jefferson, tagged	.20	.20	
a.	Booklet pane of 8	1.00	.75	
b.	Booklet pane of 4 + 2 labels	.80	.60	
c.	Untagged (Bureau precanceled)		.20	

1234   1235   1238

1236   1237   1239

1240   1241   1242   1245

1243   1244   1246

1247   1248   1249   1250

Scott No.	Description	Unused Value	Used Value	/ / / / / /
1279	1¼c Albert Gallatin.................................	.20	.20	
1280	2c Frank Lloyd Wright, tagged..........	.20	.20	
a.	Booklet pane of 5 + label..............	1.25	.80	
b.	Untagged (Bureau precanceled)		.20	
c.	Booklet pane of 6	1.00	.75	
1281	3c Francis Parkman, tagged...............	.20	.20	
a.	Untagged (Bureau precanceled)		.20	
1282	4c Abraham Lincoln, untagged	.20	.20	
a.	Tagged..	.20	.20	
1283	5c Washington, untagged....................	.20	.20	
a.	Tagged..	.20	.20	
1283B	5c Washington, redrawn, tagged........	.20	.20	
d.	Untagged (Bureau precanceled)		.20	
1284	6c Franklin D. Roosevelt, untagged....	.20	.20	
a.	Tagged..	.20	.20	
b.	Booklet pane of 8	1.50	1.00	
c.	Booklet pane of 5 + label..............	1.50	1.00	
d.	Horiz. pair, imperf. between	—		
1285	8c Albert Einstein, untagged..............	.20	.20	
a.	Tagged..	.20	.20	
1286	10c Andrew Jackson, tagged	.20	.20	
b.	Untagged (Bureau precanceled)		.20	
1286A	12c Henry Ford, tagged.......................	.25	.20	
c.	Untagged (Bureau precanceled)		.25	
1287	13c John F. Kennedy, tagged...............	.30	.20	
a.	Untagged (Bureau precanceled)		.35	
1288	15c Oliver Wendell Holmes, magenta, tagged	.30	.20	
a.	Untagged (Bureau precanceled)		.30	
d.	Type II..	.55	.20	

Type II: The necktie does not touch coat at bottom.

Perf. 10

1288B	15c Holmes (1288), magenta, (from bklt. pane)	.30	.20	
c.	Booklet pane of 8	2.80	1.75	
e.	As "c," vert. imperf. btwn.	—		

Perf. 11x10½, 10½x11

1289	20c George C. Marshall, untagged	.40	.20	
a.	Tagged..	.40	.20	
1290	25c Frederick Douglass, rose lake untagged	.55	.20	
a.	Tagged..	.45	.20	
b.	25c magenta....................................	25.00	—	
1291	30c John Dewey, untagged	.65	.20	
a.	Tagged..	.50	.20	
1292	40c Thomas Paine, untagged	.80	.20	
a.	Tagged..	.65	.20	

1251

1252

1253

1254-1257

1258

1259

1260

1262

1263

1264

1261

1265

1266

Scott No.	Description	Unused Value	Used Value	/ / / / /
1293	50c Lucy Stone, untagged	1.00	.20	
a.	Tagged..............................	.80	.20	
1294	$1 Eugene O'Neill, untagged	2.25	.20	
a.	Tagged..............................	1.65	.20	
1295	$5 John Bassett Moore, untagged	9.50	2.25	
a.	Tagged..............................	8.00	2.00	

1966-81, Coil Stamps, Tagged, Perf. 10 Horizontally

1297	3c Francis Parkman (1281)	.20	.20	
a.	Imperf., pair..................................	30.00		
b.	Untagged (Bureau precanceled)		.20	
c.	As "b," imperf. pair.......................		6.00	
1298	6c Franklin D. Roosevelt (1284)	.20	.20	
a.	Imperf., pair..................................	2,250.		

Tagged Perf. 10 Vertically

1299	1c Thomas Jefferson (1278)	.20	.20	
a.	Untagged (Bureau precanceled)		.20	
b.	Imperf., pair..................................	30.00	—	
1303	4c Abraham Lincoln (1282)...............	.20	.20	
a.	Untagged (Bureau precanceled)		.20	
b.	Imperf., pair..................................	900.00		
1304	5c George Washington (1283)	.20	.20	
a.	Untagged (Bureau precanceled)		.20	
b.	Imperf., pair..................................	175.00		
e.	As "a," imperf. pair		375.00	
1304C	5c Washington, redrawn (1283B).......	.20	.20	
d.	Imperf., pair..................................	750.00		
1305	6c Franklin D. Roosevelt....................	.20	.20	
a.	Imperf., pair..................................	75.00		
b.	Untagged (Bureau precanceled)		.20	
1305E	15c Oliver Wendell Holmes (1288), type I	.25	.20	
f.	Untagged (Bureau precanceled)		.30	
g.	Imperf., pair..................................	30.00		
h.	Pair, imperf. btwn.	200.00		
i.	Type II..	.60	.20	
j.	Imperf., pair, type II	85.00		
1305C	$1 Eugene O'Neill (1294)...................	2.00	.40	
d.	Imperf., pair..................................	2,250.		

1966

1306	5c Migratory Bird Treaty.....................	.20	.20	
1307	5c Humane Treatment of Animals......	.20	.20	
1308	5c Indiana Statehood..........................	.20	.20	
1309	5c American Circus............................	.20	.20	
1310	5c SIPEX	.20	.20	
1311	5c SIPEX Souvenir Sheet, imperf......	.20	.20	
1312	5c Bill of Rights.................................	.20	.20	

1267

1268

1269

1271

1270

1272

1273

1274

1275

1276

1278

1279

1280

1281

1282

1283

1283B

1284

1285

Redrawn

Scott No.	Description	Unused Value	Used Value	//////
1313	5c Polish Millennium	.20	.20	
1314	5c National Park Service, untagged...	.20	.20	
a.	Tagged	.30	.25	
1315	5c Marine Corps Reserve, untagged..	.20	.20	
a.	Tagged	.30	.20	
b.	Black & bister (engr.) omitted	*16,000.*		
1316	5c Women's Clubs, untagged	.20	.20	
a.	Tagged	.30	.20	
1317	5c Johnny Appleseed, untagged	.20	.20	
a.	Tagged	.30	.20	
1318	5c Beautification of America, untagged	.20	.20	
a.	Tagged	.30	.20	
1319	5c Great River Road, untagged	.20	.20	
a.	Tagged	.30	.20	
1320	5c Savings Bond, untagged	.20	.20	
a.	Tagged	.30	.20	
b.	Red, dark blue & black omitted	*4,250.*		
c.	Dark blue (engr.) omitted	*8,500.*		
1321	5c Christmas, untagged	.20	.20	
a.	Tagged	.30	.20	
1322	5c Mary Cassatt, untagged	.20	.20	
a.	Tagged	.30	.25	
1967				
1323	5c National Grange	.20	.20	
1324	5c Canada Centenary	.20	.20	
1325	5c Erie Canal	.20	.20	
1326	5c Search for Peace	.20	.20	
1327	5c Henry David Thoreau.15	.20		
1328	5c Nebraska Statehood	.20	.20	
1329	5c Voice of America	.20	.20	
1330	5c Davy Crockett	.20	.20	
a.	Vert. pair, imperf. btwn.	*6,000.*		
b.	Green (engr.) omitted	—		
c.	Black & green (engr.) omitted	—		
1331	5c Astronaut	.50	.20	
1332	5c Gemini 4 Capsule	.50	.20	
b.	Pair, #1331-1332	1.10	*1.25*	
1333	5c Urban Planning	.20	.20	
1334	5c Finnish Independence	.20	.20	
1335	5c Thomas Eakins	.20	.20	
1336	5c Christmas	.20	.20	
1337	5c Mississippi Statehood	.20	.20	
1968-71, Perf. 11				
1338	6c Flag	.20	.20	
k.	Vert. pair, imperf. btwn.	*550.00*		
Coil Stamp, Perf. 10 Vertically				
1338A	6c Flag (1338)	.20	.20	
b.	Imperf., pair	*500.00*		

1286   1286A   1287   1288   1289

1290   1291   1292   1293   1294

1295   1305   1306

1307

1308   1309

1310

1312   1313

1311

Scott No.	Description	Unused Value	Used Value	//////

Perf. 11x10½

Scott No.	Description	Unused Value	Used Value
1338D	6c Flag (1338)	.20	.20
e.	Horiz. pair, imperf. btwn.	175.00	
1338F	8c Flag (1338), red denomination	.20	.20
i.	Vert. pair, imperf.	45.00	
j.	Horiz. pair, imperf. btwn.	55.00	
p.	Slate green omitted	400.00	
t.	Horiz. pair, imperf. vertically	—	

Coil Stamp, Perf. 10 Vertically

Scott No.	Description	Unused Value	Used Value
1338G	8c Flag (1338), red denomination	.20	.20
h.	Imperf., pair	55.00	

1968

Scott No.	Description	Unused Value	Used Value
1339	6c Illinois Statehood	.20	.20
1340	6c HemisFair '68	.20	.20
a.	White omitted	1,250.	
1341	$1 Airlift	2.25	1.25
1342	6c Support our Youth	.20	.20
1343	6c Law and Order	.20	.20
1344	6c Register and Vote	.20	.20
1345	6c Fort Moultrie Flag	.40	.25
1346	6c Fort McHenry Flag	.30	.25
1347	6c Washington's Cruisers Flag	.25	.25
1348	6c Bennington Flag	.25	.25
1349	6c Rhode Island Flag	.25	.25
1350	6c First Stars and Stripes	.25	.25
1351	6c Bunker Hill Flag	.25	.25
1352	6c Grand Union Flag	.25	.25
1353	6c Philadelphia Light Horse Flag	.25	.25
1354	6c First Navy Jack	.25	.25
a.	Strip of 10, #1345-1354	2.75	3.25
1355	6c Walt Disney	.20	.20
a.	Ocher (Walt Disney, 6c, etc.) omitted	600.00	—
b.	Vert. pair, imperf. horiz.	700.00	
c.	Imperf., pair	675.00	
d.	Black omitted	1,500.	
e.	Horiz. pair, imperf. btwn.	4,750.	
f.	Blue omitted	1,750.	
1356	6c Father Marquette	.20	.20
1357	6c Daniel Boone	.20	.20
1358	6c Arkansas River Navigation	.20	.20
1359	6c Leif Erikson	.20	.20
1360	6c Cherokee Strip	.20	.20
1361	6c John Trumbull	.20	.20
b.	Black (engr.) omitted	11,000.	
1362	6c Waterfowl Conservation	.20	.20
a.	Vert. pair, imperf. btwn.	550.00	—
b.	Red & dark blue omitted	900.00	
c.	Red omitted		1,750.

1315

1317

1319

1320

1314

1316

1318

1321

1322

1324

1325

1326

1328

1323

1327

1329

1330

Scott No.	Description	Unused Value	Used Value	//////
1363	6c Christmas, tagged......................	.20	.20	
a.	Untagged	.20	.20	
b.	Imperf., pair, tagged	225.00		
c.	Light yellow omitted	65.00	—	
d.	Imperf., pair, untagged	300.00		
1364	6c Chief Joseph	.20	.20	
1969				
1365	6c Beautification - Cities	.25	.20	
1366	6c Beautification - Parks....................	.25	.20	
1367	6c Beautification - Highways............	.25	.20	
1368	6c Beautification - Streets.................	.25	.20	
a.	Block of 4, #1365-1368................	1.25	1.75	
1369	6c American Legion..........................	.20	.20	
1370	6c Grandma Moses...........................	.20	.20	
a.	Horiz. pair, imperf. btwn.	225.00	—	
b.	Black and Prussian blue omitted...	800.00		
1371	6c Apollo 8......................................	.20	.20	
1372	6c W.C. Handy	.20	.20	
1373	6c California Settlement....................	.20	.20	
1374	6c John Wesley Powell	.20	.20	
1375	6c Alabama Statehood	.20	.20	
1376	6c Douglas Fir	.35	.20	
1377	6c Lady's Slipper..............................	.35	.20	
1378	6c Ocotillo	.35	.20	
1379	6c Franklinia....................................	.35	.20	
a.	Block of 4, #1376-1379................	1.50	2.50	
1380	6c Dartmouth College Case	.20	.20	
1381	6c Professional Baseball	.65	.20	
a.	Black (1869-1969, United States, 6c, Professional Baseball) omitted....	1,100.		
1382	6c Intercollegiate Football.................	.20	.20	
1383	6c Dwight D. Eisenhower.................	.20	.20	
1384	6c Christmas.....................................	.20	.20	
	Precanceled....................................	.50	.20	
b.	Imperf., pair...................................	1,000.		
c.	Light green omitted.......................	22.50		
d.	Lt green, red & yellow omitted.....	950.00	—	
e.	Yellow omitted...............................	3,000.		
g.	Red & yellow omitted	—		
1385	6c Hope for the Crippled...................	.20	.20	
1386	6c William M. Harnett	.20	.20	
1970				
1387	6c American Bald Eagle	.20	.20	
1388	6c African Elephant Herd	.20	.20	
1389	6c Haida Ceremonial Canoe	.20	.20	
1390	6c Age of Reptiles.............................	.20	.20	
a.	Block of 4, #1387-1390.................	.55	.80	
1391	6c Maine Statehood...........................	.20	.20	

1331-1332

1333

1334

1336

1339

1335

1337

1338

1341

1342

1340

1343

1344

Scott No.	Description	Unused Value	Used Value	/ / / / / /
1392	6c Wildlife Conservation	.20	.20	☐☐☐☐☐

1970-74, Tagged, Perf. 11x10½ , 10½ x11, 11 (#1394)

1393	6c Dwight D. Eisenhower, untagged..	.20	.20	☐☐☐☐☐
a.	Booklet pane of 8	1.50	.75	☐☐☐☐☐
b.	Booklet pane of 5 + label..............	1.50	.75	☐☐☐☐☐
c.	Untagged (Bureau precanceled)....		.20	☐☐☐☐☐
1393D	7c Benjamin Franklin, tagged	.20	.20	☐☐☐☐☐
e.	Untagged (Bureau precanceled)....		.20	☐☐☐☐☐
1394	8c Eisenhower	.20	.20	☐☐☐☐☐
b.	Red omitted.	—		☐☐☐☐☐
c.	Red and blue omitted.	—		☐☐☐☐☐
1395	8c Eisenhower (1393), deep claret (from bklt. pane)	.20	.20	☐☐☐☐☐
a.	Booklet pane of 8	1.80	1.25	☐☐☐☐☐
b.	Booklet pane of 6	1.25	1.10	☐☐☐☐☐
c.	Booklet pane of 4 + 2 labels	1.65	1.00	☐☐☐☐☐
d.	Booklet pane of 7 + label..............	1.90	1.10	☐☐☐☐☐
e.	Vert. pair, imperf btwn.	600.00		☐☐☐☐☐
1396	8c Postal Service Emblem.................	.20	.20	☐☐☐☐☐
1397	14c Fiorello LaGuardia, tagged	.25	.20	☐☐☐☐☐
a.	Untagged (Bureau precanceled)....		.25	☐☐☐☐☐
1398	16c Ernie Pyle, tagged	.30	.20	☐☐☐☐☐
a.	Untagged (Bureau precanceled)....		.35	☐☐☐☐☐
1399	18c Dr. Elizabeth Blackwell................	.35	.20	☐☐☐☐☐
1400	21c Amadeo P. Giannini......................	.40	.20	☐☐☐☐☐

Coil Stamps, Perf. 10 Vertically

1401	6c Eisenhower (1393), dk bl gray, tagged	.20	.20	☐☐☐☐☐
a.	Untagged (Bureau precanceled)....		.20	☐☐☐☐☐
b.	Imperf., pair...............................	2,000.		☐☐☐☐☐
1402	8c Eisenhower (1393), dp claret, tagged	.20	.20	☐☐☐☐☐
a.	Imperf., pair.................................	45.00		☐☐☐☐☐
b.	Untagged (Bureau precanceled)....		.20	☐☐☐☐☐
c.	Pair, imperf. btwn.	6,250.		☐☐☐☐☐

1970

1405	6c Edgar Lee Masters......................	.20	.20	☐☐☐☐☐
1406	6c Woman Suffrage...........................	.20	.20	☐☐☐☐☐
1407	6c South Carolina............................	.20	.20	☐☐☐☐☐
1408	6c Stone Mountain Memorial	.20	.20	☐☐☐☐☐
1409	6c Fort Snelling...............................	.20	.20	☐☐☐☐☐
1410	6c Save Our Soil..............................	.25	.20	☐☐☐☐☐
1411	6c Save Our Cities...........................	.25	.20	☐☐☐☐☐
1412	6c Save Our Water...........................	.25	.20	☐☐☐☐☐
1413	6c Save Our Air...............................	.25	.20	☐☐☐☐☐
a.	Block of 4, #1410-1413..................	1.10	1.50	☐☐☐☐☐
1414	6c Christmas - Religious...................	.20	.20	☐☐☐☐☐
a.	Precanceled...................................	.20	.20	☐☐☐☐☐
b.	Black omitted	550.00		☐☐☐☐☐
c.	As "a," blue omitted	1,500.		☐☐☐☐☐

1345

1346

1347

1348

1349

1350

1351

1352

1353

1354

1356

1357

1358

1355

1359

1361

1363

1360

1362

Scott No.	Description	Unused Value	Used Value	/ / / / / /
1415	6c Christmas - Locomotive	.30	.20	
a.	Precanceled	.75	.20	
b.	Black omitted	2,500.		
1416	6c Christmas - Toy Horse	.30	.20	
a.	Precanceled	.75	.20	
b.	Black omitted	2,500.		
c.	Imperf., pair (#1416, 1418)		4,000.	
1417	6c Christmas - Tricycle	.30	.20	
a.	Precanceled	.75	.20	
b.	Black omitted	2,500.		
1418	6c Christmas - Doll Carriage	.30	.20	
a.	Precanceled	.75	.20	
b.	Block of 4, #1415-1418	1.25	1.75	
c.	As "b," precanceled	3.25	3.75	
d.	Black omitted	2,500.		
e.	As "b," black omitted.	10,000.		
1419	6c United Nations	.20	.20	
1420	6c Landing of the Pilgrims	.20	.20	
a.	Orange & yellow omitted	900.00		
1421	6c Disabled American Veterans	.20	.20	
1422	6c Servicemen	.20	.20	
a.	Pair, #1421-1422	.30	.40	
1971				
1423	6c Wool Industry	.20	.20	
b.	Teal blue ("United States") omitted	—		
1424	6c General Douglas MacArthur	.20	.20	
a.	Red omitted.	—		
1425	6c Blood Donors	.20	.20	
1426	8c Missouri Statehood	.20	.20	
1427	8c Trout	.20	.20	
a.	red omitted		1,250.	
1428	8c Alligator	.20	.20	
1429	8c Polar Bear	.20	.20	
1430	8c California Condor	.20	.20	
a.	Block of 4, #1427-1430	.80	1.00	
b.	As "a," lt grn & dk grn omitted from #1427-1428	4,500.		
c.	As "a," red omitted from #1427, 1429-1430	7,500.		
1431	8c Antarctic Treaty	.20	.20	
b.	Both colors omitted	500.00		
1432	8c Bicentennial Emblem	.20	.20	
a.	Gray & black omitted	500.00		
b.	Gray (U.S. Postage 8c) omitted	900.00		
1433	8c John Sloan	.20	.20	
b.	Red engr. ("John Sloan" and "8" omitted	—		
1434	8c Lunar Module	.20	.20	
1435	8c Lunar Rover	.20	.20	

1364

1365-1368

1369

1370

1371

1373

1372

1374

1375

1376-1379

Scott No.	Description	Unused Value	Used Value	/ / / / / /
b.	Pair, #1434-1435	.40	.45	
d.	As "b," blue & red (litho.) omitted	1,500.		
1436	8c Emily Dickinson...........................	.20	.20	
a.	Black & olive (engr.) omitted	750.00		
b.	Pale rose omitted	7,500.		
c.	Red omitted	—		
1437	8c San Juan....................................	.20	.20	
1438	8c Prevent Drug Abuse	.20	.20	
1439	8c CARE	.20	.20	
a.	Black omitted	4,750.		
1440	8c Decatur House	.20	.20	
1441	8c Whaler Charles W. Morgan	.20	.20	
1442	8c Cable Car..................................	.20	.20	
1443	8c San Xavier del Bac Mission..........	.20	.20	
a.	Block of 4, #1440-1443................	.75	1.00	
b.	As "a," black brown omitted	2,250.		
c.	As "a," ocher omitted	—		
1444	8c Christmas - Religious....................	.20	.20	
a.	Gold omitted.................................	550.00		
1445	8c Christmas - Partridge....................	.20	.20	
1972				
1446	8c Sidney Lanier	.20	.20	
1447	8c Peace Corps	.20	.20	
1448	2c Cape Hatteras - Ship....................	.20	.20	
1449	2c Cape Hatteras - Lighthouse..........	.20	.20	
1450	2c Cape Hatteras - Three Gulls	.20	.20	
1451	2c Cape Hatteras - Dunes................	.20	.20	
a.	Block of 4, #1448-1451................	.25	.45	
b.	As "a," black (litho.) omitted	2,250.		
1452	6c Wolf Trap Farm..........................	.20	.20	
1453	8c Yellowstone................................	.20	.20	
1454	15c Mt. McKinley	.30	.20	
b.	Yellow omitted................................	—		
1455	8c Family Planning..........................	.20	.20	
a.	Yellow omitted................................	1,250.		
b.	Dark brown & olive omitted	—		
c.	Dark brown omitted.......................	9,500.		
1456	8c Glass Blower..............................	.20	.20	
1457	8c Silversmith.................................	.20	.20	
1458	8c Wigmaker	.20	.20	
1459	8c Hatter......................................	.20	.20	
a.	Block of 4, #1456-1459................	.65	.90	
1460	6c Olympics - Bicycling...................	.20	.20	
1461	8c Olympics - Bobsledding...............	.20	.20	
1462	15c Olympics - Running	.30	.20	
1463	8c Parent Teacher Association...........	.20	.20	
1464	8c Fur Seal	.20	.20	
1465	8c Cardinal....................................	.20	.20	

1380

1381

1382

1383

1384

1385

1387-1390

1386

1391

1392

1393   1393D   1394   1396

1397   1398   1399   1400

1405   1406   1407

1408   1409

1410-1413

111

1415-1418

1414

1419

1420

1421-1422

1423

1424

1425

1426

Scott No.	Description	Unused Value	Used Value	/ / / / / /
1466	8c Brown Pelican	.20	.20	
1467	8c Bighorn Sheep	.20	.20	
a.	Block of 4, #1464-1467	.65	.90	
b.	As "a," brown omitted	4,000.		
c.	As "a," green & blue omitted	4,500.		
d.	As "a," red & brown omitted	3,000.		
1468	8c Mail Order Business	.20	.20	
1469	8c Osteopathic Medicine	.20	.20	
1470	8c Tom Sawyer	.20	.20	
a.	Horiz. pair, imperf. btwn.	4,500.		
b.	Red & black (engr.) omitted	1,800.		
c.	Yellow & tan (litho.) omitted	2,400.		
1471	8c Christmas - Religious	.20	.20	
a.	Pink omitted	140.00		
b.	Black omitted	4,000.		
1472	8c Christmas - Santa Claus	.20	.20	
1473	8c Pharmacy	.20	.20	
a.	Blue & orange omitted	800.00		
b.	Blue omitted	2,100.		
c.	Orange omitted	2,100.		
1474	8c Stamp Collecting	.20	.20	
a.	Black (litho.) omitted	600.00		
1973				
1475	8c Love	.20	.20	
1476	8c Printer	.20	.20	
1477	8c Posting a Broadside	.20	.20	
1478	8c Postrider	.20	.20	
a.	Red omitted	—		
1479	8c Drummer	.20	.20	
1480	8c Boston Tea Party - upper left	.20	.20	
1481	8c Boston Tea Party - upper right	.20	.20	
1482	8c Boston Tea Party - lower left	.20	.20	
1483	8c Boston Tea Party - lower right	.20	.20	
a.	Block of 4, #1480-1483	.65	.90	
b.	As "a," black (engr.) omitted	1,500.		
c.	As "a," black (litho.) omitted	1,400.		
1484	8c George Gershwin	.20	.20	
a.	Vert. pair, imperf. horiz.	240.00		
1485	8c Robinson Jeffers	.20	.20	
a.	Vert. pair, imperf. horiz.	250.00		
1486	8c Henry Ossawa Tanner	.20	.20	
1487	8c Willa Cather	.20	.20	
a.	Vert. pair, imperf. horiz.	275.00		
1488	8c Nicolaus Copernicus	.20	.20	
a.	Orange omitted	1,000.		
b.	Black (engraved) omitted	900.00		
1489	8c Stamp Counter	.20	.20	
1490	8c Mail Collection	.20	.20	

1427-1430

1431

1432

1433

1434-1435

1436

1437

1438

1439

Scott No.	Description	Unused Value	Used Value	/ / / / / /
1491	8c Letters on Conveyor Belt..............	.20	.20	
1492	8c Parcel Post Sorting	.20	.20	
1493	8c Mail Canceling	.20	.20	
1494	8c Manual Letter Routing	.20	.20	
1495	8c Electronic Letter Routing.............	.20	.20	
1496	8c Loading Mail on Truck.................	.20	.20	
1497	8c Mailman..	.20	.20	
1498	8c Rural Mail Delivery	.20	.20	
a.	Strip of 10, #1489-1498	1.75	2.00	
1499	8c Harry S Truman............................	.20	.20	
1500	6c Spark Coil and Spark Gap............	.20	.20	
1501	8c Transistors	.20	.20	
a.	Black (inscriptions & U.S. 8c) omitted	450.00		
b.	Tan (background) & lilac omitted.	1,250.		
1502	15c Microphone, Tubes and Speaker ...	.30	.20	
a.	Black (inscriptions & U.S. 15c) omitted	1,350.		
1503	15c Lyndon B. Johnson........................	.20	.20	
a.	Horiz. pair, imperf. vert................	350.00		
1973-74				
1504	8c Angus Cattle.................................	.20	.20	
a.	Green & red brown omitted	950.00		
b.	Vert. pair, imperf. between............	—		
1505	10c Chautauqua	.20	.20	
a.	Black (litho.) omitted		2,000.	
1506	10c Kansas Hard Winter Wheat...........	.20	.20	
a.	Black & blue (engr.) omitted.........	750.00		
1973				
1507	8c Christmas - Religious....................	.20	.20	
1508	8c Christmas - Tree	.20	.20	
a.	Vert. pair, imperf. btwn.	300.00		
1973-74, Tagged, Perf. 11x10½				
1509	10c Crossed Flags	.20	.20	
a.	Horiz. pair, imperf. btwn...............	50.00	—	
b.	Blue omitted	175.00	—	
c.	Vert. pair, imperf.	950.00		
d.	Horiz. pair, imperf. vert................	1,000.		
1510	10c Jefferson Memorial, tagged...........	.20	.20	
a.	Untagged (Bureau precanceled)....	.20		
b.	Booklet pane of 5 + label..............	1.65	.90	
c.	Booklet pane of 8	1.65	1.00	
d.	Booklet pane of 6	5.25	1.75	
e.	Vert. pair, imperf. horiz.	525.00		
f.	Vert. pair, imperf. btwn.	—		
1511	10c Zip Code.......................................	.20	.20	
a.	Yellow omitted...............................	65.00		
Coil Stamps, Perf. 10 Vertically				
1518	6.3c Liberty Bell, tagged.....................	.20	.20	
a.	Untagged (Bureau precanceled)....		.20	

1440-1443

1444

1445

1446

1447

1452

1454

1448-1451

1453

Scott No.	Description	Unused Value	Used Value	/ / / / / /
b.	Imperf., pair..................................	210.00		
c.	As "a," imperf. pair		100.00	
1519	10c Crossed Flags (1509)....................	.20	.20	
a.	Imperf., pair..................................	37.50		
1520	10c Jefferson Memorial (1510), tagged	.25	.20	
a.	Untagged (Bureau precanceled)....		.25	
b.	Imperf., pair..................................	40.00		

1974

Scott No.	Description	Unused Value	Used Value	/ / / / / /
1525	10c Veterans of Foreign Wars	.20	.20	
b.	Blue omitted..................................	—		
1526	10c Robert Frost.................................	.20	.20	
1527	10c Expo '74 World's Fair...................	.20	.20	
1528	10c Horse Racing................................	.20	.20	
a.	Blue (Horse Racing) omitted	875.00		
b.	Red (U.S. postage 10 cents) omitted	—		
1529	10c Skylab.......................................	.20	.20	
a.	Vert. pair, imperf. btwn.	—		
1530	10c Raphael......................................	.20	.20	
1531	10c Hokusai......................................	.20	.20	
1532	10c Peto..	.20	.20	
1533	10c Liotard.......................................	.20	.20	
1534	10c Terborch.....................................	.20	.20	
1535	10c Chardin......................................	.20	.20	
1536	10c Gainsborough	.20	.20	
1537	10c Goya..	.20	.20	
a.	Block or strip of 8, #1530-1537....	1.75	1.60	
b.	As "a" (block), imperf. vert.	7,000.		
1538	10c Petrified Wood............................	.20	.20	
a.	Light blue & yellow omitted	—		
1539	10c Tourmaline..................................	.20	.20	
a.	Light blue omitted	—		
b.	Black & purple omitted.................	—		
1540	10c Amethyst....................................	.20	.20	
a.	Light blue & yellow omitted	—		
1541	10c Rhodochrosite.............................	.20	.20	
a.	Block or strip of 4, #1538-1541....	.80	.90	
b.	As "a," lt blue & yellow omitted...	1,900.		
c.	Light blue omitted	—		
d.	Black & red omitted......................	—		
1542	10c Kentucky Settlement	.20	.20	
a.	Dull black (litho.) omitted.............	750.00		
b.	Green (engr. & litho.), black (engr. & litho.), & blue omitted ..	3,000.		
c.	Green (engr.) omitted	—		
d.	Green (engr.) & black (litho.) omitted	—		
f.	Blue (litho.) omitted	—		
1543	10c Carpenter's Hall...........................	.20	.20	
1544	10c "We ask but for peace . . . "..........	.20	.20	
1545	10c "Deriving their just powers . . . "..	.20	.20	
1546	10c Independence Hall........................	.20	.20	

1455

1456-1459

1460

1461

1462

1463

1464-1467

1468   1469

1470   1471   1472

1473   1474   1475

1476   1477

1478   1479

1480-1483

1484

1485

1486

1487

1488

Scott No.	Description	Unused Value	Used Value	/ / / / / /
a.	Block of 4, #1543-1546...............	.80	.90	
1547	10c Energy Conservation	.20	.20	
a.	Blue & orange omitted..................	850.00		
b.	Orange & green omitted...............	600.00		
c.	Green omitted..............................	825.00		
1548	10c Legend of Sleepy Hollow..............	.20	.20	
1549	10c Retarded Children	.20	.20	
1550	10c Christmas - Angel.........................	.20	.20	
1551	10c Christmas - Currier & Ives............	.20	.20	
a.	Buff omitted..................................	35.00		
1552	10c Christmas - Dove..........................	.20	.20	
1975				
1553	10c Benjamin West.............................	.20	.20	
1554	10c Paul Laurence Dunbar..................	.20	.20	
a.	Imperf., pair.................................	1,300.		
1555	10c D.W. Griffith................................	.20	.20	
a.	Brown (engr.) omitted	625.00		
1556	10c Pioneer 10...................................	.20	.20	
a.	Red & dark yellow omitted	1,400.		
b.	Dark blue (engr.) omitted	950.00		
d.	Dark yellow omitted......................	—		
1557	10c Mariner 10..................................	.20	.20	
a.	Red omitted	450.00	—	
b.	Ultra & bister omitted	2,000.		
1558	10c Collective Bargaining...................	.20	.20	
1559	8c Sybil Ludington............................	.20	.20	
a.	Back inscription omitted	210.00		
1560	10c Salem Poor..................................	.20	.20	
a.	Back inscription omitted	210.00		
1561	10c Haym Salomon............................	.20	.20	
a.	Back inscription omitted	210.00		
b.	Red omitted	250.00		
1562	18c Peter Francisco	.35	.20	
1563	10c Battle of Lexington & Concord	.20	.20	
a.	Vert. pair, imperf. horiz.	425.00		
1564	10c Battle of Bunker Hill....................	.20	.20	
1565	10c Continental Army.........................	.20	.20	
1566	10c Continental Navy.........................	.20	.20	
1567	10c Continental Marines	.20	.20	
1568	10c American Militia	.20	.20	
a.	Block of 4, #1565-1568................	.85	.90	
1569	10c Apollo and Soyuz Linked..............	.20	.20	
1570	10c Apollo and Soyuz Separated	.20	.20	
a.	Pair, #1569-1570	.45	.40	
c.	As "a," vert. pair, imperf. horiz.....	1,750.		
d.	As "a," yellow omitted	—		
1571	10c International Women's Year...........	.20	.20	
1572	10c Stagecoach & Truck	.20	.20	
1573	10c Locomotives	.20	.20	

1489-1493

1494-1498

1499

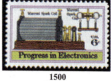

1500

1501

1502

Scott No.	Description	Unused Value	Used Value	//////
1574	10c Airplanes	.20	.20	
1575	10c Satellites	.20	.20	
a.	Block of 4, #1572-1575	.85	.90	
b.	As "a," red (10c) omitted	9,500.		
1576	10c World Peace Through Law	.20	.20	
b.	Horiz. pair, imperf. vert.	—		
1577	10c Banking	.25	.20	
1578	10c Commerce	.25	.20	
a.	Pair, #1577-1578	.50	.40	
b.	As "a," brown & blue (litho.) omitted	2,000.		
c.	As "a," brown, blue & yellow (litho.) omitted	2,500.		
1579	(10c) Christmas - Religious	.20	.20	
a.	Imperf., pair	90.00		
1580	(10c) Christmas Card, by Louis Prang, perf. 11	.20	.20	
a.	Imperf., pair	90.00		
c.	Perf. 10.9	.25	.20	
1580B	(10c) Christmas Card, by Louis Prang, 1878, perf. 10.5 x 11.3 (1580)	.65	.20	

1975-81, Perf. 11x10½

Scott No.	Description	Unused Value	Used Value	//////
1581	1c Inkwell & Quill, tagged	.20	.20	
a.	Untagged (Bureau precanceled)		.20	
1582	2c Speaker's Stand, red brn, *grnish*, tagged	.20	.20	
a.	Untagged (Bureau precanceled)		.20	
b.	Cream paper		.20	
1584	3c Ballot Box, tagged	.20	.20	
a.	Untagged (Bureau precanceled)		.20	
1585	4c Books, tagged	.20	.20	
a.	Untagged (Bureau precanceled)		1.25	
1590	9c Capitol, slate green (from bklt. pane #1623a), perf. 11 x 10½	.45	.20	
1590A	9c Capitol (from bklt. pane #1623Bc), perf. 10 x 9¾ (1590)	22.50	15.00	
1591	9c Capitol, slate green, *gray*	.20	.20	
a.	Untagged (Bureau precanceled)		.20	
1592	10c Justice, tagged	.20	.20	
a.	Untagged (Bureau precanceled)		.25	
1593	11c Printing Press	.20	.20	
1594	12c Torch	.25	.20	
1595	13c Liberty Bell (from bklt. pane)	.30	.20	
a.	Booklet pane of 6	2.25	*1.00*	
b.	Booklet pane of 7 + label	2.25	*1.00*	
c.	Booklet pane of 8	2.25	*1.00*	
d.	Booklet pane of 5 + label	1.75	*1.00*	
e.	Vert. pair, imperf. btwn.	*800.00*		

Perf. 11

Scott No.	Description	Unused Value	Used Value	//////
1596	13c Eagle & Shield	.25	.20	

123

1503

1507

1508

1504

1505

1506

1509

1510

1511

1518

1525

1526

1527

1528

1529

1530-1537

1538-1541

1543-1546

1542

1547

1548

1549

1550

1553

1554

1551

1552

1555

1556

1557

1559

1560

1561

1562

127

1558

1563

1564

1565-1568

1569-1570

Scott No.	Description	Unused Value	Used Value	/ / / / / /
a.	Imperf., pair	*50.00*	—	
b.	Yellow omitted	*160.00*		
1597	15c Flag	.30	.20	
a.	Vert. pair, imperf.	*20.00*		
b.	Gray omitted	*600.00*		
c.	Vert. strip of 3, imperf. btwn. & at top or bottom	—		

Perf. 11x10 1/2

1598	15c Flag (1597, from bklt. pane)	.40	.20	
a.	Booklet pane of 8	4.25	*.80*	
1599	16c Statue of Liberty	.35	.20	
1603	24c Old North Church, Boston	.50	.20	
1604	28c Fort Nisqually, Washington	.55	.20	
1605	29c Sandy Hook Lighthouse, N.J.	.60	.20	
1606	30c School, North Dakota	.55	.20	

Perf. 11

1608	50c Iron "Betty" Lamp	.85	.20	
a.	Black omitted	*300.00*		
b.	Vert. pair, imperf. horiz.	*1,750.*		
1610	$1 Rush Lamp & Candle Holder	2.00	.20	
a.	Brown (engraved) omitted	*250.00*		
b.	Tan, orange & yellow omitted	*350.00*		
c.	Brown inverted	*13,000.*		
1611	$2 Kerosene Lamp	3.75	.75	
1612	$5 Railroad Lantern	8.25	1.75	

Coil Stamps, Perf. 10 Vertically, Tagged

1613	3.1c Guitar	.20	.20	
a.	Untagged (Bureau precanceled)		.50	
b.	Imperf., pair	*1,400.*		
1614	7.7c Saxhorns	.20	.20	
a.	Untagged (Bureau precanceled)		.35	
b.	As "a," imperf., pair	*1,600.*		
1615	7.9c Drum	.20	.20	
a.	Untagged (Bureau precanceled)		.20	
b.	Imperf., pair	*600.00*		
1615C	8.4c Piano	.20	.20	
d.	Untagged (Bureau precanceled)	.30	.30	
e.	As "d," pair, imperf. btwn.		60.00	
f.	As "d," imperf., pair		17.50	
1616	9c Capitol (1590), slate grn, *gray*	.20	.20	
a.	Imperf., pair	*160.00*		
b.	Untagged (Bureau precanceled)		.35	
c.	As "b," imperf., pair		*700.00*	
1617	10c Justice (1592)	.20	.20	
a.	Untagged (Bureau precanceled)		.25	
b.	Imperf., pair	*60.00*		
1618	13c Liberty Bell (1595)	.25	.20	
a.	Untagged (Bureau precanceled)		.45	
b.	Imperf., pair	*25.00*		
g.	Vertical pair, imperf. btwn.	—		

1571   1576

1572-1575

1577-1578

1579   1580

1581	1582	1584	1585
1591	1592	1593	1594
1595	1596	1597	1599
1603	1604	1605	1606
1608	1610	1611	1612

1613   1614

1615

1615C

1622

1623

1629-1631

1632

Scott No.	Description	Unused Value	Used Value	/ / / / / /
h.	As "a," imperf., pair		—	
1618C 15c	Flag (1597)	.40	.20	
d.	Imperf., pair	25.00		
e.	Pair, imperf. btwn.	*150.00*		
f.	Gray omitted	*40.00*		
1619 16c	Statue of Liberty (1599)	.35	.20	
a.	Block tagging	.50	.20	

1975-81, Perf. 11x10¾

1622 13c	Flag, Independence Hall	.25	.20	
a.	Horizontal pair, imperf. btwn.	*50.00*		
b.	Vertical pair, imperf.	*1,100.*		
e.	Horiz. pair, imperf. vert.	—		
1622C 13c	Flag, Independence Hall, perf. 11¼ (1622)	1.00	.25	
d.	Vert. pair, imperf.	*150.00*		
1623 13c	Flag over Capitol (from bklt. pane) perf. 11x10½	.25	.20	
a.	Bklt. pane of 8, #1590 + 7 #1623	2.25	*1.25*	
d.	Pair, #1590 & 1623	.70	*1.00*	
1623B 13c	Flag over Capitol (from bklt. pane #1623Bc), perf. 10 x 9¾ (1623)	.80	.80	
c.	Booklet pane, 1 #1590A + 7 #1623B	29.00	—	
e.	Pair, #1590A & #1623B	24.00	22.50	

Coil Stamp, Perf. 10 Vertically

1625 13c	Flag, Independence Hall (1622)	.25	.20	
a.	Imperf., pair	25.00		

1976 , Perf. 11

1629 13c	Drummer Boy	.25	.20	
1630 13c	Old Drummer	.25	.20	
1631 13c	Fifer	.25	.20	
a.	Strip of 3, #1629-1631	.75	.75	
b.	As "a," imperf.	*1,050.*		
c.	Imperf., vert. pair, #1631	*800.00*		
1632 13c	Interphil 76	.20	.20	
a.	Dark blue and red (engr.) omitted	—		
b.	Red (engr.) omitted	—		
1633 13c	Delaware	.25	.20	
1634 13c	Pennsylvania	.25	.20	
1635 13c	New Jersey	.25	.20	
1636 13c	Georgia	.25	.20	
1637 13c	Connecticut	.25	.20	
1638 13c	Massachusetts	.25	.20	
1639 13c	Maryland	.25	.20	
1640 13c	South Carolina	.25	.20	
1641 13c	New Hampshire	.25	.20	
1642 13c	Virginia	.25	.20	
1643 13c	New York	.25	.20	
1644 13c	North Carolina	.25	.20	

1633–1682

1683

1684

1685

Scott No.	Description	Unused Value	Used Value	/ / / / / /
1645	13c Rhode Island	.25	.20	
1646	13c Vermont	.25	.20	
1647	13c Kentucky	.25	.20	
1648	13c Tennessee	.25	.20	
1649	13c Ohio	.25	.20	
1650	13c Louisiana	.25	.20	
1651	13c Indiana	.25	.20	
1652	13c Mississippi	.25	.20	
1653	13c Illinois	.25	.20	
1654	13c Alabama	.25	.20	
1655	13c Maine	.25	.20	
1656	13c Missouri	.25	.20	
1657	13c Arkansas	.25	.20	
1658	13c Michigan	.25	.20	
1659	13c Florida	.25	.20	
1660	13c Texas	.25	.20	
1661	13c Iowa	.25	.20	
1662	13c Wisconsin	.25	.20	
1663	13c California	.25	.20	
1664	13c Minnesota	.25	.20	
1665	13c Oregon	.25	.20	
1666	13c Kansas	.25	.20	
1667	13c West Virginia	.25	.20	
1668	13c Nevada	.25	.20	
1669	13c Nebraska	.25	.20	
1670	13c Colorado	.25	.20	
1671	13c North Dakota	.25	.20	
1672	13c South Dakota	.25	.20	
1673	13c Montana	.25	.20	
1674	13c Washington	.25	.20	
1675	13c Idaho	.25	.20	
1676	13c Wyoming	.25	.20	
1677	13c Utah	.25	.20	
1678	13c Oklahoma	.25	.20	
1679	13c New Mexico	.25	.20	
1680	13c Arizona	.25	.20	
1681	13c Alaska	.25	.20	
1682	13c Hawaii	.25	.20	
a.	Pane of 50	15.00	—	
1683	13c Telephone Centennial	.25	.20	
a.	Black and purple omitted	500.00		
b.	Red omitted	—		
c.	All colors omitted	—		
1684	13c Commercial Aviation	.25	.20	
1685	13c Chemistry	.25	.20	
1686	Surrender of Cornwallis, Sheet of 5	3.25	—	
a.-e.	13c Any single	.45	.40	
f.	USA/13c omitted on b, c & d, imperf.	—	2,250.	
g.	USA/13c omitted on a & e	450.00	—	

135

1686

1687

Scott No.	Description	Unused Value	Used Value	/ / / / / /
h.	Imperf., tagging omitted..............		2,250.	
i.	USA/13c omitted on b, c & d	450.00		
j.	USA/13c double on b	—		
k.	USA/13c omitted on c & d...........	750.00		
l.	USA/13c omitted on e	500.00		
m.	USA/13c omitted, imperf., tagging omitted		—	
n.	As "g," imperf., tagging omitted...		—	
1687	Declaration of Independence, Sht. of 5	4.25	—	
a.-e. 18c	Any single......................................	.55	.55	
f.	Design & margin inscriptions omitted	3,000.		
g.	USA/18c omitted on a & c............	750.00		
h.	USA/18c omitted on b, d & e	450.00		
i.	USA/18c omitted on d..................	500.00	500.00	
j.	Black omitted in design.................	2,000.		
k.	USA/18c omitted, imperf.,			
	tagging omitted	3,000.		
m.	USA/18c omitted on b & e............	500.00		
n.	USA/18c omitted on b & d	—		
p.	Imperf., tagged	—		
1688	Washington Crossing the Delaware,			
	Sheet of 5	5.25	—	
a.-e. 24c	Any single.....................................	.70	.70	
f.	USA/24c omitted, imperf.	3,500.		
g.	USA/24c omitted on d & e............	450.00	450.00	
h.	Design & margin inscriptions omitted	3,250.		
i.	USA/24c omitted on a, b & c........	500.00	—	
j.	Imperf., tagging omitted................	3,000.		
k.	USA/24c of d & e inverted	—		
l.	As "i," imperf, tagging omitted.....	3,500.		
n.	As No. 1688, perfs inverted	—		
1689	Washington Reviewing Army,			
	Sheet of 5	6.25	—	
a.-e. 31c	multi, any single	.85	.85	
f.	USA/31c omitted............................	2,750.		
g.	USA/31c omitted on a & c............	400.00		
h.	USA/31c omitted on b, d & e	450.00	—	
i.	USA/31c omitted on e..................	450.00		
j.	Black omitted in design.................	2,000.		
k.	Imperf., tagging omitted................		2,250.	
l.	USA/31c omitted on b & d	—		
m.	USA/31c omitted on a, b & e........	—		
n.	As "m," imperf., tagging omitted..	—		
p.	As "h," imperf., tagging omitted ...		2,500.	
q.	As "g," imperf., tagging omitted ...	2,750.		
r.	"USA/31c" omitted on d & e	—		
t.	USA/31c omitted on d...................	—		
v.	As No. 1689, perfs inverted..........	—		
1690	13c Benjamin Franklin	.25	.20	
a.	Light blue omitted	225.00		
1691	13c Declaration of Independence - Left	.30	.20	

Washington Crossing the Delaware
From a Painting by Emanuel Leutze / Eastman Johnson

1688

Washington Reviewing His Ragged Army at Valley Forge
From a Painting by William T. Trego

1689

1690

Scott No.	Description	Unused Value	Used Value	/ / / / / /
1692	13c Declaration of Independence - Gathered Curtains	.30	.20	
1693	13c Declaration of Independence - Table	.30	.20	
1694	13c Declaration of Independence - Right	.30	.20	
a.	Strip of 4, #1691-1694	1.20	1.10	
1695	13c Olympics - Diving	.25	.20	
1696	13c Olympics - Skiing	.25	.20	
1697	13c Olympics - Running	.25	.20	
1698	13c Olympics - Skating	.25	.20	
a.	Block of 4, #1695-1698	1.10	1.40	
b.	As "a," imperf.	700.00		
1699	13c Clara Maass	.25	.20	
a.	Horiz. pair, imperf. vert.	450.00		
1700	13c Adolph S. Ochs	.25	.20	
1701	13c Christmas - Religious	.25	.20	
a.	Imperf., pair	100.00		
1702	13c Christmas - "Winter Pastime"	.25	.20	
a.	Imperf., pair	100.00		
1703	13c Christmas - "Winter Pastime" (1702), block tagging	.25	.20	
a.	Imperf., pair	110.00		
b.	Vert. pair, imperf. btwn.	—		
1977				
1704	13c Washington at Princeton	.25	.20	
a.	Horiz. pair, imperf. vert.	550.00		
1705	13c Sound Recording	.25	.20	
1706	13c Zia Pot	.25	.20	
1707	13c San Ildefonso Pot	.25	.20	
1708	13c Hopi Pot	.25	.20	
1709	13c Acoma Pot	.25	.20	
a.	Block or strip of 4	1.00	1.00	
b.	As "a," imperf. vert.	2,500.		
1710	13c Lindbergh Flight	.25	.20	
a.	Imperf., pair	1,050.		
1711	13c Colorado Statehood	.25	.20	
a.	Horiz. pair, imperf. btwn.	600.00		
b.	Horiz. pair, imperf. vert.	900.00		
1712	13c Swallowtail Butterfly	.25	.20	
1713	13c Checkerspot Butterfly	.25	.20	
1714	13c Dogface Butterfly	.25	.20	
1715	13c Orange-tip Butterfly	.25	.20	
a.	Block of 4, #1712-1715	1.00	1.00	
b.	As "a," imperf. horiz.	15,000.		
1716	13c Marquis de Lafayette	.25	.20	
a.	Red omitted	—		
1717	13c Seamstress	.25	.20	
1718	13c Blacksmith	.25	.20	
1719	13c Wheelwright	.25	.20	
1720	13c Leatherworker	.25	.20	
a.	Block of 4, #1717-1720	1.00	1.00	

1691-1694

1699

1695-1698

1700

1701

1702

1704

1705

Scott No.	Description	Unused Value	Used Value	//////
1721	13c Peace Bridge	.25	.20	
1722	13c Battle of Oriskany	.25	.20	
1723	13c Energy Conservation	.25	.20	
a.	Pair, #1723-1724	.50	.50	
1724	13c Energy Development	.25	.20	
1725	13c Alta California	.25	.20	
1726	13c Articles of Confederation	.25	.20	
1727	13c Talking Pictures	.25	.20	
1728	13c Surrender at Saratoga	.25	.20	
1729	13c Christmas - Washington Praying	.25	.20	
a.	Imperf., pair	75.00		
1730	13c Christmas - Mailbox	.25	.20	
a.	Imperf., pair	300.00		
1978				
1731	13c Carl Sandburg	.25	.20	
1732	13c Capt. James Cook - Portrait	.25	.20	
1733	13c Capt. James Cook - Ships	.25	.20	
a.	Vert. pair, imperf. horiz.	—		
b.	Pair, #1732-1733	.50	.50	
c.	As "a," imperf. btwn.	4,500.		
1978-80				
1734	13c Indian Head Penny	.25	.20	
a.	Horiz. pair, imperf. vert.	300.00		
1735	(15c) "A" & Eagle, photogravure	.25	.20	
a.	Imperf., pair	90.00		
b.	Vert. pair, imperf. horiz.	700.00		
Booklet Stamps, Engraved				
1736	(15c) "A" & Eagle (1735)	.25	.20	
a.	Booklet pane of 8	2.25	1.25	
c.	Vert. pair, imperf. between	—		
1737	15c Roses	.25	.20	
a.	Booklet pane of 8	2.25	1.25	
b.	As "a," imperf.	—		
1738	15c Virginia Windmill	.30	.20	
1739	15c Rhode Island Windmill	.30	.20	
1740	15c Massachusetts Windmill	.30	.20	
1741	15c Illinois Windmill	.30	.20	
1742	15c Texas Windmill	.30	.20	
a.	Bklt. pane, 2 each #1738-1742	3.50	3.00	
b.	Strip of 5, #1738-1742	1.50	1.40	
Coil Stamp, Perf. 10 Vertically				
1743	(15c) "A" & Eagle (1735)	.25	.20	
a.	Imperf., pair	90.00		
1978				
1744	13c Harriet Tubman	.25	.20	
1745	13c Quilts - Orange Flowered Fabric	.25	.20	

1706-1709

1710

1711

1716

1712-1715

1717-1720

1721

1722

1725

1723-1724

1726

1727

1728

1729

1730

1731

1732-1733

1745-1748

1734

1735

1738-1742

1737

1749-1752

1744

1753

144

Scott No.	Description	Unused Value	Used Value	/ / / / / /
1747	13c Quilts - Orange Striped Fabric	.25	.20	
1748	13c Quilts - Black Plaid Fabric	.25	.20	
a.	Block of 4, #1745-1748	1.00	1.00	
1749	13c Ballet	.25	.20	
1750	13c Dance in Theater	.25	.20	
1751	13c Folk Dancing	.25	.20	
1752	13c Modern Dance	.25	.20	
a.	Block of 4, #1749-1752	1.00	1.00	
1753	13c French Alliance............................	.25	.20	
1754	13c Early Cancer Detection	.25	.20	
1755	13c Jimmie Rodgers............................	.25	.20	
1756	15c George M. Cohan	.30	.20	
1757	CAPEX, block of 8	2.00	2.00	
a.	13c Cardinal	.25	.20	
b.	13c Mallard	.25	.20	
c.	13c Canada goose...............................	.25	.20	
d.	13c Blue jay.......................................	.25	.20	
e.	13c Moose	.25	.20	
f.	13c Chipmunk	.25	.20	
g.	13c Red fox	.25	.20	
h.	13c Raccoon	.25	.20	
i.	Yellow, green, red, brown, blue, and black (litho.) omitted..................	7,000.		
j.	Strip of 4 (a.-d.), imperf. vert.	7,000.		
k.	Strip of 4 (e.-h.), imperf. vert.	4,750.		
l.	As No. 1757, 'd' and 'h' with black omitted —			
1758	15c Photography.................................	.30	.20	
1759	15c Viking Missions to Mars	.30	.20	
1760	15c Great Gray Owl	.30	.20	
1761	15c Saw-whet Owl	.30	.20	
1762	15c Barred Owl	.30	.20	
1763	15c Great Horned Owl	.30	.20	
a.	Block of 4, #1760-1763	1.25	1.25	
1764	15c Giant Sequoia	.30	.20	
1765	15c White Pine	.30	.20	
1766	15c White Oak	.30	.20	
1767	15c Gray Birch	.30	.20	
a.	Block of 4, #1764-1767	1.25	1.25	
b.	As "a," imperf. horiz.	15,000.		
1768	15c Christmas - Religious	.30	.20	
a.	Imperf., pair....................................	90.00		
1769	15c Christmas - Hobby Horse	.30	.20	
a.	Imperf., pair....................................	100.00		
b.	Vert. pair, imperf. horiz.	2,000.		
1979				
1770	15c Robert F. Kennedy........................	.35	.20	
1771	15c Dr. Martin Luther King, Jr.	.30	.20	
a.	Imperf., pair....................................	—		

1757

1754

1755

1759

1756

1760–1763

1768

1758

1769

Scott No.	Description	Unused Value	Used Value	/ / / / / /
1772	15c International Year of the Child.......	.35	.20	
1773	15c John Steinbeck	.30	.20	
1774	15c Albert Einstein	.35	.20	
1775	15c Toleware - Straight-spouted coffeepot	.30	.20	
1776	15c Toleware - Tea Caddy.......................	.30	.20	
1777	15c Toleware - Sugar Bowl......................	.30	.20	
1778	15c Toleware - Curved-spouted coffeepot	.30	.20	
a.	Block of 4, #1775-1778.................	1.25	1.25	
b.	As "a," imperf. horiz......................	*4,250.*		
1779	15c Architecture - Jefferson....................	.30	.20	
1780	15c Architecture - Latrobe......................	.30	.20	
1781	15c Architecture - Bulfinch.....................	.30	.20	
1782	15c Architecture - Strickland..................	.30	.20	
a.	Block of 4, #1779-1782.................	1.25	*1.50*	
1783	5c Persistent Trillium	.30	.20	
1784	15c Hawaiian Wild Broadbean	.30	.20	
1785	15c Contra Costa Wallflower	.30	.20	
1786	15c Antioch Dunes Evening Primrose ..	.30	.20	
a.	Block of 4, #1783-1786.................	1.25	1.25	
b.	As "a," imperf.	*600.00*		
1787	15c Seeing Eye Dogs	.30	.20	
a.	Imperf., pair...................................	*425.00*		
1788	15c Special Olympics	.30	.20	
1789	15c John Paul Jones, perf. 11x12	.30	.20	
c.	Vert. pair, imperf. horiz.................	*175.00*		
1789A	15c John Paul Jones, perf. 11 (1789)....	.55	.20	
d.	Vert. pair, imperf horiz..................	*150.00*		
1789B	15c John Paul Jones, perf. 12 (1789)....	*2,500.*	*1,000.*	
1979-80				
1790	10c Olympics - Decathlon	.20	.20	
1791	15c Olympics - Running.........................	.30	.20	
1792	15c Olympics - Women's Swimming	.30	.20	
1793	15c Olympics - Rowing	.30	.20	
1794	15c Olympics - Equestrian.....................	.30	.20	
a.	Block of 4, #1791-1794.................	1.25	*1.50*	
b.	As "a," imperf.	*1,500.*		
1795	15c Olympics - Speed Skating, perf. 11¼x10½	.35	.20	
1796	15c Olympics - Downhill Skiing, perf. 11¼x10½	.35	.20	
1797	15c Olympics - Ski Jump, perf. 11¼x10½	.35	.20	
1798	15c Olympics - Ice Hockey, perf. 11¼x10½	.35	.20	
b.	Block of 4, #1795-1798.................	1.50	1.40	
1795A	15c Olympics - Speed Skating, perf. 11 (1795)..............................	1.05	.60	
1796A	15c Olympics - Downhill Skiing, perf. 11 (1796)..............................	1.05	.60	
1797A	15c Olympics - Ski Jump, perf. 11 (1797)..............................	1.05	.60	

1764-1767

1770

1771

1772

1773

1774

1775-1778

Scott No.	Description	Unused Value	Used Value	/ / / / / /
1798A 15c	Olympics - Ice Hockey, perf. 11 (1798)	1.05	.60	☐☐☐☐☐
c.	Block of 4, #1795A-1798A (1795-1798)	4.25	3.50	☐☐☐☐☐
1979				
1799 15c	Christmas - Religious	.30	.20	☐☐☐☐☐
a.	Imperf., pair	*90.00*		☐☐☐☐☐
b.	Vert. pair, imperf. horiz.	*700.00*		☐☐☐☐☐
c.	Vert. pair, imperf. btwn.	*2,250.*		☐☐☐☐☐
1800 15c	Christmas - Santa Claus	.30	.20	☐☐☐☐☐
a.	Green & yellow omitted	*625.00*		☐☐☐☐☐
b.	Green, yellow & tan omitted	*700.00*		☐☐☐☐☐
1801 15c	Will Rogers	.30	.20	☐☐☐☐☐
a.	Imperf., pair	*225.00*		☐☐☐☐☐
1802 15c	Vietnam Veterans	.30	.20	☐☐☐☐☐
1980				
1803 15c	W.C. Fields	.30	.20	☐☐☐☐☐
a.	Imperf., pair	—		☐☐☐☐☐
1804 15c	Benjamin Banneker	.35	.20	☐☐☐☐☐
a.	Horiz. pair, imperf. vert.	*800.00*		☐☐☐☐☐
1805 15c	Letters Preserve Memories	.30	.20	
1806 15c	P.S. Write Soon, purple & multi	.30	.20	
1807 15c	Letters Lift Spirits	.30	.20	
1808 15c	P.S. Write Soon (1806), grn & multi	.30	.20	
1809 15c	Letters Shape Opinions	.30	.20	
1810 15c	P.S. Write Soon (1806), red & multi	.30	.20	
a.	Vert. strip of 6, #1805-1810	1.85	*2.25*	
1980-81, Coil Stamps, Perf. 10 Vertically				
1811 1c	Inkwell & Quill (1581)	.20	.20	☐☐☐☐☐
a.	Imperf., pair	*175.00*		☐☐☐☐☐
1813 3.5c	Violins, tagged	.20	.20	☐☐☐☐☐
a.	Untagged (Bureau precanceled, lines only)		.20	☐☐☐☐☐
b.	Imperf., pair	*225.00*		☐☐☐☐☐
1816 12c	Torch (1594), tagged	.25	.20	☐☐☐☐☐
a.	Untagged (Bureau precanceled)		.25	☐☐☐☐☐
b.	Imperf., pair	*200.00*		☐☐☐☐☐
c.	As "a," brownish red, *reddish beige*		.25	☐☐☐☐☐
1981				
1818 (18c)	"B" & Eagle, photogravure	.35	.20	☐☐☐☐☐
Booklet Stamp, Perf. 10, Engraved				
1819 (18c)	"B" & Eagle (1818)	.40	.20	☐☐☐☐☐
a.	Booklet pane of 8	3.75	2.25	☐☐☐☐☐
Coil Stamp, Perf. 10 Vertically				
1820 (18c)	"B" & Eagle (1818), engraved	.40	.20	☐☐☐☐☐
a.	Imperf., pair	*100.00*		☐☐☐☐☐

1779-1782

1783-1786

1787   1788   1789

1790

1791-1794

1795-1798

1799

1800

1802

151

1801

1803

1804

1805

1806

1807

1809

1813

1818

1821

1822

1823

1824

1825

1826

Scott No.	Description	Unused Value	Used Value	/ / / / / /
1980				
1821	15c Frances Perkins	.30	.20	
1822	15c Dolley Madison	.30	.20	
a.	Red brown omitted	—		
1823	15c Emily Bissell	.35	.20	
a.	Vert. pair, imperf. horiz.	400.00		
b.	All colors omitted.	—		
1824	15c Helen Keller, Anne Sullivan	.30	.20	
1825	15c Veterans Administration	.30	.20	
a.	Horiz. pair, imperf. vert.	450.00		
1826	15c Bernardo de Galvez	.30	.20	
a.	Red, brown & blue (engr.) omitted.	800.00		
b.	Blue, brown, red (engr.), yellow (litho.) omitted	1,400.		
1827	15c Brain Coral	.30	.20	
1828	15c Elkhorn Coral	.30	.20	
1829	15c Chalice Coral	.30	.20	
1830	15c Finger Coral	.30	.20	
a.	Block of 4, #1827-1830	1.25	1.10	
b.	As "a.," imperf.	1,000.		
c.	As "a.," vert. imperf. btwn.	—		
d.	As "a.," imperf. vert.	3,000.		
1831	15c Organized Labor	.30	.20	
a.	Imperf., pair	375.00		
1832	15c Edith Wharton	.30	.20	
1833	15c Education	.30	.20	
a.	Horiz. pair, imperf. vert.	240.00		
1834	15c Bella Bella Mask	.30	.20	
1835	15c Chilkat Tlingit Mask	.30	.20	
1836	15c Tlingit Mask	.30	.20	
1837	15c Bella Coola Mask	.30	.20	
a.	Block of 4, #1834-1837	1.25	1.25	
1838	15c Architecture - Renwick	.30	.20	
1839	15c Architecture - Richardson	.30	.20	
1840	15c Architecture - Furness	.30	.20	
1841	15c Architecture - Davis	.30	.20	
a.	Block of 4, #1838-1841	1.25	1.50	
1842	15c Christmas - Religious	.30	.20	
a.	Imperf., pair	70.00		
1843	15c Christmas - Wreath & Toys	.30	.20	
a.	Imperf., pair	70.00		
b.	Buff omitted	25.00		
c.	Vert. pair, imperf. horiz.	—		
d.	Horiz. pair, imperf. btwn.	4,000.		
1980-85				
1844	1c Dorothea Dix	.20	.20	
a.	Imperf. pair	300.00		
b.	Vert. pair, imperf. btwn. & at bottom	3,000.		

1827-1830

1831

1832

1833

1834-1837

154

Scott No.	Description	Unused Value	Used Value	/ / / / / /
e.	Vert. pair, imperf. horiz.	—		
1845	2c Igor Stravinsky	.20	.20	
1846	3c Henry Clay	.20	.20	
1847	4c Carl Schurz....................................	.20	.20	
1848	5c Pearl Buck	.20	.20	
1849	6c Walter Lippmann...........................	.20	.20	
a.	Vert. pair, imperf. btwn. & at bottom.	2,000.		
1850	7c Abraham Baldwin	.20	.20	
1851	8c Henry Knox...................................	.20	.20	
1852	9c Sylvanus Thayer	.20	.20	
1853	10c Richard Russell	.25	.20	
a.	Vert. pair, imperf. btwn. & at bottom	900.00		
b.	Horiz. pair, imperf. btwn.	2,250.		
1854	11c Alden Partridge	.30	.20	
1855	13c Crazy Horse.................................	.30	.20	
1856	14c Sinclair Lewis..............................	.25	.20	
b.	Vert. pair, imperf. horiz.	125.00		
c.	Horiz. pair, imperf. btwn.	9.00		
d.	Vert. pair, imperf. btwn.	1,500.		
e.	All color omitted.	—		
1857	17c Rachel Carson	.35	.20	
1858	18c George Mason	.35	.20	
1859	19c Sequoyah	.40	.20	
1860	20c Ralph Bunche	.40	.20	
1861	20c Thomas H. Gallaudet	.50	.20	
1862	20c Harry S Truman	.40	.20	
1863	22c John James Audubon	.75	.20	
d.	Vert. pair, imperf. horiz.	2,500.		
e.	Vert. pair, imperf. btwn.	—		
f.	Horiz. pair, imperf. btwn.	2,500.		
1864	30c Frank C. Laubach..........................	.60	.20	
1865	35c Dr. Charles R. Drew......................	.75	.20	
1866	37c Robert Millikan	.80	.20	
1867	39c Grenville Clark.............................	.90	.20	
a.	Vert. pair, imperf. horiz.	600.00		
b.	Vert. pair, imperf. btwn.	2,000.		
1868	40c Lillian M. Gilbreth	.90	.20	
1869	50c Chester W. Nimitz.........................	.95	.20	
1981				
1874	15c Everett Dirksen............................	.30	.20	
1875	15c Whitney M. Young	.35	.20	
1876	18c Rose...	.35	.20	
1877	18c Camellia......................................	.35	.20	
1878	18c Dahlia	.35	.20	
1879	18c Lily...	.35	.20	
a.	Block of 4, #1876-1879	1.40	1.25	
1880	18c Bighorn.......................................	.55	.20	
1881	18c Puma...	.55	.20	

1838-1841

1842   1843   1874   1875

1876-1879

HOW TO USE THIS BOOK

The number in the first column is its Scott number or identifying number.
Following that is the denomination of the stamp and its color. Finally, the value,
unused and used is shown.

Scott No.	Description	Unused Value	Used Value	//////
1882	18c Harbor seal	.55	.20	
1883	18c American Buffalo	.55	.20	
1884	18c Brown bear	.55	.20	
1885	18c Polar bear	.55	.20	
1886	18c Elk (wapiti)	.55	.20	
1887	18c Moose	.55	.20	
1888	18c White-tailed deer	.55	.20	
1889	18c Pronghorn	.55	.20	
a.	Bklt. pane of 10, #1880-1889	8.50	7.00	
1890	18c Flag, Grain Field	.35	.20	
a.	Imperf., pair	110.00		
b.	Vert. pair, imperf. horiz.	850.00		

Coil Stamp, Perf. 10 Vertically

Scott No.	Description	Unused Value	Used Value	//////
1891	18c Flag, Sea Coast	.35	.20	
a.	Imperf., pair	30.00	—	
b.	Pair, imperf. btwn.	—		

Booklet Stamps, Perf. 11

Scott No.	Description	Unused Value	Used Value	//////
1892	6c Stars (from bklt. pane)	.50	.20	
1893	18c Flag, Mountain (from bklt. pane)	.30	.20	
a.	Booklet pane of 8 (2 #1892, 6 #1893)	3.00	2.25	
b.	As "a.," vert. imperf. btwn.	75.00		
c.	Pair, #1892, 1893	.90	1.00	
1894	20c Flag, Supreme Court (1895)	.40	.20	
a.	Vert. pair, imperf.	35.00		
b.	Vert. pair, imperf. horiz.	550.00		
c.	Dark blue omitted	85.00		
d.	Black omitted	325.00		

Coil Stamp, Perf. 10 Vertically

Scott No.	Description	Unused Value	Used Value	//////
1895	20c Flag, Supreme Court, tagged.	.40	.20	
a.	Imperf., pair	10.00		
b.	Black omitted	50.00		
c.	Dark blue omitted	1,500.		
d.	Pair, imperf. btwn.	1,250.		
e.	Untagged (Bureau precanceled).	.50	.50	

Booklet Stamps, Perf. 11x10½

Scott No.	Description	Unused Value	Used Value	//////
1896	20c Flag, Supreme Court (1894)	.40	.20	
a.	Booklet pane of 6	3.00	2.25	
b.	Booklet pane of 10	5.25	3.25	

1981-84, Coil Stamps, Perf. 10 Vertically

Scott No.	Description	Unused Value	Used Value	//////
1897	1c Omnibus	.20	.20	
b.	Imperf., pair	675.00		
1897A	2c Locomotive	.20	.20	
e.	Imperf., pair	52.50		
1898	3c Handcar	.20	.20	
1898A	4c Stagecoach, tagged	.20	.20	
b.	Untagged (Bureau precanceled).	.20	.20	
c.	As "b.," imperf., pair	750.00		

157

1844

1845

1846

1847

Pearl Buck
USA 5c
1848

1849

Abraham Baldwin
USA 7
1850

Henry Knox
USA 8
1851

1852

Richard Russell
USA 10c
1853

1854

USA 13c
Crazy Horse
1855

Sinclair Lewis
USA 14
1856

Rachel Carson
USA 17c
1857

George Mason
USA 18c
1858

USA 19c
Sequoyah
1859

Ralph Bunche
USA 20c
1860

Thomas H Gallaudet
USA 20c
1861

Harry S Truman
USA 20c
1862

John J. Audubon
USA 22
1863

Frank C Laubach
USA 30c
1864

Charles R Drew MD
USA 35c
1865

Robert Millikan
37c USA
1866

Grenville Clark
USA 39
1867

Lillian M.Gilbreth
USA 40c
1868

USA 50
Chester W. Nimitz
1869

158

Scott No.		Description	Unused Value	Used Value	/ / / / / /
d.		No. 1898A, imperf., pair...............	850.00	—	
1899	5c	Motorcycle	.20	.20	
a.		Imperf., pair..................................	2,750.		
1900	5.2c	Sleigh, tagged................................	.20	.20	
a.		Untagged (Bureau precanceled).	.20	.20	
1901	5.9c	Bicycle, tagged..............................	.25	.20	
a.		Untagged (Bureau precanceled, lines only).....................................	.20	.20	
b.		As "a.," imperf., pair.....................	200.00		
1902	7.4c	Baby Buggy, tagged........................	.20	.20	
a.		Untagged (Bureau precanceled).	.20	.20	
1903	9.3c	Mail Wagon, tagged........................	.30	.20	
a.		Untagged (Bureau precanceled, lines only).....................................	.25	.25	
b.		As "a.," imperf., pair.....................	125.00		
1904	10.9c	Hansom Cab, tagged	.30	.20	
a.		Untagged (Bureau precanceled, lines only).....................................	.30	.25	
b.		As "a.," imperf., pair.....................	150.00		
1905	11c	Caboose, tagged..............................	.30	.20	
a.		Untagged..	.25	.20	
1906	17c	Electric Auto, tagged......................	.35	.20	
a.		Untagged (Bureau precanceled, Presorted First Class).....................	.35	.35	
b.		Imperf., pair..................................	165.00		
c.		As "a.," imperf., pair.....................	650.00		
1907	18c	Surrey	.35	.20	
a.		Imperf., pair..................................	140.00		
1908	20c	Fire Pumper	.35	.20	
a.		Imperf., pair..................................	110.00		

1983, Booklet Stamp, Perf. 10 Vertically on 1 or 2 Sides

Scott No.		Description	Unused Value	Used Value	/ / / / / /
1909		$9.35 Eagle & Moon	21.00	15.00	
a.		Booklet pane of 3............................	65.00	—	

1981

Scott No.		Description	Unused Value	Used Value	/ / / / / /
1910	18c	American Red Cross	.35	.20	
1911	18c	Savings & Loan	.35	.20	
1912	18c	Moon Walk	.40	.20	
1913	18c	Shuttle - Jettison of Boosters..........	.40	.20	
1914	18c	Shuttle - Cargo Doors Open	.40	.20	
1915	18c	Skylab	.40	.20	
1916	18c	Pioneer 11, Saturn.........................	.40	.20	
1917	18c	Shuttle - Lifting Off	.40	.20	
1918	18c	Shuttle - Landing	.40	.20	
1919	18c	Space Telescope	.40	.20	
a.		Block of 8, #1912-1919	3.25	3.00	
b.		As "a.," imperf.	8,000.		
1920	18c	Professional Management...............	.35	.20	
1921	18c	Save Wetland Habitats	.35	.20	

1897   1897A   1898   1898A

1899   1900   1901   1902

1903   1904   1905

1906   1907   1908

1909

Scott No.	Description	Unused Value	Used Value	/ / / / / /
1922	18c Save Grassland Habitats	.35	.20	
1923	18c Save Mountain Habitats................	.35	.20	
1924	18c Save Woodland Habitats	.35	.20	
a.	Block of 4, #1921-1924	1.50	1.25	
1925	18c International Year of the Disabled ..	.35	.20	
a.	Vert. pair, imperf. horiz..................	2,600.		
1926	18c Edna St. Vincent Millay................	.35	.20	
a.	Black (engr., inscriptions) omitted .	300.00	—	
1927	18c Alcoholism..........................	.40	.20	
a.	Imperf., pair.....................................	400.00		
b.	Vert. pair, imperf. horiz..................	2,500.		
1928	18c Architecture - White.......................	.40	.20	
1929	18c Architecture - Hunt	.40	.20	
1930	18c Architecture - Maybeck	.40	.20	
1931	18c Architecture - Sullivan	.40	.20	
a.	Block of 4, #1928-1931	1.65	1.75	
1932	18c Babe Zaharias...............................	.40	.20	
1933	18c Bobby Jones...............................	.40	.20	
1934	18c Frederic Remington.......................	.35	.20	
a.	Vert. pair, imperf. btwn.	275.00		
b.	Brown omitted............................	450.00		
1935	18c James Hoban	.35	.20	
1936	20c James Hoban (1935)	.35	.20	
1937	18c Battle of Yorktown.......................	.35	.20	
1938	18c Battle of Virginia Capes................	.35	.20	
a.	Pair, #1937-1938	.90	.75	
b.	As "a.," black (engr., inscriptions) omitted....................	400.00		
1939 (20c)	Christmas - Religious.......................	.40	.20	
b.	Vert. pair, imperf. horiz..................	1,650.		
1940 (20c)	Christmas - Bear on Sled................	.40	.20	
a.	Imperf., pair.....................................	275.00		
b.	Vert. pair, imperf. horiz..................	2,500.		
1941	20c John Hanson.......................................	.40	.20	
1942	20c Barrel Cactus	.35	.20	
1943	20c Agave..	.35	.20	
1944	20c Beavertail Cactus	.35	.20	
1945	20c Saguaro..	.35	.20	
a.	Block of 4, #1942-1945	1.50	1.25	
b.	As "a.," deep brown (litho.) omitted..........................	6,500.		
c.	No. 1945 imperf., vert. pair	5,250.		
1946 (20c)	"C" & Eagle	.40	.20	

Coil Stamp, Perf. 10 Vertically

1947 (20c)	"C" & Eagle (1946)	.60	.20	
a.	Imperf., pair.....................................	1,400.		
1948 (20c)	"C" & Eagle (from bklt. pane), perf. 11	.40	.20	

161

1890   1891

1892   1893

1895   1880-1889

HOW TO USE THIS BOOK

The number in the first column is its Scott number or identifying number.
Following that is the denomination of the stamp and its color. Finally, the value,
unused and used is shown.

Scott No.	Description	Unused Value	Used Value	/ / / / / /
a.	Booklet pane of 10...............	4.50	3.25	☐☐☐☐☐
1982				
1949	20c Bighorn, (from bklt. pane).............	.55	.20	☐☐☐☐☐
a.	Booklet pane of 10................	5.50	2.50	☐☐☐☐☐
b.	As "a.," imperf. btwn.	110.00		☐☐☐☐☐
c.	Type II...............................	.55	.20	☐☐☐☐☐
d.	As "c.," booklet pane of 10............	11.00	—	☐☐☐☐☐
1950	20c Franklin D. Roosevelt	.40	.20	☐☐☐☐☐
1951	20c Love, perf. 11	.40	.20	☐☐☐☐☐
b.	Imperf., pair.....................	275.00		☐☐☐☐☐
c.	Blue omitted	225.00		☐☐☐☐☐
d.	Yellow omitted	1,000.		☐☐☐☐☐
e.	Purple omitted.................	—		☐☐☐☐☐
1951A	20c Love, Perf. 11¼x10½ (1951)....	.75	.25	☐☐☐☐☐
1952	20c George Washington............	.40	.20	☐☐☐☐☐
Perf 10½ x 11¼				
1953	20c Alabama	.50	.25	☐☐☐☐☐
1954	20c Alaska..........................	.50	.25	☐☐☐☐☐
1955	20c Arizona........................	.50	.25	☐☐☐☐☐
1956	20c Arkansas.......................	.50	.25	☐☐☐☐☐
1957	20c California......................	.50	.25	☐☐☐☐☐
1958	20c Colorado.......................	.50	.25	☐☐☐☐☐
1959	20c Connecticut....................	.50	.25	☐☐☐☐☐
1960	20c Delaware.......................	.50	.25	☐☐☐☐☐
1961	20c Florida	.50	.25	☐☐☐☐☐
1962	20c Georgia	.50	.25	☐☐☐☐☐
1963	20c Hawaii.........................	.50	.25	☐☐☐☐☐
1964	20c Idaho...........................	.50	.25	☐☐☐☐☐
1965	20c Illinois.........................	.50	.25	☐☐☐☐☐
1966	20c Indiana.........................	.50	.25	☐☐☐☐☐
1967	20c Iowa............................	.50	.25	☐☐☐☐☐
1968	20c Kansas	.50	.25	☐☐☐☐☐
1969	20c Kentucky.......................	.50	.25	☐☐☐☐☐
1970	20c Louisiana	.50	.25	☐☐☐☐☐
1971	20c Maine...........................	.50	.25	☐☐☐☐☐
1972	20c Maryland.......................	.50	.25	☐☐☐☐☐
1973	20c Massachusetts..................	.50	.25	☐☐☐☐☐
1974	20c Michigan.......................	.50	.25	☐☐☐☐☐
1975	20c Minnesota......................	.50	.25	☐☐☐☐☐
1976	20c Mississippi.....................	.50	.25	☐☐☐☐☐
1977	20c Missouri.......................	.50	.25	☐☐☐☐☐
1978	20c Montana........................	.50	.25	☐☐☐☐☐
1979	20c Nebraska.......................	.50	.25	☐☐☐☐☐
1980	20c Nevada.........................	.50	.25	☐☐☐☐☐
1981	20c New Hampshire.................	.50	.25	☐☐☐☐☐
b.	Black (engr.) omitted	6,000.		☐☐☐☐☐
1982	20c New Jersey	.50	.25	☐☐☐☐☐
1983	20c New Mexico	.50	.25	☐☐☐☐☐

1910 1911

1912-1919

1921-1924

Scott No.	Description	Unused Value	Used Value	/ / / / / /
1984	20c New York	.50	.25	
1985	20c North Carolina	.50	.25	
1986	20c North Dakota	.50	.25	
1987	20c Ohio	.50	.25	
1988	20c Oklahoma	.50	.25	
1989	20c Oregon	.50	.25	
1990	20c Pennsylvania	.50	.25	
1991	20c Rhode Island	.50	.25	
b.	Black (engr.) omitted	6,000.		
1992	20c South Carolina	.50	.25	
1993	20c South Dakota	.50	.25	
1994	20c Tennessee	.50	.25	
1995	20c Texas	.50	.25	
1996	20c Utah	.50	.25	
1997	20c Vermont	.50	.25	
1998	20c Virginia	.50	.25	
1999	20c Washington	.50	.25	
2000	20c West Virginia	.50	.25	
2001	20c Wisconsin	.50	.25	
b.	Black (engr.) omitted	—		
2002	20c Wyoming	.50	.25	
b.	Pane of 50, perf. Nos. 1953-2002	25.00	—	
d.	Pane of 50, imperf.	27,500.		

Perf 11¼ x 11

Scott No.	Description	Unused Value	Used Value	/ / / / / /
1953A	20c Alabama	.55	.30	
1954A	20c Alaska	.55	.30	
1955A	20c Arizona	.55	.30	
1956A	20c Arkansas	.55	.30	
1957A	20c California	.55	.30	
1958A	20c Colorado	.55	.30	
1959A	20c Connecticut	.55	.30	
1960A	20c Delaware	.55	.30	
1961A	20c Florida	.55	.30	
1962A	20c Georgia	.55	.30	
1963A	20c Hawaii	.55	.30	
1964A	20c Idaho	.55	.30	
1965A	20c Illinois	.55	.30	
1966A	20c Indiana	.55	.30	
1967A	20c Iowa	.55	.30	
1968A	20c Kansas	.55	.30	
1969A	20c Kentucky	.55	.30	
1970A	20c Louisiana	.55	.30	
1971A	20c Maine	.55	.30	
1972A	20c Maryland	.55	.30	
1973A	20c Massachusetts	.55	.30	
1974A	20c Michigan	.55	.30	
1975A	20c Minnesota	.55	.30	
1976A	20c Mississippi	.55	.30	
1977A	20c Missouri	.55	.30	

1920

1925

1927

1926

1932

1933

1928-1931

1934

1941

1935

1937-1938

1939

1940

1942-1945

1946

1948

1949

1950

1951

1952

2005

167

State Birds and Flowers 1953-2002, 1953A-2002A

2003

2010

2004

2006-2009

Scott No.		Description	Unused Value	Used Value	/ / / / / /
1978A	20c	Montana	.55	.30	
1979A	20c	Nebraska	.55	.30	
1980A	20c	Nevada	.55	.30	
1981A	20c	New Hampshire	.55	.30	
1982A	20c	New Jersey	.55	.30	
1983A	20c	New Mexico	.55	.30	
1984A	20c	New York	.55	.30	
1985A	20c	North Carolina	.55	.30	
1986A	20c	North Dakota	.55	.30	
1987A	20c	Ohio	.55	.30	
1988A	20c	Oklahoma	.55	.30	
1989A	20c	Oregon	.55	.30	
1990A	20c	Pennsylvania	.55	.30	
1991A	20c	Rhode Island	.55	.30	
1992A	20c	South Carolina	.55	.30	
1993A	20c	South Dakota	.55	.30	
1994A	20c	Tennessee	.55	.30	
1995A	20c	Texas	.55	.30	
1996A	20c	Utah	.55	.30	
1997A	20c	Vermont	.55	.30	
1998A	20c	Virginia	.55	.30	
1999A	20c	Washington	.55	.30	
2000A	20c	West Virginia	.55	.30	
2001A	20c	Wisconsin	.55	.30	
2002A	20c	Wyoming	.55	.30	
c.		Pane of 50, Nos. 1953A-2002A	27.50	—	
2003	20c	U.S. - Netherlands	.40	.20	
a.		Imperf., pair	325.00		
2004	20c	Library of Congress	.40	.20	
Coil Stamp, Perf. 10 Vertically					
2005	20c	Consumer Education	.55	.20	
a.		Imperf., pair	100.00		
2006	20c	Solar Energy	.40	.20	
2007	20c	Synthetic Fuels	.40	.20	
2008	20c	Breeder Reactor	.40	.20	
2009	20c	Fossil Fuels	.40	.20	
a.		Block of 4, #2006-2009	1.65	1.50	
2010	20c	Horatio Alger	.40	.20	
2011	20c	Aging Together	.40	.20	
2012	20c	The Barrymores	.40	.20	
2013	20c	Dr. Mary Walker	.40	.20	
2014	20c	International Peace Garden	.40	.20	
a.		Black & green (engr.) omitted	260.00		
2015	20c	America's Libraries	.40	.20	
a.		Vert. pair, imperf. horiz.	300.00		
c.		All colors omitted.	—		
2016	20c	Jackie Robinson	1.10	.20	
2017	20c	Touro Synagogue	.40	.20	
a.		Imperf., pair	2,500.		

2011

2014

2012

2013

2015

2016

2017

2018

2019-2022

Scott No.	Description	Unused Value	Used Value	/ / / / / /
2018	20c Wolf Trap Farm Park	.40	.20	
2019	20c Architecture - Wright	.45	.20	
b.	Red omitted	—		
2020	20c Architecture - Mies van der Rohe	.45	.20	
a.	Red omitted	—		
2021	20c Architecture - Gropius	.45	.20	
2022	20c Architecture -Saarinen	.45	.20	
a.	Block of 4, #2019-2022	2.00	1.75	
2023	20c Francis of Assisi	.40	.20	
2024	20c Ponce de Leon	.40	.20	
a.	Imperf., pair	500.00		
b.	Vert. pair, imperf. between & at top	—		
2025	13c Christmas - Dog & Cat	.25	.20	
a.	Imperf., pair	650.00		
2026	20c Christmas - Religious	.40	.20	
a.	Imperf., pair	150.00		
b.	Horiz. pair, imperf. vert.	—		
c.	Vert. pair, imperf. horiz.	—		
2027	20c Christmas - Sledding	.50	.20	
2028	20c Christmas - Snowman	.50	.20	
2029	20c Christmas - Skating	.50	.20	
2030	20c Christmas - Tree	.50	.20	
a.	Block of 4, #2027-2030	2.10	1.50	
b.	As "a.," imperf.	2,750.		
c.	As "a.," imperf. horiz.	—		
1983				
2031	20c Science & Technology	.40	.20	
a.	Black (engr.) omitted	1,400.		
2032	20c Intrepid Balloon	.40	.20	
2033	20c Two Large Balloons	.40	.20	
2034	20c Large Balloon at Right	.40	.20	
2035	20c Explorer II Balloon	.40	.20	
a.	Block of 4, #2032-2035	1.65	1.50	
b.	As "a," imperf.	4,250.		
2036	20c U.S. - Sweden	.40	.20	
2037	20c Civilian Conservation Corps	.40	.20	
a.	Imperf., pair	2,900.		
2038	20c Joseph Priestley	.40	.20	
2039	20c Voluntarism	.40	.20	
a.	Imperf., pair	750.00		
2040	20c U.S. - Germany	.40	.20	
2041	20c Brooklyn Bridge	.40	.20	
b.	All color omitted.	—		
2042	20c Tennessee Valley Authority	.40	.20	
2043	20c Physical Fitness	.40	.20	
2044	20c Scott Joplin	.40	.20	
a.	Imperf., pair	475.00		
2045	20c Medal of Honor	.40	.20	
a.	Red omitted	240.00		

2023

2024

2025

2026

2031

2027-2030

2036

2037

HOW TO USE THIS BOOK

The number in the first column is its Scott number or identifying number. Following that is the denomination of the stamp and its color. Finally, the value, unused and used is shown.

Scott No.	Description	Unused Value	Used Value	/ / / / / /
2046	20c Babe Ruth	1.25	.20	
2047	20c Nathaniel Hawthorne	.45	.20	
2048	13c Olympics - Discus	.35	.20	
2049	13c Olympics - High Jump	.35	.20	
2050	13c Olympics - Archery	.35	.20	
2051	13c Olympics - Boxing	.35	.20	
a.	Block of 4, #2048-2051	1.50	1.25	
2052	20c Treaty of Paris	.40	.20	
2053	20c Civil Service	.40	.20	
2054	20c Metropolitan Opera	.40	.20	
2055	20c Charles Steinmetz	.45	.20	
2056	20c Edwin Armstrong	.45	.20	
2057	20c Nikola Tesla	.45	.20	
2058	20c Philo T. Farnsworth	.45	.20	
a.	Block of 4, #2055-2058	1.80	1.25	
b.	As "a.," black omitted	375.00		
2059	20c Streetcar - New York	.45	.20	
2060	20c Streetcar - Alabama	.45	.20	
2061	20c Streetcar - Arkansas	.45	.20	
2062	20c Streetcar - Louisiana	.45	.20	
a.	Block of 4, #2059-2062	1.80	1.40	
b.	As "a.," black omitted	425.00		
c.	As "a.," black omitted on #2059, 2061	—		
2063	20c Christmas - Religious	.40	.20	
2064	20c Christmas - Santa Claus	.40	.20	
a.	Imperf., pair	175.00		
2065	20c Martin Luther	.40	.20	
1984				
2066	20c Alaska Statehood	.40	.20	
2067	20c Olympics - Ice Dancing	.50	.20	
2068	20c Olympics - Alpine Skiing	.50	.20	
2069	20c Olympics - Nordic Skiing	.50	.20	
2070	20c Olympics - Ice Hockey	.50	.20	
a.	Block of 4, #2067-2070	2.10	1.50	
2071	20c Federal Deposit Insurance Corp.	.40	.20	
2072	20c Love	.40	.20	
a.	Horiz. pair, imperf. vert.	175.00		
2073	20c Carter G. Woodson	.40	.20	
a.	Horiz. pair, imperf. vert.	1,600.		
2074	20c Soil & Water Conservation	.40	.20	
2075	20c Credit Union Act	.40	.20	
2076	20c Wild Pink Orchid	.50	.20	
2077	20c Yellow Lady's-slipper Orchid	.50	.20	
2078	20c Spreading Pogonia Orchid	.50	.20	
2079	20c Pacific Calypso Orchid	.50	.20	
a.	Block of 4, #2076-2079	2.00	1.50	
2080	20c Hawaii Statehood	.40	.20	
2081	20c National Archives	.40	.20	

2032-2035

2039

2038

2040

2041

2042

2043

2044

2045

2046

2047

174

2048-2051

2052

2053

2054

2055-2058

HOW TO USE THIS BOOK

The number in the first column is its Scott number or identifying number. Following that is the denomination of the stamp and its color. Finally, the value, unused and used is shown.

2059-2062

2063

2064

2065

2066

2071

2067-2070

2072

2073   2074   2075

2080

2076-2079

2081   2086   2082-2085

2087   2088   2089

2091

2092

2090

2093

2094

2095

2096

2097

2098-2101

178

Scott No.	Description	Unused Value	Used Value	/ / / / / /
2082	20c Olympics - Diving	.55	.20	
2083	20c Olympics - Long Jump	.55	.20	
2084	20c Olympics - Wrestling	.55	.20	
2085	20c Olympics - Kayak	.55	.20	
a.	Block of 4, #2082-2085	2.40	1.90	
b.	As "a," imperf btwn. vertically	—		
2086	20c Louisiana World Exposition	.40	.20	
2087	20c Health Research	.40	.20	
2088	20c Douglas Fairbanks	.40	.20	
2089	20c Jim Thorpe	.40	.20	
2090	20c John McCormack	.40	.20	
2091	20c St. Lawrence Seaway	.40	.20	
2092	20c Waterfowl Preservation Act	.50	.20	
a.	Horiz. pair, imperf. vert.	400.00		
2093	20c Roanoke Voyages	.40	.20	
2094	20c Herman Melville	.40	.20	
2095	20c Horace Moses	.45	.20	
2096	20c Smokey Bear	.40	.20	
a.	Horiz. pair, imperf. btwn.	300.00		
b.	Vert. pair, imperf. btwn.	240.00		
c.	Block of 4, imperf. btwn, vert. & horiz.	5,500.		
d.	Horiz. pair, imperf. vert.	1,750.		
2097	20c Roberto Clemente	1.60	.20	
a.	Horiz. pair, imperf. vert.	2,000.		
2098	20c Beagle & Boston Terrier	.45	.20	
2099	20c Chesapeake Bay Retriever & Cocker Spaniel	.45	.20	
2100	20c Alaskan Malamute & Collie	.45	.20	
2101	20c Black & Tan Coonhound & American Foxhound	.45	.20	
a.	Block of 4, #2098-2101	1.90	1.90	
2102	20c Crime Prevention	.40	.20	
2103	20c Hispanic Americans	.40	.20	
a.	Vert. pair, imperf. horiz.	2,250.		
2104	20c Family Unity	.40	.20	
a.	Horiz. pair, imperf. vert.	550.00		
c.	Vert. pair, imperf. btwn. & at bottom	—		
2105	20c Eleanor Roosevelt	.40	.20	
2106	20c Nation of Readers	.40	.20	
2107	20c Christmas - Religious	.40	.20	
2108	20c Christmas - Santa Claus	.40	.20	
a.	Horiz. pair, imperf. vert.	950.00		
2109	20c Vietnam Veterans' Memorial	.40	.20	
1985				
2110	22c Jerome Kern	.40	.20	
2111	(22c) "D" & Eagle	.55	.20	
a.	Vert. pair, imperf.	35.00		
b.	Vert. pair, imperf. horiz.	1,350.		

2102

2103

2104

2105

2106

2107

2108

2109

2110

2111

2113

2115

2116

Scott No.	Description	Unused Value	Used Value	//////

Coil Stamp, Perf. 10 Vertically

2112 (22c)	"D" & Eagle (2111)	.60	.20	
2113 (22c)	"D" & Eagle (from bklt. pane)	.80	.20	
a.	Booklet pane of 10	8.50	3.00	
b.	As "a," imperf. btwn. horiz.	—		
2114	22c Flag Over Capitol (2115)	.40	.20	

Coil Stamp, Perf. 10 Vertically

2115	22c Flag Over Capitol	.40	.20	
b.	Inscribed "T" at bottom	.50	.40	
c.	Black field of stars	—	—	
e.	Imperf., pair	12.50	—	

Booklet Stamp, Perf. 10 Horizontal on 1 or 2 Sides

2116	22c Flag Over Capitol	.50	.20	
a.	Booklet pane of 5	2.50	1.25	

Booklet Stamps, Perf. 10

2117	22c Frilled Dogwinkle	.40	.20	
2118	22c Reticulated Helmet	.40	.20	
2119	22c New England Neptune	.40	.20	
2120	22c Calico Scallop	.40	.20	
2121	22c Lightning Whelk	.40	.20	
a.	Booklet pane of 10, 2 ea. #2117-2121	4.00	3.00	
b.	As "a.," violet omitted	800.00		
c.	As "a.," vert. imperf. btwn.	600.00		
d.	As "a.," imperf.	—	—	
e.	Strip of 5, #2117-2121	2.00	—	

Booklet Stamp, Perf. 10 Vertically on 1 or 2 Sides

2122	$10.75 Eagle & Half Moon, Type I	19.00	7.50	
a.	Booklet pane of 3	60.00	—	
b.	Type II	22.50	10.00	
c.	As "b," booklet pane of 3	70.00	—	

Type I has a washed out dull appearance. Denomination appears splotchy or grainy. (P#11111) Type II has brighter, more intense colors. Denomination appears smoother (P#22222).

1985-87, Coil Stamps, Perf. 10 Vertically

2123	3.4c School Bus, tagged	.20	.20	
a.	Untagged (Bureau Precancel)	.20	.20	
2124	4.9c Buckboard, tagged	.20	.20	
a.	Untagged (Bureau Precancel)	.20	.20	
2125	5.5c Star Route Truck, tagged	.20	.20	
a.	Untagged (Bureau precancel)	.20	.20	
2126	6c Tricycle, tagged	.20	.20	
a.	Untagged (Bureau Precancel)	.20	.20	
b.	As "a.," imperf., pair	200.00		
2127	7.1c Tractor, tagged	.20	.20	
a.	Untagged (Bureau Precancel)	.20	.20	
2128	8.3c Ambulance, tagged	.20	.20	
a.	Untagged (Bureau Precancel)	.20	.20	

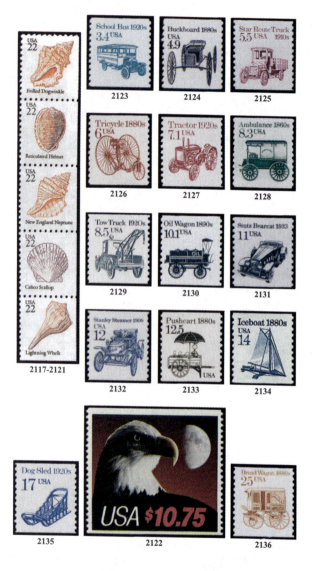

USA 22 Frilled Dogwinkle	
USA 22 Reticulated Helmet	
USA 22 New England Neptune	
USA 22 Calico Scallop	
USA 22 Lightning Whelk	

2117-2121

School Bus 1920s 3.4 USA
2123

Buckboard 1880s USA 4.9
2124

Star Route Truck 5.5 USA 1910s
2125

Tricycle 1880s 6 USA
2126

Tractor 1920s 7.1 USA
2127

Ambulance 1860s 8.3 USA
2128

Tow Truck 1920s 8.5 USA
2129

Oil Wagon 1890s 10.1 USA
2130

Stutz Bearcat 1933 11 USA
2131

Stanley Steamer 1909 USA 12
2132

Pushcart 1880s 12.5 USA
2133

Iceboat 1880s USA 14
2134

Dog Sled 1920s 17 USA
2135

USA $10.75
2122

Bread Wagon 1880s 25 USA
2136

HOW TO USE THIS BOOK

The number in the first column is its Scott number or identifying number.
Following that is the denomination of the stamp and its color. Finally, the value,
unused and used is shown.

Scott No.	Description	Unused Value	Used Value	//////
2129 8.5c	Tow Truck, tagged...........................	.20	.20	
a.	Untagged (Bureau Precancel).........	.20	.20	
2130 10.1c	Oil Wagon, tagged...........................	.25	.20	
a.	Untagged (Bureau Precancel).........	.25	.25	
b.	As "a.," imperf., pair.....................	15.00		
2131 11c	Stutz Bearcat	.25	.20	
2132 12c	Stanley Steamer, Type I, tagged......	.25	.20	
a.	Untagged (Bureau Precancel).........	.25	.25	
b.	Type II, untagged (Bureau Precancel)	.40	.30	

Type II has "Stanley Steamer 1909" 17½ mm. On Type I it is 18 mm.

2133 12.5c	Pushcart, tagged..............................	.25	.20	
a.	Untagged (Bureau Precancel).........	.25	.25	
b.	As "a.," imperf., pair.....................	50.00		
2134 14c	Iceboat, Type I.................................	.30	.20	
a.	Imperf., pair....................................	100.00		
b.	Type II..	.30	.20	

Type I design is 17½ mm wide, has overall tagging.
Type II is 17¼ mm wide, has block tagging.

2135 17c	Dog Sled...	.30	.20	
a.	Imperf., pair....................................	500.00		
2136 25c	Bread Wagon....................................	.45	.20	
a.	Imperf., pair....................................	10.00		
b.	Pair, imperf. btwn............................	750.00		

1985

2137 22c	Mary McLeod Bethune....................	.40	.20	
2138 22c	Broadbill Decoy	.65	.20	
2139 22c	Mallard Decoy..................................	.65	.20	
2140 22c	Canvasback Decoy	.65	.20	
2141 22c	Redhead Decoy	.65	.20	
a.	Block of 4, #2138-2141	4.00	2.75	
2142 22c	Winter Special Olympics	.40	.20	
a.	Vert. pair, imperf. horiz.................	550.00		
2143 22c	Love...	.40	.20	
a.	Imperf., pair....................................	1,500.		
2144 22c	Rural Electrification Administration	.45	.20	
2145 22c	AMERIPEX '86...............................	.40	.20	
a.	Red, black & blue omitted..............	200.00		
b.	Red & black omitted.......................	1,250.		
c.	Red omitted	—		
d.	Black omitted	—		
2146 22c	Abigail Adams..................................	.40	.20	
a.	Imperf., pair....................................	275.00		
2147 22c	Frederic Auguste Bartholdi.............	.40	.20	

Coil Stamps, Perf. 10 Vertically

2149 18c	George Washington, tagged.............	.35	.20	
a.	Untagged (Bureau Precancel).........	.35	.35	
b.	Imperf., pair....................................	950.00		
c.	As "a.," imperf., pair......................	800.00		

2137

2138-2141

2142

2143

2144

2145

2146

2147

2149

2150

2152

2153

2154

2155-2158

2160-2163

HOW TO USE THIS BOOK

The number in the first column is its Scott number or identifying number. Following that is the denomination of the stamp and its color. Finally, the value, unused and used is shown.

| 2168 | 2169 | 2170 | 2171 | 2172 |

| 2173 | 2175 | 2176 | 2177 | 2178 |

| 2179 | 2180 | 2181 | 2182 | 2183 |

| 2184 | 2185 | 2186 | 2187 | 2188 |

| 2189 | 2190 | 2191 | 2192 |

| 2193 | 2194 | 2195 | 2196 |

186

Scott No.		Description	Unused Value	Used Value	/ / / / / /
2150	21.1c	Envelopes, tagged	.40	.20	
a.		Untagged (Bureau Precancel)	.40	.40	
1985					
2152	22c	Korean War Veterans	.40	.20	
2153	22c	Social Security Act	.40	.20	
2154	22c	World War I Veterans	.40	.20	
a.		Red omitted	—		
2155	22c	Quarter Horse	1.00	.20	
2156	22c	Morgan Horse	1.00	.20	
2157	22c	Saddlebred Horse	1.00	.20	
2158	22c	Appaloosa Horse	1.00	.20	
a.		Block of 4, #2155-2158	6.00	5.00	
2159	22c	Public Education	.45	.20	
2160	22c	YMCA Youth Camping	.65	.20	
2161	22c	Boy Scouts	.65	.20	
2162	22c	Big Brothers/Big Sisters	.65	.20	
2163	22c	Camp Fire	.65	.20	
a.		Block of 4, #2160-2163	3.00	2.25	
2164	22c	Help End Hunger	.45	.20	
2165	22c	Christmas - Religious	.40	.20	
a.		Imperf., pair	100.00		
2166	22c	Christmas - Poinsettias	.40	.20	
a.		Imperf., pair	130.00		
1986-93					
2167	22c	Arkansas Statehood	.40	.20	
a.		Vert. pair, imperf. horiz.	—		
2168	1c	Margaret Mitchell	.20	.20	
2169	2c	Mary Lyon, tagged	.20	.20	
2170	3c	Dr. Paul Dudley White	.20	.20	
2171	4c	Father Edward Flanagan, tagged	.20	.20	
a.		4c grayish violet	.20	.20	
b.		4c deep grayish blue	.20	.20	
2172	5c	Hugo L. Black	.20	.20	
2173	5c	Luis Munoz Marin, tagged	.20	.20	
a.		Untagged	.20	.20	
2175	10c	Red Cloud, lake	.20	.20	
e.		10c carmine	.20	.20	
2176	14c	Julia Ward Howe	.25	.20	
2177	15c	Buffalo Bill Cody	.35	.20	
2178	17c	Belva Ann Lockwood	.30	.20	
2179	20c	Dr. Virginia Apgar, red brown	.40	.20	
a.		20c orange brown	.40	.20	
2180	21c	Chester Carlson	.40	.20	
2181	23c	Mary Cassatt	.45	.20	
2182	25c	Jack London, perf. 11	.45	.20	
a.		Booklet pane of 10	4.50	3.75	
d.		Horiz. pair, imperf btwn	—		
2183	28c	Sitting Bull	.50	.20	
2184	29c	Earl Warren	.55	.20	

2159

2164

2165

2166

2167

2202

2203

2204

2211

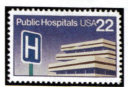

2210

2205-2209

188

Scott No.	Description	Unused Value	Used Value	/ / / / / /
2185	29c Thomas Jefferson	.50	.20	
2186	35c Dennis Chavez	.65	.20	
2187	40c Claire Chennault, dark blue	.70	.20	
2188	45c Dr. Harvey Cushing, bright blue	.85	.20	
a.	45c blue	1.65	.20	
2189	52c Hubert H. Humphrey	1.10	.20	
2190	56c John Harvard	1.10	.20	
2191	65c H.H. 'Hap' Arnold	1.20	.20	
2192	75c Wendell Willkie	1.30	.20	
2193	$1 Bernard Revel	2.50	.50	
2194	$1 Johns Hopkins, intense deep blue	1.75	.50	
b.	$1 deep blue	1.75	.50	
d.	$1 dark blue	1.75	.50	
e.	$1 blue	1.75	.60	
2195	$2 William Jennings Bryan	4.00	.50	
2196	$5 Bret Harte	8.50	1.00	
Booklet Stamp, Perf. 10 on 2 or 3 Sides				
2197	25c Jack London (2182)	.45	.20	
a.	Booklet pane of 6	3.00	2.25	
1986				
2198	22c Handstamped Cover	.45	.20	
2199	22c Boy, Stamp Collection	.45	.20	
2200	22c No. 836 Magnified	.45	.20	
2201	22c No. 2216 on First Day Cover	.45	.20	
a.	Booklet pane of 4, #2198-2201	2.00	1.75	
b.	As "a.," black omitted on #2198, 2201	50.00	—	
c.	As "a.," blue (litho.) omitted on #2198-2200	2,500.		
d.	As "a.," buff (litho.) omitted	—		
2202	22c Love	.40	.20	
2203	22c Sojourner Truth	.40	.20	
2204	22c Republic of Texas	.40	.20	
a.	Horiz. pair, imperf. vert.	1,100.		
b.	Dark red omitted	2,750.		
c.	Dark blue omitted	8,500.		
2205	22c Muskellunge	.60	.20	
2206	22c Atlantic Cod	.60	.20	
2207	22c Largemouth Bass	.60	.20	
2208	22c Bluefin Tuna	.60	.20	
2209	22c Catfish	.60	.20	
a.	Booklet pane of 5, #2205-2209	5.50	2.75	
2210	22c Public Hospitals	.40	.20	
a.	Vert. pair, imperf. horiz.	325.00		
b.	Horiz. pair, imperf. vert.	1,350.		
2211	22c Duke Ellington	.40	.20	
a.	Vert. pair, imperf. horiz.	1,000.		
2216	Washington-Harrison, sheet of 9	4.25		
a.-i.	22c Any single	.45	.25	
j.	Blue omitted	3,250.		

2216

2217

2218

2219

2198-2201

2220-2223

2235-2238

2225

2224

2226

2240-2243

2239

2246

Scott No.	Description	Unused Value	Used Value	/ / / / / /
k.	Black inscription omitted..............	*2,000.*		
l.	Imperf.	*10,500.*		
2217	Tyler-Grant, sheet of 9	4.25	—	
a.-i. 22c	Any single	.45	.25	
j.	Black inscription omitted..............	*3,750.*		
2218	Hayes-Wilson, sheet of 9	4.25		
a.-i. 22c	Any single	.45	.25	
j.	Brown omitted................................	—		
k.	Black inscription omitted..............	*2,900.*		
2219	Harding-Johnson, White House, sht. of 9	4.25	—	
a.-i. 22c	Any single	.45	.25	
j.	Blkish blue (engr.) inscription omitted on a.-b., d.-e., g.-h.	—		
l.	Blackish blue (engr.) omitted on all stamps....................................	—		
2220 22c	Elisha Kent Kane	.65	.20	
2221 22c	Adolphus W. Greely	.65	.20	
2222 22c	Vilhjalmur Stefansson..................	.65	.20	
2223 22c	Robert E. Peary & Matthew Henson	.65	.20	
a.	Block of 4, #2220-2223	2.75	2.25	
b.	As "a," black (engr.) omitted	*8,500.*		
2224 22c	Statue of Liberty	.40	.20	
a.	Scarlet omitted	—		

1986-87, Coil Stamps, Perf. 10 Vertically

Scott No.	Description	Unused Value	Used Value	/ / / / / /
2225 1c	Omnibus, tagged	.20	.20	
a.	Untagged	.20	.20	
c.	Imperf., pair...................................	*2,000.*		
2226 2c	Locomotive, tagged........................	.20	.20	
a.	Untagged	.20	.20	
2228 4c	Stagecoach (1898A).......................	.20	.20	
b.	Imperf., pair...................................	300.00		
2231 8.3c	Ambulance (2128), (Bureau precancel)......................	.20	.20	

On No. 2228 "Stagecoach 1890s" is 17 mm long, on No. 1898A 19¹/₂ mm long. On No. 2231 "Ambulance 1860s" is 18 mm long, on No. 2128 18¹/₂ mm long.

1986

Scott No.	Description	Unused Value	Used Value	/ / / / / /
2235 22c	Navajo Art - Stripes & Diamonds ..	.50	.20	
2236 22c	Navajo Art - 2 Diamonds Across....	.50	.20	
2237 22c	Navajo Art - 5 Diamonds Across....	.50	.20	
2238 22c	Navajo Art - 4 Diamonds Across....	.50	.20	
a.	Block of 4, #2235-2238	2.50	2.25	
b.	As "a," black (engr.) omitted	*350.00*		
2239 22c	T.S. Eliot......................................	.40	.20	
2240 22c	Highlander Figure	.40	.20	
2241 22c	Ship Figurehead	.40	.20	
2242 22c	Nautical Figure..............................	.40	.20	
2243 22c	Cigar Store Indian.........................	.40	.20	

2244   2245   2247

2248   2249   2250   2251

2268   2267   2269

2271   2272   2274

2270   2273

Scott No.	Description	Unused Value	Used Value	—/—/—/—/—/—/
a.	Block of 4, #2240-2243	1.75	1.75	
b.	As "a.," imperf. vert.	*1,500.*		
2244	22c Christmas - Religious....................	.40	.20	
2245	22c Christmas - Village........................	.40	.20	

1987
2246	22c Michigan Statehood	.40	.20	
2247	22c Pan-American Games	.40	.20	
a.	Silver omitted........................	*1,500.*		
2248	22c Love	.40	.20	
2249	22c Jean Baptiste Pointe du Sable	.40	.20	
2250	22c Enrico Caruso................................	.40	.20	
a.	Black (engr.) omitted	*5,000.*		
2251	22c Girl Scouts....................................	.40	.20	
a.	All litho. colors omitted.................	*2,500.*		
b.	Red & black (engr.) omitted	*2,000.*		

1987-88, Coil Stamps, Perf. 10 Vertically
2252	3c Conestoga Wagon, tagged..............	.20	.20	
a.	Untagged	.20	.20	
2253	5c Milk Wagon..................................	.20	.20	
2254	5.3c Elevator (Bureau precancel in scarlet)	.20	.20	
2255	7.6c Carretta (Bureau precancel in scarlet)	.20	.20	
2256	8.4c Wheelchair (Bureau precancel in red)	.20	.20	
a.	Imperf., pair.................................	*700.00*		
2257	10c Canal Boat.....................................	.20	.20	
e.	Imperf., pair.................................	—		
2258	13c Patrol Wagon (Bureau precancel in red)	.25	.25	
2259	13.2c Coal Car (Bureau precancel in red)	.25	.25	
a.	Imperf., pair.................................	*100.00*		
2260	15c Tugboat..	.25	.20	
c.	Imperf., pair.................................	*800.00*		
2261	16.7c Popcorn Wagon (Bureau precancel in blk)	.30	.30	
a.	Imperf., pair.................................	*225.00*		
2262	17.5c Racing Car, tagged.......................	.30	.20	
a.	Untagged (Bureau precancel)	.30	.30	
b.	Imperf., pair.................................	*2,250.*		
2263	20c Cable Car.......................................	.35	.20	
a.	Imperf., pair.................................	*75.00*		
2264	20.5c Fire Engine (Bureau precancel in black)	.40	.40	
2265	21c Railroad Mail Car (Bureau precancel in red)	.40	.40	
a.	Imperf., pair.................................	*65.00*		
2266	24.1c Tandem Bicycle (Bureau precancel in red)	.45	.45	

1987, Booklet Stamps
2267	22c Congratulations	.65	.20	
2268	22c Get Well..	.80	.20	
2269	22c Thank You......................................	.80	.20	

Scott No.	Description	Unused Value	Used Value	/ / / / / /
2270	22c Love You, Dad	.80	.20	
2271	22c Best Wishes	.80	.20	
2272	22c Happy Birthday	.65	.20	
2273	22c Love You, Mother	1.25	.20	
2274	22c Keep in Touch	.80	.20	
a.	Booklet pane of 10 (#2268-2271, 2273-2274, 2 each #2267, 2272)	10.00	5.00	

1987

Scott No.	Description	Unused Value	Used Value	/ / / / / /
2275	22c United Way	.40	.20	
2276	22c Flag & Fireworks	.40	.20	
a.	Booklet pane of 20	8.50	—	
2277	(25c) "E" & Earth, perf 11	.45	.20	
2278	25c Flag & Clouds, perf 11	.45	.20	

Coil Stamps, Perf. 10 Vertically

Scott No.	Description	Unused Value	Used Value	/ / / / / /
2279	(25c) "E" & Earth (2277)	.45	.20	
a.	Imperf., pair	85.00	—	
2280	25c Flag Over Yosemite, Green Trees	.45	.20	
c.	Imperf., pair	15.00		
e.	Black trees	100.00	—	
f.	Pair, imperf. btwn.	800.00		
2281	25c Honeybee	.45	.20	
a.	Imperf., pair	50.00		
b.	Black (engr.) omitted	60.00		
c.	Black (litho.) omitted	450.00		
d.	Pair, imperf. between	1,000.		
e.	Yellow (litho.) omitted	1,200.		

Booklet Stamps

Scott No.	Description	Unused Value	Used Value	/ / / / / /
2282	(25c) "E" & Earth (2277), perf. 10	.50	.20	
a.	Booklet pane of 10	6.50	3.50	
2283	25c Pheasant, multicolored	.50	.20	
a.	Booklet pane of 10	6.00	3.50	
b.	25c multi, red removed from sky	6.25	.20	
c.	As "b," booklet pane of 10	67.50	—	
d.	As "a," horiz. imperf. btwn.	2,250.		
2284	25c Grosbeak	.50	.20	
2285	25c Owl	.50	.20	
b.	Bklt. pane of 10, 5 each #2284-2285	5.00	3.50	
d.	Pair, #2284-2285	1.10	.25	
2285A	25c Flag & Clouds (2278), perf. 10	.50	.20	
c.	Booklet pane of 6	3.00	2.00	

1987

Scott No.	Description	Unused Value	Used Value	/ / / / / /
2286	22c Barn swallow	.85	.20	
2287	22c Monarch butterfly	.85	.20	
2288	22c Bighorn sheep	.85	.20	
2289	22c Broad-tailed hummingbird	.85	.20	
2290	22c Cottontail	.85	.20	

Scott No.	Description	Unused Value	Used Value	/ / / / / /
2291	22c Osprey	.85	.20	
2292	22c Mountain lion	.85	.20	
2293	22c Luna moth	.85	.20	
2294	22c Mule deer	.85	.20	
2295	22c Gray squirrel	.85	.20	
2296	22c Armadillo	.85	.20	
2297	22c Eastern chipmunk	.85	.20	
2298	22c Moose	.85	.20	
2299	22c Black bear	.85	.20	
2300	22c Tiger swallowtail	.85	.20	
2301	22c Bobwhite	.85	.20	
2302	22c Ringtail	.85	.20	
2303	22c Red-winged blackbird	.85	.20	
2304	22c American lobster	.85	.20	
2305	22c Black-tailed jack rabbit	.85	.20	
2306	22c Scarlet tanager	.85	.20	
2307	22c Woodchuck	.85	.20	
2308	22c Roseate spoonbill	.85	.20	
2309	22c Bald eagle	.85	.20	
2310	22c Alaskan brown bear	.85	.20	
2311	22c Iiwi	.85	.20	
2312	22c Badger	.85	.20	
2313	22c Pronghorn	.85	.20	
2314	22c River otter	.85	.20	
2315	22c Ladybug	.85	.20	
2316	22c Beaver	.85	.20	
2317	22c White-tailed deer	.85	.20	
2318	22c Blue jay	.85	.20	
2319	22c Pika	.85	.20	
2320	22c American Buffalo	.85	.20	
2321	22c Snowy egret	.85	.20	
2322	22c Gray wolf	.85	.20	
2323	22c Mountain goat	.85	.20	
2324	22c Deer mouse	.85	.20	
2325	22c Black-tailed prairie dog	.85	.20	
2326	22c Box turtle	.85	.20	
2327	22c Wolverine	.85	.20	
2328	22c American elk	.85	.20	
2329	22c California sea lion	.85	.20	
2330	22c Mockingbird	.85	.20	
2331	22c Raccoon	.85	.20	
2332	22c Bobcat	.85	.20	
2333	22c Black-footed ferret	.85	.20	
2334	22c Canada goose	.85	.20	
2335	22c Red fox	.85	.20	
a.	Pane of 50, #2286-2335	47.50		
	2286b-2335b, any single, red omitted	—		

Conestoga Wagon 1800s — USA 3 — 2252	Milk Wagon 1900s — 5 USA — 2253	Elevator 1900s — 5.3 USA — Nonprofit Carrier Route Sort — 2254	Carreta 1770s — 7.6 USA — Nonprofit — 2255
Wheel Chair 1920s — 8.4 USA — Nonprofit — 2256	Canal Boat 1880s — 10 USA — 2257	Patrol Wagon 1880s — USA 13 — Presorted First-Class — 2258	Coal Car 1870s — 13.2 USA — Bulk Rate — 2259
Tugboat 1900s — USA 15 — 2260	Popcorn Wagon 16.7 USA 1902 — Bulk Rate — 2261	Racing Car 1911 — USA 17.5 — ZIP+4 Presort — 2262	USA 20 — Cable Car 1880s — 2263
	Fire Engine 1900s — 20.5 USA — ZIP+4 Presort — 2264	Railroad Mail Car 1920s — Presorted First-Class — 21 USA — 2265	Tandem Bicycle — 1890s 24.1 — USA — ZIP+4 — 2266

HOW TO USE THIS BOOK

The number in the first column is its Scott number or identifying number. Following that is the denomination of the stamp and its color. Finally, the value, unused and used is shown.

Scott No.	Description	Unused Value	Used Value	/ / / / / /
1987-90				
2336	22c Delaware Ratification	.60	.20	
2337	22c Pennsylvania Ratification	.60	.20	
2338	22c New Jersey Ratification	.60	.20	
a.	Black (engr.) omitted	5,500.		
2339	22c Georgia Ratification	.60	.20	
2340	22c Connecticut Ratification	.60	.20	
2341	22c Massachusetts Ratification	.60	.20	
2342	22c Maryland Ratification	.60	.20	
2343	25c South Carolina Ratification	.60	.20	
a.	Strip of 3, vert. imperf. btwn.	—		
b.	Red omitted.	—		
2344	25c New Hampshire Ratification	.60	.20	
2345	25c Virginia Ratification	.60	.20	
2346	25c New York Ratification	.60	.20	
2347	25c North Carolina Ratification	.60	.20	
2348	25c Rhode Island Ratification	.60	.20	
1987				
2349	22c U.S.-Morocco Diplomatic Relations	.40	.20	
a.	Black (engr.) omitted	275.00		
2350	22c William Faulkner	.40	.20	
2351	22c Lacemaking - Upper Left	.45	.20	
2352	22c Lacemaking - Upper Right	.45	.20	
2353	22c Lacemaking - Lower Left	.45	.20	
2354	22c Lacemaking - Lower Right	.45	.20	
a.	Block of 4, #2351-2354	1.90	1.90	
b.	As "a," white omitted	950.00		
2355	22c "The Bicentennial . . ."	.55	.20	
a.	Grayish green (background) omitted	—		
2356	22c "We the People . . ."	.55	.20	
a.	Grayish green (background) omitted	—		
2357	22c "Establish Justice, . . ."	.55	.20	
a.	Grayish green (background) omitted	—		
2358	22c "And Secure . . ."	.55	.20	
a.	Grayish green (background) omitted	—		
2359	22c "Do Ordain . . ."	.55	.20	
a.	Bklt. pane of 5, #2355-2359	2.75	2.25	
b.	Grayish green (background) omitted	—		
2360	22c Signing of the Constitution	.45	.20	
2361	22c Certified Public Accounting	1.50	.20	
a.	Black (engr.) omitted	725.00		
2362	22c Stourbridge Lion	.55	.20	
2363	22c Best Friend of Charleston	.55	.20	
2364	22c John Bull	.55	.20	
2365	22c Brother Jonathan	.55	.20	
a.	Red omitted	—		
2366	22c Gowan and Marx	.55	.20	
a.	Booklet pane of 5, #2362-2366	2.75	2.50	
b.	As "a," black omitted on #2366	—		

2275

2276

2277

2278

2280

2281

2283

2284

2285

2286-2335

Scott No.	Description	Unused Value	Used Value	/ / / / / /
2367	22c Christmas - Religious......................	.40	.20	
2368	22c Christmas - Ornaments	.40	.20	
1988				
2369	22c Olympics - Skiing	.40	.20	
2370	22c Australia Bicentennial....................	.40	.20	
2371	22c James Weldon Johnson	.40	.20	
2372	22c Siamese, Exotic Shorthair Cats	.45	.20	
2373	22c Abyssinian, Himalayan Cats...........	.45	.20	
2374	22c Maine Coon, Burmese Cats.............	.45	.20	
2375	22c American Shorthair, Persian Cats....	.45	.20	
a.	Block of 4, #2372-2375	1.90	1.90	
2376	22c Knute Rockne................................	.40	.20	
2377	25c Francis Ouimet..............................	.45	.20	
2378	25c Rose..	.45	.20	
a.	Imperf., pair..................................	3,000.		
2379	45c Roses	.65	.20	
2380	25c Olympics - Gymnastics Rings	.45	.20	
2381	25c 1928 Locomobile	.60	.20	
2382	25c 1929 Pierce-Arrow.........................	.60	.20	
2383	25c 1931 Cord......................................	.60	.20	
2384	25c 1932 Packard..................................	.60	.20	
2385	25c 1935 Duesenberg	.60	.20	
a.	Booklet pane of 5, #2381-2385	6.00	2.25	
2386	25c Nathaniel Palmer...........................	.65	.20	
2387	25c Lt. Charles Wilkes.........................	.65	.20	
2388	25c Richard E. Byrd	.65	.20	
2389	25c Lincoln Ellsworth	.65	.20	
a.	Block of 4, #2386-2389	2.75	2.00	
b.	Black (engr.) omitted	1,500.		
c.	As "a.," imperf. horiz.	3,000.		
2390	25c Deer	.65	.20	
2391	25c Horse	.65	.20	
2392	25c Camel..	.65	.20	
2393	25c Goat	.65	.20	
a.	Block of 4, #2390-2393	3.00	2.00	
2394	$8.75 Eagle and Moon	13.50	8.00	
2395	25c Happy Birthday	.50	.20	
2396	25c Best Wishes	.50	.20	
a.	Bklt. pane, 3 #2395 + 3 #2396 with gutter btwn.	3.50	3.25	
2397	25c Thinking of You.............................	.50	.20	
2398	25c Love You.......................................	.50	.20	
a.	Bklt. pane of 6, 3 #2397 + 3 #2398 with gutter btwn.	3.50	3.25	
b.	As "a.," imperf. horiz.	—		
2399	25c Christmas - Religious......................	.45	.20	
a.	Gold omitted	30.00		
2400	25c Christmas - Sleigh..........................	.45	.20	

Dec 7,1787   USA
Delaware 22

Dec 12,1787
Pennsylvania

Dec 18,1787   USA
New Jersey 22

2336   2337   2338

January 2, 1788
Georgia

January 9,1788
Connecticut

Feb 6, 1788
Massachusetts

2339   2340   2341

April 28, 1788   USA
Maryland 22

May 23, 1788
South Carolina

June 21,1788
New Hampshire

2342   2343   2344

June 25, 1788   USA
Virginia 25

July 26, 1788   USA
New York 25

November 21,1789
North Carolina

May 29, 1790
Rhode Island

2345   2346   2347   2348

Scott No.	Description	Unused Value	Used Value	/ / / / / /
1989				
2401	25c Montana Statehood	.45	.20	
2402	25c A. Philip Randolph	.45	.20	
2403	25c North Dakota Statehood	.45	.20	
2404	25c Washington Statehood	.45	.20	
2405	25c Experiment	.45	.20	
2406	25c Phoenix	.45	.20	
2407	25c New Orleans	.45	.20	
2408	25c Washington	.45	.20	
2409	25c Walk in the Water	.45	.20	
a.	Booklet pane of 5, #2405-2409	2.25	1.75	
2410	25c World Stamp Expo '89	.45	.20	
2411	25c Arturo Toscanini	.45	.20	
1989-90				
2412	25c House of Representatives	.50	.20	
2413	25c Senate	.50	.20	
2414	25c Executive Branch	.50	.20	
2415	25c Supreme Court	.50	.20	
1989				
2416	25c South Dakota Statehood	.45	.20	
2417	25c Lou Gehrig	.50	.20	
2418	25c Ernest Hemingway	.45	.20	
a.	Vert. pair, imperf. horiz.	—		
2419	$2.40 Moon Landing	4.00	2.00	
a.	Black (engr.) omitted	2,500.		
b.	Imperf., pair	750.00		
c.	Black (litho.) omitted	3,250.		
2420	25c Letter Carriers	.45	.20	
2421	25c Bill of Rights	.45	.20	
a.	Black (engr.) omitted	325.00		
2422	25c Tyrannosaurus Rex	.65	.20	
2423	25c Pteranodon	.65	.20	
2424	25c Stegosaurus	.65	.20	
2425	25c Brontosaurus	.65	.20	
a.	Block of 4, #2422-2425	3.00	2.00	
b.	As "a.," black (engr.) omitted	750.00		
2426	25c Columbian Artifacts	.45	.20	
2427	25c Christmas - Religious	.45	.20	
a.	Booklet pane of 10	4.75	3.50	
b.	Red (litho.) omitted	850.00		
2428	25c Christmas - Sleigh, perf. 11	.45	.20	
a.	Vert. pair, imperf. horiz.	2,000.		
Booklet Stamps, Perf. 11½ on 2 or 3 Sides				
2429	25c Christmas - Sleigh (2428)	.45	.20	
a.	Booklet pane of 10	4.75	3.50	
b.	As "a.," horiz. imperf. btwn.	—		
d.	As "a.," red omitted	—		

2349

2351-2354

2355-2359

2350   **2360**

2367   **2368**

2361   **2369**

2362-2366

2370

2371

2376

2372-2375

2377 2378 2379

2381-2385

2380

2390-2393

Scott No.	Description	Unused Value	Used Value	/ / / / / /
Die cut, Self-adhesive				
2431	25c Eagle and Shield	.50	.20	☐☐☐☐☐
a.	Booklet pane of 18	11.00		☐☐☐☐☐
b.	Vert. pair, no die cutting btwn.	*850.00*		
1989				
2433	World Stamp Expo '89, sheet of 4 ..	14.00	9.00	☐☐☐☐☐
a.	90c like No. 122	2.00	1.75	☐☐☐☐☐
b.	90c like No. 132TC (blue frame, brown center)	2.00	1.75	☐☐☐☐☐
c.	90c like No. 132TC (green frame, blue center)	2.00	1.75	☐☐☐☐☐
d.	90c like No. 132TC (scarlet frame, blue center)	2.00	1.75	☐☐☐☐☐
2434	25c Stagecoach	.45	.20	☐☐☐☐☐
2435	25c Paddlewheel Steamer	.45	.20	☐☐☐☐☐
2436	25c Biplane	.45	.20	☐☐☐☐☐
2437	25c Automobile	.45	.20	☐☐☐☐☐
a.	Block of 4, #2434-2437	2.00	1.75	☐☐☐☐☐
b.	As "a.," dark blue (engr.) omitted....	*700.00*		
2438	UPU Congress, sheet of 4, imperf.	4.00	1.75	☐☐☐☐☐
a.	25c Stagecoach (2434)	.65	.25	☐☐☐☐☐
b.	25c Paddlewheel Steamer (2435)	.65	.25	☐☐☐☐☐
c.	25c Biplane (2436)	.65	.25	☐☐☐☐☐
d.	25c Automobile (2437)	.65	.25	☐☐☐☐☐
e.	Dark blue & gray (engr.) omitted....	*5,500.*		
1990				
2439	25c Idaho Statehood	.45	.20	☐☐☐☐☐
2440	25c Love, perf. 12$\frac{1}{2}$x13	.45	.20	☐☐☐☐☐
a.	Imperf., pair	*800.00*		
Booklet Stamp, Perf. 11½ on 2 or 3 Sides				
2441	25c Love (2440)	.45	.20	☐☐☐☐☐
a.	Booklet pane of 10	4.75	*3.50*	☐☐☐☐☐
b.	As "a.," bright pink omitted	*1,900.*		☐☐☐☐☐
c.	As "b.," single stamp	180.00		
2442	25c Ida B. Wells	.45	.20	☐☐☐☐☐
2443	15c Beach Umbrella	.30	.20	☐☐☐☐☐
a.	Booklet pane of 10	3.00	*2.00*	☐☐☐☐☐
b.	As "a.," blue omitted	*1,400.*		☐☐☐☐☐
c.	As 2443, blue omitted	*140.00*		
2444	25c Wyoming Statehood	.45	.20	☐☐☐☐☐
a.	Black (engr.) omitted	*2,100.*	—	☐☐☐☐☐
2445	25c The Wizard of Oz	1.00	.20	☐☐☐☐☐
2446	25c Gone With the Wind	1.00	.20	☐☐☐☐☐
2447	25c Beau Geste	1.00	.20	☐☐☐☐☐
2448	25c Stagecoach	1.00	.20	☐☐☐☐☐
a.	Block of 4, #2445-2448	4.50	3.50	☐☐☐☐☐
2449	25c Marianne Moore	.45	.20	☐☐☐☐☐

2386-2389

2394

2395

2396

2397

2398

2399

2400

2401

2402

2403

2404

2410

2411

2405-2409

2412

2413

2414

2415

2416

2417

2418

2419

2420

2421

2422-2425

2426

Scott No.	Description	Unused Value	Used Value	/ / / / / /

1990-95, Coil Stamps, Perf. 10 Vertically

2451	4c Steam Carriage, tagged..................	.20	.20	
a.	Imperf., pair.................................	700.00		
b.	Untagged.......................................	.20	.20	
2452	5c Circus Wagon, engr., tagged...........	.20	.20	
a.	Untagged.......................................	.20	.20	
c.	Imperf., pair.................................	900.		
2452B	5c Circus Wagon (2452), photo...........	.20	.20	
2452D	5c Circus Wagon with cent sign (2452).	.20	.20	
2453	5c Canoe, brown, engr. (Bureau precancel in gray).....................................	.20	.20	
a.	Imperf., pair.................................	300.00		
2454	5c Canoe (2453), red, photo. (Bureau precancel in gray)............	.20	.20	
2457	10c Tractor Trailer, engr. (Bureau precancel in gray).....................................	.20	.20	
a.	Imperf., pair.................................	250.00		
b.	All color omitted...........................	—		
2458	10c Tractor Trailer (2457), photo. (Bureau precancel in black)...........	.20	.20	
2463	20c Cog Railway (2451)......................	.40	.20	
a.	Imperf., pair.................................	12500		
2464	23c Lunch Wagon...............................	.45	.20	
a.	Imperf., pair.................................	150.00		
2466	32c Ferryboat (2451)...........................	.60	.20	
a.	Imperf., pair.................................	600.00		
b.	Bright blue....................................	6.00	—	
2468	$1 Seaplane....................................	1.75	.50	
a.	Imperf., pair.................................	2,500.	—	

1990, Booklet Stamps

2470	25c Admiralty Head Lighthouse............	1.00	.20	
2471	25c Cape Hatteras Lighthouse..............	1.00	.20	
2472	25c West Quoddy Head Lighthouse......	1.00	.20	
2473	25c American Shoals Lighthouse..........	1.00	.20	
2474	25c Sandy Hook Lighthouse.................	1.00	.20	
a.	Bklt. pane of 5, #2470-2474...........	5.50	2.00	
b.	As "a.," white (USA 25).................	80.00		

Die cut, Self-adhesive

2475	25c Flag...	.50	.25	
a.	Pane of 12.....................................	6.00		
a.	Pane of 18.....................................	9.00		

1990-95

2476	1c American Kestrel...........................	.20	.20	
2477	1c American Kestrel with cent sign....	.20	.20	
2478	3c Eastern Bluebird, no cent sign........	.20	.20	
a.	Vert. pair, imperf. horiz..................	—		
b.	Double impression of all colors except yellow......................................	—		
2479	19c Fawn..	.35	.20	

2427

2428

2431

2433

2439

2434-2437

2442

2440

2443

Scott No.	Description	Unused Value	Used Value	//////
2480	30c Cardinal	.50	.20	
2481	45c Pumpkinseed Sunfish	.80	.20	
a.	Black (engr.) omitted	525.00	—	
2482	$2 Bobcat	3.00	1.25	
a.	Black (engr.) omitted	300.00		

1991-95, Booklet Stamps

2483	20c Blue Jay	.50	.20	
a.	Booklet pane of 10	5.25	2.25	
b.	As "a," imperf	200.00		
2484	29c Wood Duck, black denomination	.50	.20	
a.	Booklet pane of 10	5.50	3.75	
b.	Vert. pair, imperf. btwn.	—		
2485	29c Wood Duck (2484), red denomination	.50	.20	
a.	Booklet pane of 10	5.50	4.00	
b.	Vert. pair, imperf. btwn.	—		
c.	Imperf., pair.	—		
2486	29c African Violets	.50	.20	
a.	Booklet pane of 10	5.50	4.00	
2487	32c Peach	.60	.20	
2488	32c Pear	.60	.20	
a.	Booklet pane, 5 each #2487-2488	6.00	4.25	
b.	Pair, #2487-2488	1.25	.30	

1993-95, Booklet Stamps, Die cut, Self-adhesive

2489	29c Red Squirrel	.50	.20	
a.	Booklet pane of 18	10.00		
b.	As "a," die cutting omitted	—		
2490	29c Rose, red, green & black	.50	.20	
a.	Booklet pane of 18	10.00		
2491	29c Pine Cone	.50	.20	
a.	Booklet pane of 18	11.00		

Serpentine Die Cut

2492	32c Rose (2490), pink, green & black	.60	.20	
a.	Bklt. pane of 20 + label	12.00		
b.	Bklt. pane of 15 + label	8.75		
c.	Horiz. pair, no die cutting btwn.	—		
d.	As "a," 2 stamps and parts of 7 others printed on backing liner	—		
e.	Booklet pane of 14	21.00		
f.	Booklet pane of 16	21.00		
h.	Vertical pair, no die cutting btwn	—		
2493	32c Peach (2487)	.60	.20	
2494	32c Pear (2488)	.60	.20	
a.	Bklt. pane, 10 each #2493-2494 + label	12.50		
b.	Pair, #2493-2494	1.20		

1995, Coil Stamps, Serpentine Die Cut, Vert.

2495	32c Peach (2487)	.60	.20	
2495A	32c Pear (2488)	.60	.20	

2444   2449

2445-2448   2451   2452

2453   2457

2464   2468

2470-2474

214

Scott No.	Description	Unused Value	Used Value	/ / / / / /
1990				
2496	25c Jesse Owens	.60	.20	
2497	25c Ray Ewry	.60	.20	
2498	25c Hazel Wightman	.60	.20	
2499	25c Eddie Eagan	.60	.20	
2500	25c Helene Madison	.60	.20	
a.	Strip of 5, #2496-2500	3.25	2.50	
b.	As "a," blue omitted	—		
2501	25c Assiniboin	.80	.20	
2502	25c Cheyenne	.80	.20	
2503	25c Comanche	.80	.20	
2504	25c Flathead	.80	.20	
2505	25c Shoshone	.80	.20	
a.	Bklt. pane, 2 each #2501-2505	8.50	3.50	
b.	As "a," black (engr.) omitted	3,250.		
c.	Strip of 5, #2501-2505	2.75	1.00	
d.	As "a," horiz. imperf. btwn.	—		
2506	25c Micronesia	.45	.20	
2507	25c Marshall Islands	.45	.20	
a.	Pair, #2506-2507	.90	.60	
b.	As "a," black (engr.) omitted	2,750.		
2508	25c Killer Whale	.45	.20	
2509	25c Northern Sea Lion	.45	.20	
2510	25c Sea Otter	.45	.20	
2511	25c Common Dolphin	.45	.20	
a.	Block of 4, #2508-2511	1.90	1.90	
b.	As "a," black (engr.) omitted	700.00		
2512	25c Grand Canyon	.45	.20	
2513	25c Dwight D. Eisenhower	.60	.20	
a.	Imperf., pair	2,250.		
2514	25c Christmas - Religious	.45	.20	
a.	Booklet pane of 10	5.00	3.25	
2515	25c Christmas - Tree, perf. 11	.45	.20	
a.	Vert. pair, imperf. horiz.	1,100.		
b.	All colors missing.	—		
Booklet Stamp, Perf. 11½ x11 on 2 or 3 Sides				
2516	25c Christmas - Tree (2515)	.45	.20	
a.	Booklet pane of 10	5.00	3.25	
1991				
2517	(29c) "F" & Flower, perf. 13, yellow, black, red & yellow green	.50	.20	
a.	Imperf., pair	700.00		
b.	Horiz. pair, imperf. vert.	1,250.		
Coil Stamp, Perf. 10 Vertically				
2518	(29c) "F" & Flower (2517), yellow, black, dull red & dark yellow green	.50	.20	
a.	Imperf., pair	42.50		

2475

2476   2477

2478

2482

2483   2487

2488   2489

2490   2491

2496-2500

2501-2505

216

Scott No.	Description	Unused Value	Used Value	/ / / / / /
Booklet Stamps, Perf. 11 on 2 or 3 Sides				
2519	(29c) "F" & Flower (2517), yellow, black, dull red & dk green, bullseye perfs.	.50	.20	☐☐☐☐☐
a.	Booklet pane of 10	6.50	*4.50*	☐☐☐☐☐
2520	(29c) "F" & Flower (2517), pale yellow, black, red & brt green	.50	.20	☐☐☐☐☐
a.	Booklet pane of 10	18.00	*4.50*	☐☐☐☐☐
b.	As "a," imperf. horiz.	—		☐☐☐☐☐
1991				
2521	(4c) Text	.20	.20	☐☐☐☐☐
a.	Vert. pair, imperf. horiz.	*110.00*		☐☐☐☐☐
Die cut, Self-adhesive				
2522	(29c) "F" & Flag	.55	.25	☐☐☐☐☐
a.	Pane of 12	7.00		☐☐☐☐☐
Coil Stamps, Perf. 10 Vertically				
2523	29c Flag over Mt. Rushmore, blue, red & claret, engraved	.50	.20	☐☐☐☐☐
b.	Imperf., pair	*25.00*		☐☐☐☐☐
c.	Blue, red & brown	5.00	—	☐☐☐☐☐
2523A	29c Flag over Mt. Rushmore (2523), blue, red & brown, photogravure	.50	.20	☐☐☐☐☐
1991-92, Perf. 11				
2524	29c Flower, dull yellow, black, red & yellow green	.50	.20	☐☐☐☐☐
Perf. 13 x 12½				
2524A	29c Flower, dull yellow, black, red & yellow green (2524)	.75	.20	☐☐☐☐☐
Coil Stamps, Rouletted 10 Vertically				
2525	29c Flower (2524), pale yellow, black, red & yellow green	.50	.20	☐☐☐☐☐
Perf. 10 Vertically				
2526	29c Flower (2524), pale yellow, black, red & yellow green	.50	.20	☐☐☐☐☐
Booklet Stamp, Perf. 11 on 2 or 3 sides				
2527	29c Flower (2524), pale yellow, black, red & bright green	.50	.20	☐☐☐☐☐
a.	Booklet pane of 10	5.50	*3.50*	☐☐☐☐☐
b.	As "a," vert. imperf. btwn.	*1,500.*		☐☐☐☐☐
d.	As "a," imperf. horiz.	*2,750.*		☐☐☐☐☐
1991				
2528	29c Flag & Olympic Rings	.50	.20	☐☐☐☐☐
a.	Booklet pane of 10	5.25	*3.50*	☐☐☐☐☐
b.	As "a," horiz. imperf. btwn., perfed at top and bottom	—		☐☐☐☐☐
c.	Vert. pair, imperf. btwn., perfed at top and bottom	—		☐☐☐☐☐

2479

2480

2481

2484

2486

2506-2507

2508-2511

2512

2513

2514

2515

2517

2521

2522

Scott No.	Description	Unused Value	Used Value	/ / / / / /
d.	Vert. strip of 3, top or bottom pair imperf. btwn............................	—		
e.	Vert. pair, imperf. horiz....................	2,000.		

1991-94, Coil Stamps, Perf. 9.8 Vertically

2529	19c Fishing Boat, tagged........................	.35	.20	
a.	Type II (finer dot pattern)...............	.35	.20	
b.	As "a.," untagged	1.00	.40	
2529C	19c Fishing Boat (2529), one loop of rope	.50	.20	

Booklet Stamp, Perf. 10 on 2 or 3 Sides

2530	19c Balloon	.35	.20	
a.	Booklet pane of 10............................	3.50	2.75	

1991

2531	29c Flags on Parade	.50	.20	

Die cut, Self-adhesive

2531A	29c Liberty Torch................................	.55	.25	
b.	Pane of 18..	10.50		
c.	Pair, imperf.	—		

1991

2532	50c Switzerland..................................	1.00	.25	
a.	Vert. pair, imperf. horiz..................	2,250.		
2533	29c Vermont Statehood........................	.55	.20	
2534	29c Savings Bonds.............................	.50	.20	

Perf. 12½ x13

2535	29c Love..	.50	.20	
b.	Imperf., pair......................................	—		

Perf. 11

2535A	29c Love (2535).....................................	.75	.20	

Booklet Stamp, Perf. 11 on 2 or 3 Sides

2536	29c Love (2535).................................	.50	.20	
a.	Booklet pane of 10...........................	5.25	3.50	
2537	52c Love...	.90	.20	
2538	29c William Saroyan............................	.50	.20	
2539	$1 Eagle & Olympic Rings..................	1.75	.50	

1991-95

2540	$2.90 Eagle..	5.00	2.50	
a.	Vert. pair, imperf. horiz..................	—		
2541	$9.95 Eagle..	15.00	7.50	
2542	$14 Eagle...	22.50	10.00	
2543	$2.90 Futuristic Space Shuttle	5.00	2.25	
2544	$3 Space Shuttle *Challenger*	5.25	2.25	

2523

2524

2528

2529

2530

2531

2531A

2532

2533

2534

2535

2537

2538

2544

2544A

Scott No.	Description	Unused Value	Used Value	/ / / / / /
c.	Horiz. pair, imperf. btwn.	—		
d.	Imperf, pair.	2,250.		
2544A	$10.75 Space Shuttle *Endeavour*	17.50	7.50	
1991				
2545	29c Royal Wulff	1.00	.20	
2546	29c Jock Scott	1.00	.20	
2547	29c Apte Tarpon Fly	1.00	.20	
2548	29c Lefty's Deceiver	1.00	.20	
2549	29c Muddler Minnow	1.00	.20	
a.	Booklet pane of 5, #2545-2549	5.50	2.50	
2550	29c Cole Porter	.50	.20	
a.	Vert. pair, imperf. horiz.	650.00		
2551	29c Desert Shield & Desert Storm	.50	.20	
a.	Vert. pair, imperf. horiz.	1,500.		
2552	29c Desert Shield & Desert Storm (2551) 20½ mm wide (from bklt. pane)	.50	.20	
a.	Booklet pane of 5	2.75	2.25	
2553	29c Olympics - Pole Vault	.50	.20	
2554	29c Olympics - Discus	.50	.20	
2555	29c Olympics - Women's Sprints	.50	.20	
2556	29c Olympics - Javelin	.50	.20	
2557	29c Olympics - Women's Hurdles	.50	.20	
a.	Strip of #2553-2557	2.75	2.25	
2558	29c Numismatics	.50	.20	
2559	World War II, block of 10	5.25	5.00	
a.-j.	29c Any single	.50	.30	
k.	Black (engr.) omitted	10,000.		
2560	29c Basketball	.50	.20	
2561	29c District of Columbia	.50	.20	
a.	Black (engr.) omitted	110.00		
2562	29c Laurel and Hardy	.55	.20	
2563	29c Bergen and McCarthy	.55	.20	
2564	29c Jack Benny	.55	.20	
2565	29c Fanny Brice	.55	.20	
2566	29c Abbott and Costello	.55	.20	
a.	Booklet pane, 2 each #2562-2566	6.00	3.50	
b.	As "a.," scarlet & bright violet (engr.) omitted	700.00		
c.	Strip of 5, #2562-2566	2.75	—	
2567	29c Jan E. Matzeliger	.50	.20	
a.	Horiz. pair, imperf. vert.	1,500.		
b.	Vert. pair, imperf. horiz.	1,500.		
c.	Imperf. pair.	1,250.		
2568	29c Mercury	.85	.20	
2569	29c Venus	.85	.20	
2570	29c Earth	.85	.20	
2571	29c Moon	.85	.20	

2539

2540

2541

2542

2543

2550

2545-2549

2551

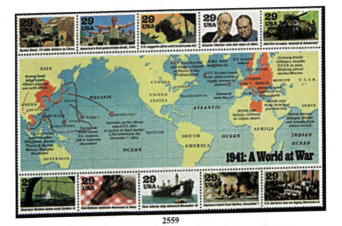

2559

2558

2560

2567

2561

223

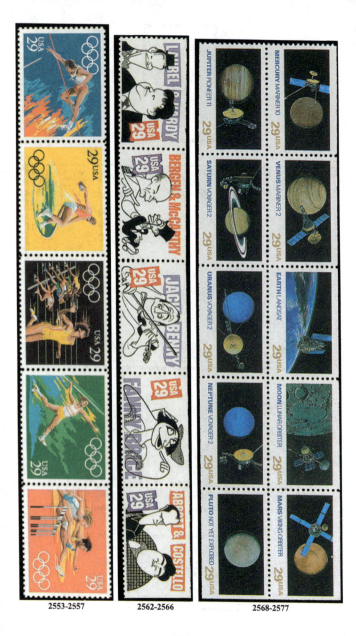

2553-2557   2562-2566   2568-2577

Scott No.	Description	Unused Value	Used Value	/ / / / / /
2572	29c Mars	.85	.20	
2573	29c Jupiter	.85	.20	
2574	29c Saturn	.85	.20	
2575	29c Uranus	.85	.20	
2576	29c Neptune	.85	.20	
2577	29c Pluto	.85	.20	
a.	Booklet pane of 10, #2568-2577	9.00	3.50	
2578	(29c) Christmas - Religious	.50	.20	
a.	Booklet pane of 10	5.50	3.25	
b.	As "a.," single, red & black (engr.) omitted	3,500.		
2579	(29c) Christmas - Santa in Chimney, perf 11	.50	.20	
a.	Horiz. pair, imperf. vert.	300.00		
b.	Vert. pair, imperf. horiz.	500.00		

Booklet Stamps, Size: 25x18½ mm, Perf. 11 on 2 or 3 sides

2580	(29c) Christmas - Santa in Chimney (2579), Type I	1.75	.20	
2581	(29c) Christmas - Santa in Chimney (2579), Type II.	1.75	.20	
a.	Pair, #2580, 2581	3.50	.25	
b.	Bklt. pane, 2 each #2580, 2581	7.50	1.25	
	The extreme left brick in the top row of chimney is missing on Type II, No. 2581.			
2582	(29c) Christmas - Santa Checking List	.50	.20	
a.	Booklet pane of 4	2.00	1.25	
2583	(29c) Christmas - Santa with Presents	.50	.20	
a.	Booklet pane of 4	2.00	1.25	
2584	(29c) Christmas - Santa at Fireplace	.50	.20	
a.	Booklet pane of 4	2.00	1.25	
2585	(29c) Christmas - Santa and Sleigh	.50	.20	
a.	Booklet pane of 4	2.00	1.25	

1995, Perf. 11.2

2587	32c James K. Polk	.60	.20	

1994, Perf. 11.5

2590	$1 Surrender of Gen. John Burgoyne	1.90	.50	
2592	$5 Washington and Jackson	8.00	2.50	

1992-93, Booklet Stamps
Perf. 10 on 2 or 3 sides

2593	29c Flag, black denomination	.50	.20	
a.	Booklet pane of 10	5.25	4.25	

Perf. 11 x 10 on 2 or 3 sides

2593B	29c Flag, black denomination (2593)	1.00	.50	
c.	Booklet pane of 10	10.00	6.00	

Perf. 11x10 on 2 or 3 Sides

2594	29c Flag (2593), red denomination	.50	.20	
a.	Booklet pane of 10	5.25	4.25	

2578 2579 2582

2583 2584 2585

2587 2592 2590

2593 2595

Scott No.	Description	Unused Value	Used Value	/ / / / / /
1992-94, Die cut, Self-adhesive				
2595	29c Eagle & Shield, brown denomination	.50	.25	
a.	Booklet pane of 17 + label	13.00		
b.	Pair, no die cutting	200.00		
c.	Brown (engr.) omitted....................	450.00		
d.	As "a," no die cutting.....................	1,750.		
2596	29c Eagle & Shield (2595), green denom.	.50	.25	
a.	Booklet pane of 17 + label	12.00		
2597	29c Eagle & Shield (2595), red denom..	.50	.25	
a.	Booklet pane of 17 + label	10.00		
2598	29c Eagle	.50	.20	
a.	Booklet pane of 18.........................	10.00		
2599	29c Statue of Liberty	.50	.20	
a.	Booklet pane of 18.........................	10.00		
1991-93, Coil Stamps, Perf. 10 Vertically				
2602	(10c) Eagle & Shield (Bureau precancel, Bulk Rate, in blue)........................	.20	.20	
a.	Imperf. pair.....................................	—		
2603	(10c) Eagle & Shield, orange yellow & multi (Bureau precancel, Bulk Rate, in red)	.20	.20	
a.	Imperf., pair....................................	30.00		
2604	(10c) Eagle & Shield (2603), gold & multi (Bureau precancel, Bulk Rate, in red)	.20	.20	
2605	23c Flag (Bureau precancel in blue)	.40	.40	
2606	23c Reflected Flag (Bureau precanceled)	.40	.40	
2607	23c Reflected Flag (2606), multi (Bureau precanceled)....................	.40	.40	
c.	Imperf., pair....................................	90.00		
2608	23c Reflected Flag (2606), violet blue, red & black (Bureau precanceled).	.40	.40	
	On No. 2607 "First Class" is 9mm long. On No. 2608 "First Class" is 8 1/2 mm long.			
2609	29c Flag over White House.	.50	.20	
a.	Imperf. pair.....................................	20.00		
b.	Pair, imperf. btwn...........................	100.00		
1992				
2611	29c Olympics - Ice Hockey	.50	.20	
2612	29c Olympics - Figure Skating..............	.50	.20	
2613	29c Olympics - Speed Skating	.50	.20	
2614	29c Olympics - Skiing	.50	.20	
2615	29c Olympics - Bobsledding	.50	.20	
a.	Strip of 5, #2611-2615.....................	2.75	2.50	
2616	29c World Columbian Stamp Expo........	.50	.20	
2617	29c W.E.B. DuBois	.50	.20	
2618	29c Love	.50	.20	
a.	Horiz. pair, imperf. vert.	750.00		
b.	As "a," green omitted on right stamp	—		

2598

2599

2602

2603

2605

2606

2609

2618

2616

2617

2619

2611-2615

Scott No.	Description	Unused Value	Used Value	/ / / / / /
2619	29c Olympic Baseball............................	.50	.20	
2620	29c Seeking Queen Isabella's Support ...	.50	.20	
2621	29c Crossing the Atlantic.......................	.50	.20	
2622	29c Approaching Land	.50	.20	
2623	29c Coming Ashore	.50	.20	
a.	Block of 4, #2620-2623	2.00	2.00	
2624	First Sighting of Land, sheet of 3	1.75	—	
a.	1c deep blue (like No. 230)................	.20	.20	
b.	4c ultramarine (like No. 233)	.20	.20	
c.	$1 salmon (like No. 241)	1.65	1.00	
2625	Claiming a New World (2624), sht. of 3	6.75	—	
a.	2c brown violet (like No. 231)	.20	.20	
b.	3c green (like No. 232)........................	.20	.20	
c.	$4 crimson lake (like No. 244).............	6.50	4.00	
2626	Seeking Royal Support (2624), sheet of 3	1.40	—	
a.	5c chocolate (like No. 234)	.20	.20	
b.	30c orange brown (like No. 239)...........	.50	.30	
c.	50c slate blue (like No. 240).................	.80	.50	
2627	Royal Favor Restored (2624), sheet of 3	5.25	—	
a.	6c purple (like No. 235)	.20	.20	
b.	8c magenta (like No. 236)	.20	.20	
c.	$3 yellow green (like No. 243).............	4.75	3.00	
2628	Reporting Discoveries (2624) Sht. of 3	3.75	—	
a.	10c black brown (like No. 237).............	.20	.20	
b.	15c dark green (like No. 238)................	.25	.20	
c.	$2 brown red (like No. 242)	3.25	2.00	
2629	$5 Christopher Columbus (2624), sheet of 1 (like No. 245)................	8.50	—	
a.	$5 black, single stamp..........................	8.00	5.00	
2630	29c New York Stock Exchange	.50	.20	
a.	Black omitted.	—		
c.	Center inverted.	—		
2631	29c Cosmonaut.......................................	.50	.20	
2632	29c Astronaut	.50	.20	
2633	29c Apollo Modules	.50	.20	
2634	29c Soyuz	.50	.20	
a.	Block of 4, #2631-2634	2.00	1.90	
2635	29c Alaska Highway	.50	.20	
a.	Black (engr.) omitted	500.00		
2636	29c Kentucky Statehood	.50	.20	
a.	Dark blue omitted.	—		
b.	Dark blue and red omitted.	—		
c.	All colors omitted.	—		
2637	29c Olympics - Soccer............................	.50	.20	
2638	29c Olympics - Gymnastics....................	.50	.20	
2639	29c Olympics - Volleyball	.50	.20	

2620-2623

2624-2629

2630

2635

2636

2631-2634

2637-2641

2642-2646

2698   2699

2700-2703

Scott No.	Description	Unused Value	Used Value	/ / / / / /
2640	29c Olympics - Boxing	.50	.20	
2641	29c Olympics - Swimming	.50	.20	
a.	Strip of 5, #2637-2641	2.50	2.25	
2642	29c Ruby-Throated Hummingbird	.50	.20	
2643	29c Broad-billed Hummingbird	.50	.20	
2644	29c Costa's Hummingbird	.50	.20	
2645	29c Rufous Hummingbird	.50	.20	
2646	29c Calliope Hummingbird	.50	.20	
a.	Booklet pane of 5, #2642-2646	2.75	2.25	
2647	29c Indian Paintbrush	.50	.20	
2648	29c Fragrant Water Lily	.50	.20	
2649	29c Meadow Beauty	.50	.20	
2650	29c Jack-in-the-Pulpit	.50	.20	
2651	29c California Poppy	.50	.20	
2652	29c Large-flowered Trillium	.50	.20	
2653	29c Tickseed	.50	.20	
2654	29c Shooting Star	.50	.20	
2655	29c Stream Violet	.50	.20	
2656	29c Bluets	.50	.20	
2657	29c Herb Robert	.50	.20	
2658	29c Marsh Marigold	.50	.20	
2659	29c Sweet White Violet	.50	.20	
2660	29c Claret Cup Cactus	.50	.20	
2661	29c White Mountain Avens	.50	.20	
2662	29c Sessile Bellwort	.50	.20	
2663	29c Blue Flag	.50	.20	
2664	29c Harlequin Lupine	.50	.20	
2665	29c Twinflower	.50	.20	
2666	29c Common Sunflower	.50	.20	
2667	29c Sego Lily	.50	.20	
2668	29c Virginia Bluebells	.50	.20	
2669	29c Ohia Lehua	.50	.20	
2670	29c Rosebud Orchid	.50	.20	
2671	29c Showy Evening Primrose	.50	.20	
2672	29c Fringed Gentian	.50	.20	
2673	29c Yellow Lady's Slipper	.50	.20	
2674	29c Passionflower	.50	.20	
2675	29c Bunchberry	.50	.20	
2676	29c Pasqueflower	.50	.20	
2677	29c Round-lobed Hepatica	.50	.20	
2678	29c Wild Columbine	.50	.20	
2679	29c Fireweed	.50	.20	
2680	29c Indian Pond Lily	.50	.20	
2681	29c Turk's Cap Lily	.50	.20	
2682	29c Dutchman's Breeches	.50	.20	
2683	29c Trumpet Honeysuckle	.50	.20	
2684	29c Jacobs Ladder	.50	.20	
2685	29c Plains Prickly Pear	.50	.20	
2686	29c Moss Campion	.50	.20	

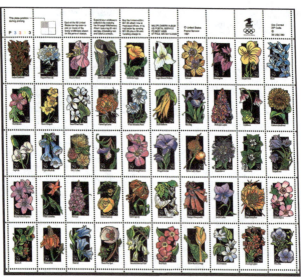

2647-2696

2697

Scott No.	Description	Unused Value	Used Value	/ / / / / /
2687	29c Bearberry	.50	.20	
2688	29c Mexican Hat	.50	.20	
2689	29c Harebell	.50	.20	
2690	29c Desert Five Spot	.50	.20	
2691	29c Smooth Solomon's Seal	.50	.20	
2692	29c Red Maids	.50	.20	
2693	29c Yellow Skunk Cabbage	.50	.20	
2694	29c Rue Anemone	.50	.20	
2695	29c Standing Cypress	.50	.20	
2696	29c Wild Flax	.50	.20	
a.	Pane of 50, #2647-2696	25.00	—	
2697	World War II, block of 10	5.25	4.50	
a.-j.	29c Any single	.50	.30	
k.	Red (litho.) omitted	10,000.		
2698	29c Dorothy Parker	.50	.20	
2699	29c Theodore von Karman	.50	.20	
2700	29c Azurite	.50	.20	
2701	29c Copper	.50	.20	
2702	29c Variscite	.50	.20	
2703	29c Wulfenite	.50	.20	
a.	Block or strip of 4, #2700-2703	2.00	1.75	
b.	As "a.," silver (litho.) omitted	8,500.		
c.	As "a.," red (litho.) omitted	—		
d.	As "a.," silver (litho.) omitted	—		
2704	29c Juan Rodriguez Cabrillo	.50	.20	
2705	29c Giraffe	.50	.20	
2706	29c Giant Panda	.50	.20	
2707	29c Flamingo	.50	.20	
2708	29c King Penguins	.50	.20	
2709	29c White Bengal Tiger	.50	.20	
a.	Booklet pane of 5, #2705-2709	2.50	2.00	
b.	As "a.," imperforate	3,000.		
2710	29c Christmas - Religious	.50	.20	
a.	Booklet pane of 10	5.25	3.50	
2711	29c Christmas - Horse	.50	.20	
2712	29c Christmas - Locomotive	.50	.20	
2713	29c Christmas - Fire Pumper	.50	.20	
2714	29c Christmas - Boat	.50	.20	
a.	Block of 4, #2711-2714	2.00	1.10	

Booklet Stamps, Perf. 11 on 2 or 3 sides

Scott No.	Description	Unused Value	Used Value	/ / / / / /
2715	29c Christmas - Horse (2711)	.50	.20	
2716	29c Christmas - Locomotive (2712)	.50	.20	
2717	29c Christmas - Fire Pumper (2713)	.50	.20	
2718	29c Christmas - Boat (2714)	.50	.20	
a.	Booklet pane of 4, #2715-2718	2.25	1.25	
b.	As "a.," imperf. horiz.	—		
c.	As "a.," imperf.	—		

2704

2710

2720

Giraffe

Giant Panda

Flamingo

King Penguins

White Bengal Tiger

2705-2709

2724-2730

2722

2723

GREETINGS GREETINGS

GREETINGS GREETINGS

2711-2714

Scott No.	Description	Unused Value	Used Value	/ / / / / /
Die cut, Self-adhesive				
2719	29c Christmas - Locomotive (2712).......	.60	.20	☐☐☐☐☐
a.	Booklet pane of 18...........................	11.00	—	☐☐☐☐☐
1992				
2720	29c Year of the Rooster...........................	.50	.20	☐☐☐☐☐
1993				
2721	29c Elvis Presley, "Elvis" only (2724)...	.50	.20	☐☐☐☐☐
a.	Imperf, pair.....................................	—		☐☐☐☐☐
2722	29c Oklahoma!, no frameline	.50	.20	☐☐☐☐☐
Perf. 10				
2723	29c Hank Williams, 27½ mm inscription,	.50	.20	☐☐☐☐☐
Perf. 11.2 x 11.5				
2723A	29c Hank Williams, 27½ mm inscription (2723)........................	22.50	—	☐☐☐☐☐
Perf. 10				
2724	29c Elvis Presley, with "Presley," no frameline	.60	.20	☐☐☐☐☐
2725	29c Bill Haley	.60	.20	☐☐☐☐☐
2726	29c Clyde McPhatter	.60	.20	☐☐☐☐☐
2727	29c Ritchie Valens	.60	.20	☐☐☐☐☐
2728	29c Otis Redding	.60	.20	☐☐☐☐☐
2729	29c Buddy Holly	.60	.20	☐☐☐☐☐
2730	29c Dinah Washington	.60	.20	☐☐☐☐☐
a.	Vert. strip of 7, #2724-2730.............	4.25		☐☐☐☐☐
Booklet stamps, Perf. 11 Horiz., with Framelines				
2731	29c Presley (2724)	.55	.20	☐☐☐☐☐
2732	29c Haley (2725)...................................	.55	.20	☐☐☐☐☐
2733	29c McPhatter (2726)	.55	.20	☐☐☐☐☐
2734	29c Valens (2727)	.55	.20	☐☐☐☐☐
2735	29c Redding (2728)	.55	.20	☐☐☐☐☐
2736	29c Holly (2729)	.55	.20	☐☐☐☐☐
2737	29c Washington (2730).........................	.55	.20	☐☐☐☐☐
a.	Booklet pane, 2 #2731, 1 each #2732-2737	5.00	2.25	☐☐☐☐☐
b.	Booklet pane, #2731, 2735-2737 + tab	2.25	1.50	☐☐☐☐☐
2741	29c Ringed Planet....................................	.55	.20	☐☐☐☐☐
2742	29c Craft without Wings.........................	.55	.20	☐☐☐☐☐
2743	29c Astronauts...	.55	.20	☐☐☐☐☐
2744	29c Craft with Long Wings	.55	.20	☐☐☐☐☐
2745	29c Craft with Short Wings....................	.55	.20	☐☐☐☐☐
a.	Booklet pane of 5, #2741-2745	2.75	2.25	☐☐☐☐☐
2746	29c Percy Lavon Julian..........................	.50	.20	☐☐☐☐☐
2747	29c Oregon Trail	.50	.20	☐☐☐☐☐
2748	29c World University Games.................	.50	.20	☐☐☐☐☐
2749	29c Grace Kelly	.50	.20	☐☐☐☐☐

2741-2745

2746

2749

2755

2747

2748

2754

2750-2753

2756-2759

2766

2760-2764

2765

239

2772-2774

2767-2770

2779-2782

2783-2784

2785-2788

2789

2791-2794

2804

2805

2806

2807-2811

2812

2813

2814

2815

2816

2817

Scott No.	Description	Unused Value	Used Value	/ / / / / /
2750	29c Clown	.55	.20	
2751	29c Ringmaster	.55	.20	
2752	29c Trapeze Artist	.55	.20	
2753	29c Elephant	.55	.20	
a.	Block of 4, #2750-2753	2.25	1.75	
2754	29c Cherokee Strip Land Run	.50	.20	
2755	29c Dean Acheson	.50	.20	
2756	29c Steeplechase	.50	.20	
2757	29c Thoroughbred Racing	.50	.20	
2758	29c Harness Racing	.50	.20	
2759	29c Polo	.50	.20	
a.	Block of 4, #2756-2759	2.00	1.75	
b.	As "a.," black (engr.) omitted	1,250.		
2760	29c Hyacinth	.50	.20	
2761	29c Daffodil	.50	.20	
2762	29c Tulip	.50	.20	
2763	29c Iris	.50	.20	
2764	29c Lilac	.50	.20	
a.	Booklet pane of 5, #2760-2764	2.50	2.00	
b.	As "a.," black (engr.) omitted	240.00		
c.	As "a.," imperf.	2,500.		
2765	World War II, block of 10	5.25	5.00	
a.-j.	29c Any single	.50	.30	
2766	29c Joe Louis	.50	.20	
2767	29c Show Boat	.50	.20	
2768	29c Porgy & Bess	.50	.20	
2769	29c Oklahoma! with frameline	.50	.20	
2770	29c My Fair Lady	.50	.20	
a.	Booklet pane of 4, #2767-2770	2.50	2.00	
2771	29c Hank Williams (2723), 27mm inscription	.55	.20	
2772	29c Patsy Cline	.55	.20	
2773	29c Carter Family	.55	.20	
2774	29c Bob Wills	.55	.20	
a.	Block or horiz. strip of 4, #2771-2774	2.20	1.75	

Booklet stamps, Perf. 11 Horiz., with Frameline

2775	29c Hank Williams (2723), 22mm inscript.	.50	.20	
2776	29c Carter Family	.50	.20	
2777	29c Patsy Cline	.50	.20	
2778	29c Bob Wills	.50	.20	
a.	Booklet pane of 4, #2775-2778	2.50	2.00	
2779	29c Benjamin Franklin	.50	.20	
2780	29c Civil War Soldier	.50	.20	
2781	29c Charles Lindbergh	.50	.20	
2782	29c Stamps	.50	.20	
a.	Block or strip of 4, #2779-2782	2.00	1.75	
b.	As "a.," black and maroon omitted	—		
c.	As "a.," imperf.	3,500.		

2819-2828

2829-2833

2818   2834   2835   2836

Scott No.	Description	Unused Value	Used Value	/ / / / /
2783	29c Recognizing Deafness......................	.50	.20	
2784	29c American Sign Language	.50	.20	
a.	Pair, #2783-2784	1.00	.65	
2785	29c Rebecca of Sunnybrook Farm	.50	.20	
2786	29c Little House on the Prairie..............	.50	.20	
2787	29c Adventures of Huckleberry Finn.....	.50	.20	
2788	29c Little Women...................................	.50	.20	
a.	Block or horiz. strip of 4, #2785-2788	2.00	2.00	
b.	As "a.," imperf.	*3,000.*		
2789	29c Christmas - Religious......................	.50	.20	

Booklet Stamp, Perf. 11½x11 on 2 or 3 Sides, 18x25 mm

2790	29c Christmas - Religious (2789)..........	.50	.20	
a.	Booklet pane of 4............................	2.25	*1.75*	
b.	Pair, imperf.	—		
c.	As "a.," imperf.	—		

Perf. 11½

2791	29c Christmas - Jack-in-the-Box	.50	.20	
2792	29c Christmas - Reindeer......................	.50	.20	
2793	29c Christmas - Snowman......................	.50	.20	
2794	29c Christmas - Toy Soldier	.50	.20	
a.	Block or strip of 4, #2791-2794	2.00	2.00	

Booklet Stamps, Perf. 11x10 on 2 or 3 Sides

2795	29c Christmas - Toy Soldier (2794)	.85	.20	
2796	29c Christmas - Snowman (2793)..........	.85	.20	
2797	29c Christmas - Reindeer (2792)	.85	.20	
2798	29c Christmas - Jack-in-the-Box (2791).50	.85		
a.	Booklet pane, 3 each #2795-2796, 2 each #2797-2798............	8.50	*4.00*	
b.	Booklet pane, 3 each #2797-2798, 2 each #2795-2796.....................	8.50	*4.00*	
c.	Block of 4, #2795-2798..................	3.40	1.75	

Die cut, Self-adhesive, 19½x26½mm

2799	29c Christmas - Snowman (2793)..........	.50	.20	
2800	29c Christmas - Toy Soldier (2794)	.50	.20	
2801	29c Christmas - Jack-in-the-Box (2791).50		.20	
2802	29c Christmas - Reindeer (2792)	.50	.20	
a.	Booklet pane, 3 each #2799-2802....	7.00		
b.	Block of 4, #2799-2802..................	2.00		

Die cut, Self-adhesive, 17x20 mm

2803	29c Christmas - Snowman (2793)..........	.50	.20	
a.	Booklet pane of 18........................	10.00		

Perf. 11

2804	29c Mariana Islands	.50	.20	

Perf. 11.2

2805	29c Columbus' Landing in Puerto Rico.	.50	.20	

2837

Allied forces retake New Guinea, 1944

2838a

2839

First Moon Landing, 1969

2841

2840

2843-2847

Scott No.	Description	Unused Value	Used Value	/ / / / / /
2806	29c AIDS Awareness	.50	.20	
a.	Perf. 11 vert. on 1 or 2 sides	.50	.20	
b.	As "a," booklet pane of 5	2.50	2.00	

1994

2807	29c Olympics - Slalom	.50	.20	
2808	29c Olympics - Luge	.50	.20	
2809	29c Olympics - Ice Dancing	.50	.20	
2810	29c Olympics - Cross-Country Skiing	.50	.20	
2811	29c Olympics - Ice Hockey	.50	.20	
a.	Strip of 5, #2807-2811	2.50	2.50	
2812	29c Edward R. Murrow	.50	.20	

Die cut, Self-adhesive

2813	29c Love	.50	.20	
a.	Pane of 18	11.00		

Booklet stamp, Perf. 10.9x11.1

2814	29c Love, photogravure	.50	.20	
a.	Booklet pane of 10	5.50	3.50	
b.	As "a," imperf.	—		
e.	Horiz. pair, imperf btwn.	—		

Perf. 11.1

2814C	29c Love (2814), litho. & engr.	.50	.20	
2815	52c Love	1.00	.20	
2816	29c Dr. Allison Davis	.50	.20	
2817	29c Year of the Dog	.55	.20	
2818	29c Buffalo Soldier	.50	.20	
a.	Double impression of red brown (engr. inscriptions).	—		
2819	29c Rudolph Valentino	.50	.20	
2820	29c Clara Bow	.50	.20	
2821	29c Charlie Chaplin	.50	.20	
2822	29c Lon Chaney	.50	.20	
2823	29c John Gilbert	.50	.20	
2824	29c Zasu Pitts	.50	.20	
2825	29c Harold Lloyd	.50	.20	
2826	29c Keystone Cops	.50	.20	
2827	29c Theda Bara	.50	.20	
2828	29c Buster Keaton	.50	.20	
a.	Block of 10, #2819-2828	5.00	4.00	
b.	As "a," black (litho.) omitted	—		
c.	As "a," red, black & bright violet (litho.) omitted	—		
2829	29c Lily	.50	.20	
2830	29c Zinnia	.50	.20	
2831	29c Gladiola	.50	.20	
2832	29c Marigold	.50	.20	
2833	29c Rose	.50	.20	

Scott No.	Description	Unused Value	Used Value	/ / / / / /
a.	Booklet pane of 5, #2829-2833	2.50	—	
b.	As "a.," imperf.	*2,250.*		
c.	As "a.," black (engr.) omitted	*250.00*		
2834	29c World Cup Soccer..........................	.50	.20	
2835	40c World Cup Soccer..........................	.80	.20	
2836	50c World Cup Soccer..........................	1.00	.20	
2837	World Cup Soccer, Sheet of 3, #a.-c. (like #2834-2836)	2.50	2.00	
2838	World War II, block of 10 (2765)....	6.00	5.50	
a.-j.	29c Any single	.60	.30	
2839	29c Norman Rockwell..........................	.50	.20	
2840	Norman Rockwell, sheet of 4..........	4.00	2.75	
a.	50c Freedom from Want......................	1.00	.65	
b.	50c Freedom from Fear.......................	1.00	.65	
c.	50c Freedom of Speech	1.00	.65	
d.	50c Freedom of Worship.....................	1.00	.65	
2841	Moon Landing, sheet of 12..............	7.50	—	
a.	29c Single stamp.................................	.60	.60	
2842	$9.95 Moon Landing..............................	17.50	7.50	
2843	29c Hudson's General..........................	.55	.20	
2844	29c McQueen's Jupiter.........................	.55	.20	
2845	29c Eddy's No. 242..............................	.55	.20	
2846	29c Ely's No. 10..................................	.55	.20	
2847	29c Buchanan's No. 999	.55	.20	
a.	Booklet pane of 5, #2843-2847	2.75	*2.00*	
2848	29c George Meany................................	.50	.20	
2849	29c Al Jolson......................................	.60	.20	
2850	29c Bing Crosby	.60	.20	
2851	29c Ethel Waters	.60	.20	
2852	29c Nat "King" Cole............................	.60	.20	
2853	29c Ethel Merman................................	.60	.20	
a.	Vert. strip of 5, #2849-2853.............	3.00	2.00	
2854	29c Bessie Smith.................................	.60	.20	
2855	29c Muddy Waters...............................	.60	.20	
2856	29c Billie Holiday...............................	.60	.20	
2857	29c Robert Johnson.............................	.60	.20	
2858	29c Jimmy Rushing..............................	.60	.20	
2859	29c "Ma" Rainey.................................	.50	.20	
2860	29c Mildred Bailey..............................	.50	.20	
2861	29c Howlin' Wolf	.50	.20	
a.	Block of 9, #2854-2861 +1 additional stamp	5.50	4.50	
2862	29c James Thurber	.50	.20	
2863	29c Motorboat.....................................	.50	.20	
2864	29c Ship..	.50	.20	
2865	29c Ship's Wheel................................	.50	.20	

2854–2861

2849–2853

2842

2848   2862

2863–2866

2951-2954

2867

2868

2871

2872

2869

2873

2874

2876

Scott No.	Description	Unused Value	Used Value	/ / / / / /
2866	29c Coral	.50	.20	
a.	Block of 4, #2963-2966	2.00	1.50	
b.	As "a.," imperf..............................	1,750.		
2867	29c Black-necked Crane	.50	.20	
2868	29c Whooping Crane	.50	.20	
a.	Pair, #2867-2868	1.00	.65	
b.	Black and magenta (engr.) omitted	2,000.		
2869	Legends of the West, pane of 20.....	12.00	—	
a.-t.	29c Any single.......................................	.60	.20	
2870	29c Legends of the West (2869), pane of 20....................................	190.00	—	

Nos. 2869 and 2870 have different Bill Pickett stamps. Framelines on No. 2870 are thinner than on No. 2869.

2871	29c Christmas - Religious, perf. 11¼....	1.50	.20	
2871A	29c Christmas-Religious, perf. 9¾x11 (2871)	.60	.20	
b.	Booklet Pane of 10	6.25	3.50	
c.	As "b," imperf.	2,500.		
2872	29c Christmas - Stocking......................	.50	.20	
a.	Booklet pane of 20	10.50	3.00	
b.	Imperf., pair..................................	—		
c.	As "a," imperf horiz.	—		
d.	Quadruple impression of black, triple impression of blue, double impression of red and yellow, green normal...	—		
2873	29c Christmas - Santa Claus.................	.50	.20	
a.	Booklet pane of 12	6.25		
2874	29c Christmas - Cardinal	.50	.20	
a.	Booklet pane of 18	9.50		
2875	$2 Bureau of Engraving & Printing, Sheet of 4, perf. 11	15.00	—	
a.	Single stamp (like No. 262)...........	3.00	1.25	
2876	29c Year of the Boar	.55	.20	
2877	(3c) Dove, tan, brt bl & red, thin inscript.	.20	.20	
a.	Imperf., pair..................................	200.00		
b.	Double impression of red...............	—		
2878	(3c) Dove (2877), tan, dk blue & red, heavy inscriptions	.20	.20	
2879	(20c) Flag, black "G," yellow & multi.....	.40	.20	
a.	Imperf pair....................................	—		
2880	(20c) Flag (2879), red "G," yellow & multi	.50	.20	
2881	(32c) Flag, black "G" & multi, perf 11.2x11.1	.75	.20	
a.	Booklet pane of 10	6.00	3.75	
2882	(32c) Flag (2881), red "G" & multi	.60	.20	

Distance on No. 2882 from bottom of red G to top of flag immediately above is 13 ¾ mm, on No. 2885 13 ½ mm.

2875

2877

2879

2881

2888

2893

2897

2902

2905

2907

2908

2911

2919

2933

2934

2938

2940

2941

2942

2943

2948

2949

Scott No.	Description	Unused Value	Used Value	/ / / / / /

Booklet stamps

2883 (32c)	Flag (2881), black "G" & multi, perf.10x9.9..............................	.60	.20	☐☐☐☐☐
a.	Booklet pane of 10	6.25	3.75	
2884 (32c)	Flag (2881), blue "G" & multi	.60	.20	☐☐☐☐☐
a.	Booklet pane of 10........................	6.00	3.75	
b.	As "a.," imperf.	—		
2885 (32c)	Flag (2881), red "G" & multi	.65	.20	☐☐☐☐☐
a.	Booklet pane of 10........................	6.50	3.75	
b.	Pair, imperf. vert.	—		
c.	Pair, imperf btwn...........................	—		

Self-adhesive, Die Cut

2886 (32c)	Flag (2881), gray, blue, light blue, red & black..............................	.60	.20	☐☐☐☐☐
a.	Booklet pane of 18........................	11.50		
2887 (32c)	Flag (2881), black, blue & red........	.60	.20	☐☐☐☐☐
a.	Booklet pane of 18........................	11.50		

No. 2886 has a small number of blue shading dots in white stripes immediately below the blue field. No. 2887 has noticeable blue shading.

1994-95, Coil Stamps, Perf. 9.8 Vert.

2888 (25c)	Flag, blue & multi	.50	.20	☐☐☐☐☐
2889 (32c)	Flag (2881), black "G" & multi......	.60	.20	☐☐☐☐☐
a.	Imperf., pair..................................	325.00		
2890 (32c)	Flag (2881), blue "G" & multi	.60	.20	☐☐☐☐☐
2891 (32c)	Flag (2881), red "G" & multi	.60	.20	

Rouletted 9.8 Vert.

2892 (32c)	Flag (2881), red "G" & multi	.60	.20	☐☐☐☐☐

Perf. 9.8 Vert.

2893 (5c)	Flag, green & multi (Bureau precancel)	.20	.20	☐☐☐☐☐

1995

2897	32c Flag over Porch................................	.60	.20	☐☐☐☐☐

Coil Stamps

2902 (5c)	Butte, perf....................................	.20	.20	☐☐☐☐☐
a.	Imperf., pair..................................	750.00		
2902B (5c)	Butte (2902), Serpentine Die Cut Vert.	.20	.20	
2903 (5c)	Mountain, perf, purple & multi	.20	.20	☐☐☐☐☐
2904 (5c)	Mountain (2903), perf, blue & multi	.20	.20	
2904A (5c)	Mountain (2903), Serpentine Die Cut Vert., purple, multi.................................	.20	.20	☐☐☐☐☐
2905 (10c)	Auto, perf.	.20	.20	☐☐☐☐☐
2906 (10c)	Auto (2905), Serpentine Die Cut Vert.	.20	.20	
2907 (10c)	Eagle and Shield (2603), Serpentine Die Cut Vert., gold & multi	.20	.20	☐☐☐☐☐
2908 (15c)	Auto Tail Fin, perf., dk org yel & multi	.30	.30	
2909 (15c)	Auto Tail Fin (2908), perf., buff & multi	.30	.30	☐☐☐☐☐

2950

2955

2956

2975

2999

3001

Scott No.	Description	Unused Value	Used Value	/ / / / / /
2910 (15c)	Auto Tail Fin (2908), Serpentine Die Cut Vert., buff & multi	.30	.30	☐☐☐☐☐

No. 2908 has dark bold colors and heavy shading lines, and heavily shaded chrome. No. 2909 has shinier chrome, more subdued colors and finer details.

2911 (25c)	Juke Box, dark red, dark yellow green & multi, perf.	.50	.50	☐☐☐☐☐
a.	Imperf., pair	—		☐☐☐☐☐
2912 (25c)	Juke Box (2911), brt org red, brt yel grn & multi, perf.	.50	.50	☐☐☐☐☐
2912A(25c)	Juke Box (2911), brt org red, brt yel grn & multi, Serpentine Die Cut Vert.	.50	.50	☐☐☐☐☐

No. 2911 has dark saturated colors, dark blue lines in music selection board. No. 2912 has bright colors, less shading and light blue lines in music selection board.

2913	32c Flag (2897), blue, tan, brown, red & lt blue, perf.	.60	.20	☐☐☐☐☐
a.	Imperf., pair	60.00		☐☐☐☐☐
2914	32c Flag (2897), blue, yellow brown, red & gray, perf.	.60	.20	☐☐☐☐☐

No. 2913 has light blue shading in flag, No. 2914 has pale gray shading.

Self-Adhesive, Serpentine Die Cut Vert.

2915	32c Flag (2897), cut 8.7 vert.	.60	.30	☐☐☐☐☐
2915A	32c Flag (2897), cut 9.8 vert., 10 or 11 "peaks" on each side	.60	.20	☐☐☐☐☐
h.	Imperf., pair	40.00		☐☐☐☐☐
i.	Tan omitted		2,000.	☐☐☐☐☐
j.	Double die cutting, one through center of stamp	30.00	—	☐☐☐☐☐
2915B	32c Flag (2897), cut 11.5 vert.	.60	.20	☐☐☐☐☐
2915C	32c Flag (2897), cut 10.9 vert.	.60	.20	☐☐☐☐☐
2915D	32c Flag (2897), cut 9.8 vert., 9 and/or 10 "peaks" on each side	.60	.20	☐☐☐☐☐

Booklet Stamps, Perf. 10.8x9.8 on 2 or 3 sides

2916	32c Flag (2897), blue, tan, brn, red & lt blue	.60	.20	☐☐☐☐☐
a.	Booklet pane of 10	6.00	3.25	☐☐☐☐☐
b.	As "a.," imperf.	—		☐☐☐☐☐

Self-Adhesive

2919	32c Flag over Field, Die Cut	.60	.20	☐☐☐☐☐
a.	Booklet pane of 18	11.00		☐☐☐☐☐
2920	32c Flag (2897), large date, Serpentine Die Cut 8.7	.60	.20	☐☐☐☐☐
a.	Booklet pane of 20 + label	12.00		☐☐☐☐☐
b.	Small date	3.00	.20	☐☐☐☐☐
c.	As "b.," booklet pane of 20 + label	110.00		☐☐☐☐☐
f.	As No. 2920, pane of 15 + label	9.00	.20	☐☐☐☐☐
h.	As No. 2920, booklet pane of 15	35.00		☐☐☐☐☐
i.	As No. 2920, imperf pair	—		☐☐☐☐☐

2976-2979

2980

2998

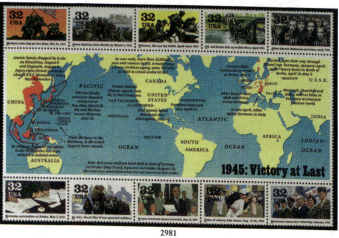

2981

Scott No.	Description	Unused Value	Used Value	/ / / / / /
2920D	32c Flag, Large date, Serpentine die cut 11.3 (2897)............................	.70	.25	
e.	Booklet pane of 10	7.50		
2921	32c Flag (2897), dk blue, tan, brn, red & lt bl, Serpentine Die Cut 9.8 on 2 or 3 sides	.75	.20	
a.	Booklet pane of 10, dated red "1996"	7.50		
d.	Booklet pane of 5 + label, dated red "1997"...................................	3.75		
e.	As "a," imperf.................................	300.00		

1995-96

2933	32c Milton S. Hershey	.60	.20	
2934	32c Cal Farley	.60	.20	
2935	32c Henry R. Luce...........................	.60	.20	
2936	32c Lila and Dewitt Wallace..............	.60	.20	
2938	46c Ruth Benedict	.90	.20	
2940	55c Dr. Alice Hamilton	1.10	.20	
2941	55c Justin S. Morrill, Self-adhesive	1.10	.20	
2942	77c Mary Breckinridge, Self-adhesive..	1.50	.20	
2943	78c Alice Paul	1.60	.20	

Perf. 11.2

2948	(32c) Love.................................	.60	.20	

Self-Adhesive

2949	(32c) Love.................................	.60	.20	
a.	Booklet pane of 20 + label.............	12.00		
b.	Red (engr.) omitted	450.00		
2950	32c Florida Statehood	.60	.20	
2951	32c Earth in Tub................................	.60	.20	
2952	32c Solar Energy..............................	.60	.20	
2953	32c Tree Planting..............................	.60	.20	
2954	32c Beach Clean-up	.60	.20	
a.	Block of 4, #2951-2954	2.40	1.75	
2955	32c Richard M. Nixon........................	.60	.20	
a.	Red (engr.) omitted	1,400.		
2956	32c Bessie Coleman...........................	.60	.20	
2957	32c Love	.60	.20	
2958	55c Love	1.10	.20	

Booklet stamps

2959	32c Love (2957), Perf 9.8x10.8	.60	.20	
a.	Booklet pane of 10	6.00	3.25	

Self-Adhesive

2960	55c Love...................................	1.10	.20	
a.	Booklet pane of 20 + label.............	22.50		

1995

2961	32c Volleyball..............................	.60	.20	
2962	32c Softball	.60	.20	
2963	32c Bowling	.60	.20	
2964	32c Tennis...................................	.60	.20	

2983-2992

3003

3002

3012

3013

2993-2997

Scott No.	Description	Unused Value	Used Value	/ / / / / /
2965	32c Golf...	.60	.20	
a.	Vert. strip of 5, #2961-2965............	3.00	2.00	
b.	As "a.," imperf.	2,500.		
c.	As "a.," yellow omitted	2,500.		
d.	As "a.," yellow, blue & mag. omitted	2,500.		
2966	32c Prisoners of War & Missing in Action	.60	.20	
2967	32c Marilyn Monroe	.60	.20	
a.	Imperf., pair	600.00		
2968	32c Texas Statehood............................	.60	.20	
2969	32c Split Rock Lighthouse	.60	.20	
2970	32c St. Joseph Lighthouse	.60	.20	
2971	32c Spectacle Reef Lighthouse.............	.60	.20	
2972	32c Marblehead Lighthouse	.60	.20	
2973	32c Thirty Mile Point Lighthouse	.60	.20	
a.	Booklet pane of 5, #2969-2973	3.00	2.75	
2974	32c United Nations	.60	.20	
2975	Civil War, pane of 20	12.00	—	
a.-t.	32c Any single....................................	.60	.20	
2976	32c Carousel Horses, upper left............	.60	.20	
2977	32c Carousel Horses, upper right	.60	.20	
2978	32c Carousel Horses, lower left............	.60	.20	
2979	32c Carousel Horses, lower right..........	.60	.20	
a.	Block of 4, #2976-2979	2.40	2.00	
2980	32c Woman Suffrage.............................	.60	.20	
a.	Black (engr.) omitted	425.00		
b.	Imperf., pair	1,500.		
2981	World War II, block of 10	6.00	5.50	
a.-j.	32c Any single....................................	.60	.30	
2982	32c Louis Armstrong, white denomination(2984)	.60	.20	
2983	32c Coleman Hawkins	.80	.20	
2984	32c Louis Armstrong, black denom.	.80	.20	
2985	32c James P. Johnson	.80	.20	
2986	32c Jelly Roll Morton	.80	.20	
2987	32c Charlie Parker...............................	.80	.20	
2988	32c Eubie Blake	.80	.20	
2989	32c Charles Mingus	.80	.20	
2990	32c Thelonious Monk	.80	.20	
2991	32c John Coltrane	.80	.20	
2992	32c Erroll Garner................................	.80	.20	
a.	Vertical block of 10, #2983-2992 ...	8.00	—	
b.	As "a.," dark blue omitted..............	—		
2993	32c Aster..	.60	.20	
2994	32c Chrysanthemum	.60	.20	
2995	32c Dahlia..	.60	.20	
2996	32c Hydrangea	.60	.20	
2997	32c Rudbeckia.....................................	.60	.20	
a.	Booklet pane of 5, #2993-2997	3.00	2.25	
b.	As "a.," imperf.	—		
2998	60c Eddie Rickenbacker	1.25	.25	

259

3000

3030 3032 3033

3036 3051 3052

Scott No.	Description	Unused Value	Used Value	/ / / / / /
a.	60c Large date, small date	1.25	.25	
2999	32c Republic of Palau	.60	.20	
3000	Comic Strips, pane of 20	12.00	—	
a.-t.	32c Any single....................................	.60	.20	
u.	As No. 3000 a.-h. imperf., i.-l. part perf	—		
v.	As No. 3000 m.-t. imperf., i.-l. part perf	—		
w.	As No. 3000 a.-l. imperf., m.-t. imperf. vertically....................................	—		
3001	32c Naval Academy	.60	.20	
3002	32c Tennessee Williams	.60	.20	
3003	32c Christmas - Religious, perf. 11.2....	.60	.20	
c.	Blk (engr., denomination) omitted	250.00		
3003A	32c Christmas -Religious, Perf. 9.8 x 10.9 from bklt pane (3003).	.65	.20	
b.	Booklet pane of 10	6.50	4.00	
3004	32c Christmas - Santa, Chimney	.60	.20	
3005	32c Christmas - Child, Jumping Jack....	.60	.20	
3006	32c Christmas - Child, Tree	.60	.20	
3007	32c Christmas - Santa, Sled	.60	.20	
b.	Booklet pane of 10, 3 ea. #3004-3005, 2 ea. #3006-3007......................	6.00	4.00	
c.	Booklet pane of 10, 2 ea. #3004-3005, 3 ea. #3006-3007......................	6.00	4.00	
d.	As "a.," imperf.	700.00		

Booklet stamps, Serpentine Die Cut

Scott No.	Description	Unused Value	Used Value	/ / / / / /
3008	32c Christmas - Santa, Sled (3007).......	.75	.20	
3009	32c Christmas - Child, Jumping Jack (3005)	.75	.20	
3010	32c Christmas - Santa, Chimney (3004)	.75	.20	
3011	32c Christmas - Child, Tree (3006)	.75	.20	
a.	Booklet pane of 20, 5 ea. #3008-3011 + label....................................	15.00	—	
3012	32c Christmas - Angel............................	.60	.20	
a.	Booklet pane of 20 + label...............	12.00	—	
b.	Vert. pair, no die cutting btwn.	—		
3013	32c Christmas - Children Sledding	.60	.20	
a.	Booklet pane of 18........................	11.00	—	

Coil stamps, Serpentine Die Cut Vert.

Scott No.	Description	Unused Value	Used Value	/ / / / / /
3014	32c Christmas - Santa, Sled (3007).......	.60	.30	
3015	32c Christmas - Child, Jumping Jack (3005)	.60	.30	
3016	32c Christmas - Santa, Chimney (3004)	.60	.30	
3017	32c Christmas - Child, Tree (3006)	.60	.30	
3018	32c Christmas - Angel (3012)................	.60	.30	
3019	32c 1893 Duryea..................................	.60	.30	
3020	32c 1894 Haynes..................................	.60	.20	
3021	32c 1898 Columbia...............................	.60	.20	
3022	32c 1899 Winton..................................	.60	.20	

1893 Duryea

1894 Haynes

1898 Columbia

1899 Winton

1901 White

3019-3023

3004-3007

Utah 1896

3024

BLACK HERITAGE

Ernest E. Just

3058

Crocus Winter Aconite Pansy Snowdrop Anemone

3025-3029

SMITHSONIAN INSTITUTION
1846-1996

3059

HAPPY NEW YEAR!

3060

262

Scott No.	Description	Unused Value	Used Value	//////
3023	32c 1901 White....................................	.60	.20	
a.	Vert. or horiz. strip of 5, #3019-3023	3.00	2.00	
1996				
3024	32c Utah Statehood............................	.60	.20	
3025	32c Crocus..	.60	.20	
3026	32c Winter Aconite	.60	.20	
3027	32c Pansy..	.60	.20	
3028	32c Snowdrop....................................	.60	.20	
3029	32c Anemone	.60	.20	
a.	Booklet pane of 5, #3025-3029	3.00	2.50	

Serpentine Die Cut 11.3, Self-adhesive

3030	32c Love	.60	.20	
a.	Booklet pane of 20 + label.............	12.00		
b.	Booklet pane of 15 + label.............	9.00		
c.	Red omitted	350.00		

Serpentine Die Cut

3031	1c American Kestrel, Self-adhesive (2477)	.20	.20	
3031A	American Kestrel, blue inscription and year	.20	.20	

1996-98

3032	2c Red-headed Woodpecker	.20	.20	
3033	3c Eastern Bluebird with cent sign......	.20	.20	
3036	$1 Red Fox, Self-adhesive	2.00	.50	

Coil Stamp, Perf. 9³/₄ Vert.

3044	1c American Kestrel (2477) with cent sign	.20	.20	
a.	Large date, small date	.20	.20	
3045	2c Red-headed Woodpecker, Coil........	.20	.20	

Serpentine Die Cut 10¹/₂x10³/₄, Booklet Stamp, Self-Adhesive

3048	20c Blue Jay (2483)	.40	.20	
a.	Booklet pane of 10...........................	4.00		
b.	Booklet pane of 4.............................	1.60		
c.	Booklet pane of 6.............................	2.40		
3049	32c Rose, serp. die cut 11¹/₄x11³/₄ (2490)	.60	.20	
a.	Booklet pane of 20 + label.............	12.00		
b.	Booklet pane of 4	2.75		
c.	Booklet pane of 5 + label...............	3.20		
d.	Booklet pane of 6	3.60		
3050	20c Ring-necked Pheasant, serp. die cut 11.25	.40	.20	
a.	Booklet pane of 10	4.00		
3051	20c Ring-Necked Pheasant, serp. die cut 10.5x11, Self adhesive bklt. stamps (3050)......................	.60	.20	
3051A	20c Ring-Necked Pheasant, serp. die cut 10.6 x 10.4................................	.30	.20	

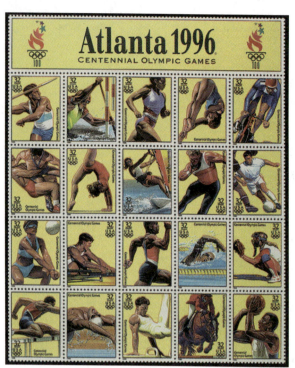

3068

3061-3064

3065

3066

3067   3069   3070

3072-3076

3077-3080

3081   3082   3087   3088

3083-3086

3090

3095

3096-3099

Scott No.	Description	Unused Value	Used Value	/ / / / / /
b.	Booklet pane of 5, 4 #3051, 1 #3051A turned sideways at top .	3.75		☐☐☐☐☐
c.	Booklet pane of 5, 4 #3051, 1 #3051A turned sideways at bottom	3.75		☐☐☐☐☐

Booklet Stamp, Serpentine Die Cut 11½ x 11¼

3052	33c Coral Pink Rose, serp. die cut 11.5x11.25	.80	.20	☐☐☐☐☐
a.	Booklet pane of 4	3.20		☐☐☐☐☐
b.	Booklet pane of 5 + label	4.00		☐☐☐☐☐
c.	Booklet pane of 6	4.80		☐☐☐☐☐
d.	Booklet pane of 20 + label	13.00		☐☐☐☐☐
i.	Imperf., pair	—		☐☐☐☐☐

Serpentine Die Cut 10¾ x10½ on 2 or 3 sides, Booklet Stamp

3052E	33c Coral Pink Rose (3052)	.65	.20	☐☐☐☐☐
f.	Booklet pane of 20	13.00		☐☐☐☐☐
g.	As "f," all 12 stamps on one side with black ("33 USA," etc.) omitted	—		☐☐☐☐☐
h.	Horiz. pair, imperf btwn	—		☐☐☐☐☐

Coil Stamp, Serpentine Die Cut 11½ Vert.

3053	20c Blue Jay (2483)	.40	.20	☐☐☐☐☐
3054	32c Yellow Rose, serp. die cut 9.75 vert.	.60	.20	☐☐☐☐☐
3055	20c Ring-Necked Pheasant, serp. die cut 9.75 vert. (3051)	.40	.20	☐☐☐☐☐

1996

3058	32c Ernest E. Just	.60	.20	☐☐☐☐☐
3059	32c Smithsonian Institution	.60	.20	☐☐☐☐☐
3060	32c Year of the Rat	.60	.20	☐☐☐☐☐
3061	32c Eadweard Muybridge	.60	.20	☐☐☐☐☐
3062	32c Ottmar Mergenthaler	.60	.20	☐☐☐☐☐
3063	32c Frederic E. Ives	.60	.20	☐☐☐☐☐
3064	32c William Dickson	.60	.20	☐☐☐☐☐
a.	Block or strip of 4, #3061-3064	2.40	2.00	☐☐☐☐☐
3065	32c Fulbright Scholarship	.60	.20	☐☐☐☐☐
3066	50c Jacqueline Cochran	1.00	.20	☐☐☐☐☐
a.	Black (engr.) omitted	70.00		☐☐☐☐☐
3067	32c Marathon	.60	.20	☐☐☐☐☐
3068	Olympic Games, pane of 20	12.00		☐☐☐☐☐
a.-t.	Any single	.60	.20	☐☐☐☐☐
u.	As No. 3068, imperf.	1,400.		☐☐☐☐☐
3069	32c Georgia O'Keeffe	.65	.20	☐☐☐☐☐
a.	Imperf., pair	175.00		☐☐☐☐☐
3070	32c Tennessee Statehood, perf.	.60	.20	☐☐☐☐☐
3071	32c Tennessee Statehood (3070), Serpentine Die Cut	.60	.30	☐☐☐☐☐
a.	Booklet pane of 20	12.00		☐☐☐☐☐
b.	Horiz. pair, no die cutting btwn	—		☐☐☐☐☐
c.	Imperf., pair	—		☐☐☐☐☐
d.	Horiz. pair, imperf. vert.	—		☐☐☐☐☐

3104

3100-3103

3106

3105

3107

3117

3108-3111

3118

Scott No.	Description	Unused Value	Used Value	/ / / / / /
3072	32c Fancy Dance	.60	.20	
3073	32c Butterfly Dance	.60	.20	
3074	32c Traditional Dance	.60	.20	
3075	32c Raven Dance	.60	.20	
3076	32c Hoop Dance	.60	.20	
a.	Strip of 5, #3072-3076	3.00	2.00	
3077	32c Eohippus	.60	.20	
3078	32c Woolly Mammoth	.60	.20	
3079	32c Mastodon	.60	.20	
3080	32c Saber-tooth Cat	.60	.20	
a.	Block or Strip of 5, #3077-3080	2.40	1.50	
3081	32c Breast Cancer Awareness	.60	.20	
3082	32c James Dean	.60	.20	
a.	Imperf., pair	325.00		
b.	As "a," red (USA 32c) and tan omitted	—		
c.	As "a," tan (James Dean) omitted	—		
d.	As "a," top stamp red and tan omitted, bottom stamp tan omitted	—		
3083	32c Mighty Casey	.60	.20	
3084	32c Paul Bunyan	.60	.20	
3085	32c John Henry	.60	.20	
3086	32c Pecos Bill	.60	.20	
a.	Block or Strip of 5, #3083-3086	2.40	2.00	
3087	32c Centennial Olympic Games	.65	.20	
3088	32c Iowa Statehood, perf.	.60	.20	
3089	32c Iowa Statehood, Self-adhesive (3088)	.60	.30	
a.	Booklet pane of 20	12.00		
3090	32c Rural Free Delivery, Centenary	.60	.20	
3091	32c Riverboats - "Robert E. Lee"	.60	.20	
3092	32c Riverboats - "Sylvan Dell"	.60	.20	
3093	32c Riverboats - "Far West"	.60	.20	
3094	32c Riverboats - "Rebecca Everingham"	.60	.20	
3095	32c Riverboats - "Bailey Gatzert"	.60	.20	
a.	Vertical strip of 5, #3091-3095	3.00		
3096	32c Count Basie	.60	.20	
3097	32c Tommy and Jimmy Dorsey	.60	.20	
3098	32c Glenn Miller	.60	.20	
3099	32c Benny Goodman	.60	.20	
a.	Block or Strip of 4, #3096-3099	2.40	1.75	
3100	32c Harold Arlen	.70	.20	
3101	32c Johnny Mercer	.70	.20	
3102	32c Dorothy Fields	.70	.20	
3103	32c Hoagy Carmichael	.70	.20	
a.	Block or Strip of 4, #3100-3103	2.80	1.75	
3104	23c F. Scott Fitzgerald	.45	.20	
3105	Endangered Species, Pane of 15	9.00	—	
a.-o.	32c Any single	.60	.20	

3119

3120

3121

3123

3124

3125

3126

3127

3130-3131

Scott No.	Description	Unused Value	Used Value	/ / / / / /
3106	32c Computer Technology	.60	.20	
3107	32c Christmas - Madonna and Child.....	.60	.20	
3108	32c Christmas - Family at Fireplace......	.60	.20	
3109	32c Christmas - Decorating Tree...........	.60	.20	
3110	32c Christmas - Dreaming of Santa Claus	.60	.20	
3111	32c Christmas - Holiday Shopping........	.60	.20	
a.	Block or Strip of 4, #3108-3111.....	2.40	1.75	

Serpentine Die Cut 10, Self-Adhesive Booklet Stamps

3112	32c Christmas - Madonna and Child (3107)	.60	.20	
a.	Booklet pane of 20 + label.............	12.00		
3113	32c Christmas - Family at Fireplace (3108)	.60	.20	
3114	32c Christmas - Decorating Tree (3109)	.60	.20	
3115	32c Christmas - Dreaming of Santa Claus (3110)..................	.60	.20	
3116	32c Christmas - Holiday Shopping (3111)	.60	.20	
a.	Booklet pane of 20, 5 ea. #3113-3116	12.00		

Self-Adhesive, Die Cut

3117	32c Christmas - Skaters	.60	.20	
a.	Booklet pane of 18.........................	11.00		
3118	32c Hanukkah..	.60	.20	

Perf. 11x11.1

3119	Cycling, Souvenir Sheet of 2, ...	2.00	2.00	
a.	50c Orange and multi...........................	1.00	1.00	
b.	50c Blue green and multi.....................	1.00	1.00	

1997

3120	32c Year of the Ox	.60	.20	
3121	32c Brig. Gen. Benjamin O. Davis, Sr. .			
	Self-adhesive	.60	.20	
3122	32c Statue of Liberty, Self-adhesive (2599)	.60	.20	
a.	Booklet pane of 20 + label.............	12.00		
b.	Booklet pane of 4	2.50		
c.	Booklet pane of 5 + label...............	3.20		
d.	Booklet pane of 6	3.60		
3122E	32c Statue of Liberty, Self-adhesive booklet stamp	1.10	.20	
f.	Booklet pane of 20 + label.............	35.00		
g.	Booklet pane of 6	7.00		
3123	32c Love - Swans Self-adhesive booklet stamp	.60	.20	
a.	Booklet pane of 20 + label.............	12.00		
3124	55c Love - Swans Self-adhesive booklet stamp	1.00	.20	
a.	Booklet pane of 20 + label.............	21.00		
3125	32c Helping Children Learn, Self-adhesive	.60	.20	
3126	32c Merian Prints, (citron) Self-adhesive booklet stamp	.60	.20	

3134

3137

3139a

3140a

3143-3146

3141

3151

3152

3153

3154-57

3158-3165

3168-3172

3166

3167

3173

3174

3175

3176

3177

3179

3180

3178

3181

3182

3183

3184

Scott No.	Description	Unused Value	Used Value	//////
3127	32c Merian Prints, (pineapple) Self-adhesive booklet stamp	.60	.20	□□□□□
a.	Booklet pane, 10 ea. #3126-3127 + label	12.00		□□□□□ □□□□□
b.	Pair, #3126-3127	1.20		
c.	Vert. pair, imperf between	*500.00*		
3128	32c Merian Botanical Prints, Self-adhesive booklet stamp 18.5 x 24mm (3126)	.75	.20	□□□□□
a.	Perf. 11.2 broken on right	1.25	.25	□□□□□
b.	Booklet pane, 2 ea. #3128-3129 + 3128a	3.00		□□□□□
3129	32c Merian Botanical Prints, Self-adhesive booklet stamp 18.5 x 24mm (3127)	.75	.20	□□□□□
a.	Perf. 11.2 broken on right	1.25	.25	□□□□□
b.	Booklet pane, 2 ea. #3128-3129 + 3129a	4.50		□□□□□
c.	Pair, #3128-3129	1.50		□□□□□
3130	32c Sailing Ship - Pacific '97	.60	.20	□□□□□
3131	32c Stagecoach - Pacific '97	.60	.20	□□□□□
a.	Pair, #3130-3131	1.25	.60	□□□□□
3132	32c Juke Box, Imperf Coil (2911)	.50	.50	□□□□□
3133	32c Flag Over Porch, Linerless Coil, serpentine die cut 9.9 vert. (2897)	.60	.20	□□□□□
3134	32c Thornton Wilder - Literary Arts	.60	.20	□□□□□
3135	32c Raoul Wallenberg	.60	.20	□□□□□
3136	Dinosaurs	9.00	—	□□□□□
a.-o.	32c Any single	.60	.20	
p.	As No. 3136, bottom seven stamps imperf.	*6,500.*		□□□□□ □□□□□
q.	As No. 3136, top 8 stamps imperf..	—		
r.	As No. 3136, all colors and tagging omitted	—		□□□□□
3137	Bugs Bunny, Self-adhesive pane of 10, Die cutting does not extend through backing	6.00		□□□□□
a.	32c Single stamp	.60	.20	□□□□□
b.	Booklet pane of 9 #3137a	5.40		□□□□□
c.	Booklet pane of 1 #3137a	.60		
3138	Bugs Bunny, Self-adhesive pane of 10, Die cut through backing (3137)	*125.00*		□□□□□
a.	32c Single stamp	*2.00*		□□□□□
b.	Booklet pane of 9 #3138a	—		□□□□□
c.	Booklet pane of 1, imperf.	—		
3139	$6 Benjamin Franklin - Pacific '97, Pane of 12	12.00	—	□□□□□
a.	50c Single stamp	1.00	.50	□□□□□

3185

3186

3187

3188

3193-3197

3198-3202

3192

276

Scott No.	Description	Unused Value	Used Value	/ / / / /
3140	$7.20 Washington - Pacific '97, Pane of 12	14.50	—	☐☐☐☐☐
a.	60c Single stamp	1.20	.60	☐☐☐☐☐
3141	32c Marshall Plan, 50th Anniversary	.60	.20	☐☐☐☐☐
3142	Classic American Aircraft, Pane of 20	12.00	—	☐☐☐☐☐
a.-t.	32c Any single	.60	.20	☐☐☐☐☐

1997 Perf. 11.2

3143	32c Bear Bryant	.60	.20	☐☐☐☐☐
3144	32c Pop Warner	.60	.20	☐☐☐☐☐
3145	32c Vince Lombardi	.60	.20	☐☐☐☐☐
3146	32c George Halas	.60	.20	☐☐☐☐☐
a.	Block or strip of 4, #3143-3146	2.40	1.75	☐☐☐☐☐

With Red Bar Above Coach's Name Perf. 11

3147	32c Vince Lombardi	.60	.30	☐☐☐☐☐
3148	32c Bear Bryant	.60	.30	☐☐☐☐☐
3149	32c Pop Warner	.60	.30	☐☐☐☐☐
3150	32c George Halas	.60	.30	☐☐☐☐☐

1997, July 28 Perf. 10.9x11.1

3151	American Dolls, Pane of 15	11.00	—	☐☐☐☐☐
a.-o.	32c Any single	.70	.20	☐☐☐☐☐

1997, July 31 Perf. 11.1

3152	32c Humphrey Bogart (1899-1957)	.60	.20	☐☐☐☐☐

1997, Aug. 21 Perf. 11.1

3153	32c *The Stars And Stripes Forever!*	.60	.20	☐☐☐☐☐

1997 Perf. 11

3154	32c Lily Pons	.65	.20	☐☐☐☐☐
3155	32c Richard Tucker	.65	.20	☐☐☐☐☐
3156	32c Lawrence Tibbett	.65	.20	☐☐☐☐☐
3157	32c Rosa Ponselle	.65	.20	☐☐☐☐☐
a.	Block or strip of 4, #3154-3157	2.60	1.75	☐☐☐☐☐
3158	32c Leopold Stokowski	.65	.20	☐☐☐☐☐
3159	32c Arthur Fiedler	.65	.20	☐☐☐☐☐
3160	32c George Szell	.65	.20	☐☐☐☐☐
3161	32c Eugene Ormandy	.65	.20	☐☐☐☐☐
3162	32c Samuel Barber	.65	.20	☐☐☐☐☐
3163	32c Ferde Grofe	.65	.20	☐☐☐☐☐
3164	32c Charles Ives	.65	.20	☐☐☐☐☐
3165	32c Louis Moreau Gottschalk	.65	.20	☐☐☐☐☐
a.	Block of 8, #3158-3165	5.25	4.00	☐☐☐☐☐

1997, Sept. 15 Perf. 11.2

3166	32c Padre Felix Varela (1788-1853)	.60	.20	☐☐☐☐☐

1997, Sept. 18 Perf. 11.2x11.1

3167	32c Department Of The Air Force, 50th Anniv.	.60	.20	☐☐☐☐☐

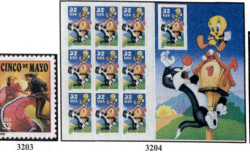

3203

3204

3206

3207

3208

3209

3211

3212-3215

3216-3219

3220

3221

Scott No.	Description	Unused Value	Used Value	/ / / / /
1997, Sept. 30 Perf. 10.2				
3168	32c Lon Chaney as The Phantom of the Opera	.60	.20	
3169	32c Bela Lugosi as Dracula	.60	.20	
3170	32c Boris Karloff as Frankenstein's Monster	.60	.20	
3171	32c Boris Karloff as The Mummy	.60	.20	
3172	32c Lon Chaney, Jr. as The Wolf Man ..	.60	.20	
a.	Strip of 5, #3168-3172	3.00	2.25	
1997, Oct. 14 Serpentine Die Cut 11.4, Self-Adhesive				
3173	32c First Supersonic Flight, 50th Anniv.	.60	.20	
1997, Oct. 18 Perf. 11.1				
3174	32c Women In Military Service	.60	.20	
1996, Oct. 22 Serpentine Die Cut 11, Self-Adhesive				
3175	32c Kwanzaa	.60	.20	
1997 Serpentine Die Cut 9.9 Booklet Stamps, Self-Adhesive				
3176	32c Madonna and Child, by Sano di Pietro Self-adhesive booklet stamp	.60	.20	
a.	Booklet pane of 20 + label	12.00		
Serpentine Die Cut 11.2x11.8 on 2, 3 or 4 Sides				
3177	32c Holly	.60	.20	
a.	Booklet pane of 20 + label	12.00		
b.	Booklet pane of 4	2.50		
c.	Booklet pane of 5 + label	3.00		
d.	Booklet pane of 6	3.75		
Souvenir Sheet 1997, Dec. 10 Perf. 11x11.1				
3178	$3 Mars Pathfinder	6.00	3.00	
a.	$3 Single stamp	5.50	2.75	
1998, Jan. 5 Perf. 11.2				
3179	32c Year of the Tiger	.60	.20	
1998, Jan. 22 Perf. 11.2				
3180	32c Alpine Skiing	.60	.20	
1998, Jan. 28 Serpentine Die Cut 11.6x11.3, Self-Adhesive				
3181	32c Madam C.J. Walker (1867-1919), Entrepreneur	.60	.20	
1998 Perf. 11.6				
3182	Celebrate The Century, 1900s, Pane of 15	9.00	—	
a.-o.	32c any single	.60	.30	
p.	Engraved red (No. 3182m, Gibson girl) omitted, in pane of 15	—		
3183	Celebrate The Century, 1910s, Pane of 15	9.00	—	

3230-3234

3222-3225

3226

3228

3235

3237

Scott No.	Description	Unused Value	Used Value	/ / / / /
a.-o.	32c any single......................................	.60	.30	☐☐☐☐☐
p.	Nos. 3183g, 3183l-3183o imperf. in pane of 15	—		☐☐☐☐☐
3184	Celebrate The Century, 1920s, Pane of 15	9.00	—	☐☐☐☐☐
a.-o.	32c any single......................................	.60	.30	
3185	32c Celebrate The Century, 1930s, Pane of 15	9.00	—	☐☐☐☐☐
a.-o.	32c any single......................................	.60	.30	
3186	Celebrate The Century, 1940s, Pane of 15	9.75	—	☐☐☐☐☐
a.-o.	33c any single......................................	.65	.30	
3187	Celebrate The Century, 1950s, Pane of 15	9.75	—	☐☐☐☐☐
a.-o.	33c any single......................................	.65	.30	

1998-2000, Lithographed, Engraved (#3182m, 3183f, 3184m, 3185b, 3186k, 3187a, 3188c, 3189h), Perf. 11½

Scott No.	Description	Unused Value	Used Value	/ / / / /
3188	Celebrate The Century, 1960s, Pane of 15....................................	9.75	—	☐☐☐☐☐
a.-o.	33c any single......................................	.65	.30	
3189	Celebrate The Century, 1970s, Pane of 15....................................	9.75	—	☐☐☐☐☐
a.-o.	33c any single......................................	.65	.30	
3190	Celebrate The Century, 1980s, Pane of 15....................................	9.75	—	☐☐☐☐☐
a.-o.	33c any single......................................	.65	.30	
3191	Celebrate The Century, 1990s, Pane of 15....................................	9.75	—	☐☐☐☐☐
a.-o.	33c any single......................................	.65	.30	

1998, Feb. 15 Perf. 11.2x11

Scott No.	Description	Unused Value	Used Value	/ / / / /
3192	32c Remember The Maine	.60	.20	☐☐☐☐☐

1998, Mar. 19 Die Cut Perf 11.3, Self-Adhesive

Scott No.	Description	Unused Value	Used Value	/ / / / /
3193	32c Southern Magnolia	.60	.20	☐☐☐☐☐
3194	32c Blue Paloverde	.60	.20	☐☐☐☐☐
3195	32c Yellow Poplar	.60	.20	☐☐☐☐☐
3196	32c Prairie Crab Apple	.60	.20	☐☐☐☐☐
3197	32c Pacific Dogwood	.60	.20	☐☐☐☐☐
a.	Strip of 5, #3193-3197	3.00		☐☐☐☐☐

1998, Mar. 25 Perf. 10.2 Alexander Calder

Scott No.	Description	Unused Value	Used Value	/ / / / /
3198	32c Black Cascade, 13 Verticals, 1959 .	.60	.20	☐☐☐☐☐
3199	32c Untitled, 1965...............................	.60	.20	☐☐☐☐☐
3200	32c Rearing Stallion, 1928	.60	.20	☐☐☐☐☐
3201	32c Portrait of a Young Man, c. 1945....	.60	.20	☐☐☐☐☐
3202	32c Un Effet du Japonais, 1945.............	.60	.20	☐☐☐☐☐
a.	Strip of 5, #3198-3202	3.00	2.25	☐☐☐☐☐

1998, Apr. 16 Serpentine Die Cut 11.7x10.9, Self-Adhesive

Scott No.	Description	Unused Value	Used Value	/ / / / /
3203	32c Cinco De Mayo	.60	.20	☐☐☐☐☐

3238-3242

3236

3243

3244

3245

3246

3247

3248

3257

3259

3260

Scott No.	Description	Unused Value	Used Value	/ / / / / /

1998, Apr. 27 Serpentine Die Cut 11.1, Self-Adhesive

3204	Sylvester & Tweety, Pane of 10	6.00		
a.	32c any single...	.60	.20	
b.	Booklet pane of 9 #3204a...............	5.40		
c.	Booklet pane of 1 #3204a...............	.60		
3205	Pane of 10, right stamp imperforate	10.00		
a.	32c single...	.60		
b.	Booklet pane of 9 #3205a...............	—		
c.	Booklet pane of 1, imperf.	—		

1998, May 29 Serpentine Die Cut 10.8x10.9, Self-Adhesive

3206	32c Wisconsin Statehood......................	.60	.30	

1998, June 5 Perf. 10 Vert., Coil Stamps

3207	(5c) Wetlands	.20	.20	
3207A	(5c) Wetlands, Self-adhesive Coil	.20	.20	
3208	(25c) Diner..	.50	.50	
3208A	(25c) Diner, Self-adhesive Coil	.50	.50	

1998, June 18 Perf. 12x12.4

3209	1898 Trans-Mississippi Stamps, Cent., Pane of 9..	7.75	5.00	
a.	1c green & black	.20	.20	
b.	2c red brown & black...........................	.20	.20	
c.	4c orange & black	.20	.20	
d.	5c blue & black	.20	.20	
e.	8c dark lilac & black...........................	.20	.20	
f.	10c purple & black...............................	.20	.20	
g.	50c green & black	1.00	.60	
h.	$1 red & black	2.00	1.25	
i.	$2 red brown & black...........................	4.00	2.50	
3210	$1 Pane of 9, #3209h	18.00	—	

1998, June 26 Perf. 11.2

3211	32c Berlin Airlift, 50th Anniv.	.60	.20	

1998, June 26 Perf. 10.1x10.2

3212	32c Huddie "Leadbelly" Ledbetter (1888-1949)	.60	.20	
3213	32c Woody Guthrie (1912-67)...............	.60	.20	
3214	32c Sonny Terry (1911-86).....................	.60	.20	
3215	32c Josh White (1908-69)......................	.60	.20	
a.	Block or strip of 4, #3212-3215	2.50	2.00	

1998, July 15 Perf. 10.1x10.3

3216	32c Mahalia Jackson (1911-72).............	.60	.20	
3217	32c Roberta Martin (1917-69)...............	.60	.20	
3218	32c Clara Ward (1924-73)	.60	.20	
3219	32c Sister Rosetta Tharpe (1921-73).....	.60	.20	
a.	Block or strip of 4, #3216-3219	2.40	2.00	

3261

3262

3272

3273

3274

3275

3276

3277

3283

3286

3270

3287

3288-3292

Scott No.	Description	Unused Value	Used Value	/ / / / / /

1998, June 26 Perf. 11.2

3220	32c La Mision de San Miguel de San Gabriel, Espanola, NM.....	.60	.20	☐☐☐☐☐

1998, July 22 Perf. 11.2

3221	32c Stephen Vincent Benet (1898-43)...	.60	.20	☐☐☐☐☐

1998, July 29 Perf. 11.2

3222	32c Antillean Euphonia	.60	.20	☐☐☐☐☐
3223	32c Green-throated Carib.....................	.60	.20	☐☐☐☐☐
3224	32c Crested Honeycreeper	.60	.20	☐☐☐☐☐
3225	32c Cardinal Honeyeater.....................	.60	.20	☐☐☐☐☐
a.	Block of 4, #3222-3225	2.40	2.00	☐☐☐☐☐

1998, Aug. 3 Perf. 11.1

3226	32c Alfred Hitchcock (1899-1980)	.60	.20	☐☐☐☐☐

1998, Aug. 5 Serpentine Die Cut 11.7, Self-Adhesive

3227	32c Organ & Tissue Donation	.60	.20	☐☐☐☐☐
3228	(10c) Modern Bicycle, Self-adhesive Coil	.20	.20	☐☐☐☐☐
3228a	Modern Bicycle, Large Date, Self-adhesive	0.2	0.2	☐☐☐☐☐
3229	(10c) Modern Bicycle coil.......................	.20	.20	☐☐☐☐☐
3230	32c Bright Eyes - Dog, Self-adhesive ...	.60	.20	☐☐☐☐☐
3231	32c Bright Eyes - Fish, Self-adhesive ...	.60	.20	☐☐☐☐☐
3232	32c Bright Eyes - Cat, Self-adhesive.....	.60	.20	☐☐☐☐☐
3233	32c Bright Eyes - Parakeet, Self-adhesive	.60	.20	☐☐☐☐☐
3234	32c Bright eyes - Hamster, Self-adhesive	.60	.20	☐☐☐☐☐
a.	Strip of 5, #3230-3234	3.00		☐☐☐☐☐
3235	32c Klondike Gold Rush Centennial.....	.60	.20	☐☐☐☐☐
3236	32c American Art, pane of 20	12.00	-	☐☐☐☐☐
a.-t.	any single..	.60	.20	☐☐☐☐☐
3237	32c American Ballet	.60	.20	☐☐☐☐☐
3238	32c Space Discovery - Space City	.60	.20	☐☐☐☐☐
3239	32c Space Discovery - Space ship landing	.60	.20	☐☐☐☐☐
3240	32c Space Discovery - Person in space suit	.60	.20	☐☐☐☐☐
3241	32c Space Discovery - Space ship taking off	.60	.20	☐☐☐☐☐
3242	32c Space Discovery - Large domed structure	.60	.20	☐☐☐☐☐
a.	Strip of 5, #3238-3242....................	3.00	2.25	☐☐☐☐☐
3243	32c Giving and Sharing, Self-adhesive .	.60	.20	☐☐☐☐☐
3244	32c Christmas - Madonna and Child, Self-adhesive booklet stamp.........	.60	.20	☐☐☐☐☐
a.	Booklet pane of 20 + label..............	12.00		☐☐☐☐☐
b.	Imperf., pair....................................	—		☐☐☐☐☐
3245	32c Wreath - Evergreen, Self-adhesive booklet stamp	1.50	.20	☐☐☐☐☐
3246	32c Wreath - Victorian, Self-adhesive booklet stamp	1.50	.20	☐☐☐☐☐
3247	32c Wreath - Chili Pepper, Self-adhesive booklet stamp	1.50	.20	☐☐☐☐☐

3293

3308

3306

3314

3315

3310-3313

3316

3317-3320

3321-3324

3329

3330

3331

Honoring Those Who Served

The United States of America 33

3325-3328

3189

3190

3191

3332

3338

3333-3337

3339-3344

Scott No.		Description	Unused Value	Used Value	/ / / / / /
3248	32c	Wreath - Tropical, Self-adhesive booklet stamp	1.50	.20	
a.		Booklet pane of 4, #3245-3248	12.50		
b.		Booklet pane of 5, #3245-3246, 3248, 2 #3247 + label	15.00		
c.		Booklet pane of 6, #3247-3248, 2 each #3245-3246	17.50		
3249	32c	Wreath (Large) - Evergreen, Self-adhesive	.60	.20	
3250	32c	Wreath (Large) - Victorian, Self-adhesive	.60	.20	
3251	32c	Wreath (Large) - Chili Pepper, Self-adhesive	.60	.20	
3252	32c	Wreath (Large) - Tropical, Self-adhesive	.60	.20	
a.		Block of 4, #3249-3252	2.40		
b.		Booklet pane, 5 each #3249-3252	12.00		
c.		Block or strip of 4, red ("Greetings 32 USA" and "1998") omitted on #3249, 3252	—		
3257	(1c)	Weather Vane, white "USA"	.20	.20	
3258	(1c)	Weather Vane, pale blue "USA"	.20	.20	
3259	22c	Uncle Sam, Self-adhesive	.45	.20	
3260	(33c)	Uncle Sam's Hat	.65	..20	
3261	$3.20	Space Shuttle Landing, Self-adhesive Priority Mail Rate	6.00	3.00	
3262	$11.75	Piggyback Space Shuttle, Self-adhesive Express Mail Rate	22.50	11.50	
3263	22c	Uncle Sam, Self-adhesive Coil	.45	.20	
a.		Imperf, pair	—		
3264	(33c)	Uncle Sam's Hat, coil	.65	.20	
3265	(33c)	Uncle Sam's Hat, Self-adhesive Coil, square corners	.65	.20	
a.		Imperf, pair	—		
b.		Red, omitted	—		
c.		Black omitted	—		
d.		Black omitted, imperf pair	—		
3266	(33c)	Uncle Sam's Hat, Self-adhesive Coil, rounded corners	.65	.20	
3267	(33c)	Uncle Sam's Hat, Self-adhesive booklet stamp, serp die cut 9.9	.65	.20	
a.		Booklet pane of 10	6.50		
3268	(33c)	Uncle Sam's Hat, Self-adhesive booklet stamp, serp. die cut 11 1/4	.65	.20	
a.		Booklet pane of 10	6.50		
b.		Booklet pane of 20 + label	13.00		
3269	(33c)	Uncle Sam's Hat, Self-adhesive booklet stamp, serp. die cut 8	.65	.20	
a.		Booklet pane of 18	12.00		
3270	(10c)	Eagle & Shield, Coil	.20	.20	

3345-3350

3351

3356-3359

3355

Scott No.	Description	Unused Value	Used Value	/ / / / / /
3270a	Eagle and Shield, Large Date, Coil stamp	.20	.20	
3271 (10c)	Eagle & Shield, Self-adhesive coil	.20	.20	
3271b	Eagle and Shield, Large Date, Self-adhesive	.20	.20	
3272	33c Year of the Rabbit - Chinese New Year	.65	.20	
3273	33c Malcolm X - Black Heritage, Self-adhesive	.65	.20	
3274	33c Love, Self-adhesive booklet stamp	.65	.20	
a.	Booklet pane of 20	13.00		
b.	Imperf pair	—		
3275	55c Love, Self-adhesive	1.10	.20	
3276	33c Hospice Care	.65	.20	
3277	33c Flag and City	.65	.20	
3278	33c Flag and City, Self-adhesive (3277)	.65	.20	
a.	Booklet pane of 4	2.60		
b.	Booklet pane of 5 + label	3.25		
c.	Booklet pane of 6	3.90		
d.	Booklet pane of 10	6.50		
e.	Booklet pane of 20 + label	13.00		
h.	As "e," imperf	—		
Serpentine Die Cut 11½ x 11¾, Booklet Stamp				
3278F	33c Flag and City (3277)	.65	.20	
g.	Booklet pane of 20 + label	13.00		
3279	33c Flag and City, Self-adhesive booklet stamp, red date	.65	.20	
a.	Booklet pane of 10	6.50		
3280	33c Flag and City, Coil, Small Date	.65	.20	
a.	Large Date	.65	.20	
b.	Imperf, pair	—		
3281	33c Flag and City, Self-adhesive coil, square corners, large date	.65	.20	
a.	Imperf., pair	27.50		
b.	Lt. blue and yellow omitted	600.00		
c.	Flag & City, small date	—		
3282	33c Flag and City, Self-adhesive coil, rounded corners	.65	.20	
3283	33c Flag and Chalkboard, Self-adhesive booklet stamp	.65	.20	
a.	Booklet pane of 18	12.00		
3286	33c Irish Immigration	.65	.20	
3287	33c Alfred Lunt and Lynn Fontanne, Actors	.65	.20	
3288	33c Arctic Hare	.65	.20	
3289	33c Arctic Fox	.65	.20	
3290	33c Snowy Owl	.65	.20	
3291	33c Polar Bear	.65	.20	
3292	33c Gray Wolf	.65	.20	
a.	Strip of 5, #3288-3292	3.25		
3293	33c Sonoran Desert, Self-adhesive pane of 10	6.50		

3369

3370

3371

3375a

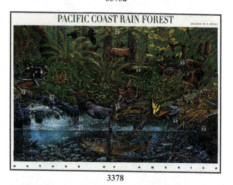

3378

3379-3383

Scott No.	Description	Unused Value	Used Value	/ / / / / /
a.-j.	any single...	.65	.20	☐☐☐☐☐
3294	33c Blueberries, Self-adhesive			
	booklet stamp, dated 1999...........	.65	.20	☐☐☐☐☐
a.	Dated 2000	.65	.20	☐☐☐☐☐
3295	33c Raspberries, Self-adhesive			
	booklet stamp, dated 1999...........	.65	.20	☐☐☐☐☐
a.	Dated 2000	.65	.20	☐☐☐☐☐
3296	33c Strawberries, Self-adhesive			
	booklet stamp, dated 1999...........	.65	.20	☐☐☐☐☐
a.	Dated 2000	.65	.20	☐☐☐☐☐
3297	33c Blackberries, Self-adhesive			
	booklet stamp, dated 1999...........	.65	.20	☐☐☐☐☐
a.	Dated 2000	.65	.20	☐☐☐☐☐
b.	Booklet pane, 5 each #3294-3297			
	+ label...................................	13.00		☐☐☐☐☐
c.	Block of 4, #3294-3297	2.60		☐☐☐☐☐
d.	Booklet pane, 5 #3297e	13.00		
e.	Block of 4, #3294a-3297a............	2.60		
3298	33c Blueberries Self-adhesive booklet stamp	.65	.20	☐☐☐☐☐
3299	33c Raspberries, Self-adhesive booklet stamp	.65	.20	☐☐☐☐☐
3300	33c Strawberries, Self-adhesive booklet stamp	.65	.20	☐☐☐☐☐
3301	33c Blackberries, Self-adhesive booklet stamp	.65	.20	☐☐☐☐☐
a.	Booklet pane of 4, #3298-3301, ...	10.00		☐☐☐☐☐
b.	Booklet pane of 5, #3298, 3299,			
	3301, 2 #3300 + label...................	3.25		☐☐☐☐☐
c.	Booklet pane of 6, #3300, 3301, 2			
	#3298, 3299..............................	4.00		☐☐☐☐☐
d.	Block of 4, #3298-3301	2.60		
3302	33c Blueberries, Self-adhesive coil	.65	.20	☐☐☐☐☐
3303	33c Raspberries, Self-adhesive coil.......	.65	.20	☐☐☐☐☐
3304	33c Strawberries, Self-adhesive coil......	.65	.20	☐☐☐☐☐
3305	33c Blackberries, Self-adhesive coil	.65	.20	☐☐☐☐☐
a.	Strip of 4, # 3302-3305	2.60		☐☐☐☐☐
3306	Daffy Duck, Self-adhesive pane of 10	6.50		☐☐☐☐☐
a.	33c any single..	.65	.20	☐☐☐☐☐
b.	Booklet pane of 9 #3306a..............	5.85		☐☐☐☐☐
c.	Booklet pane of 1 #3306a..............	.65		☐☐☐☐☐
3307	Daffy Duck, Self-adhesive pane of 10,			
	right stamp imperforate................	6.50		☐☐☐☐☐
a.	33c single..	.65		☐☐☐☐☐
b.	Booklet pane of 9 #3307a..............	—		☐☐☐☐☐
c.	Booklet pane of 1, imperf..............	—		☐☐☐☐☐
3308	33c Ayn Rand - Literary Arts	.65	.20	☐☐☐☐☐
3309	33c Cinco de Mayo, Self-adhesive	.65	.20	☐☐☐☐☐
3310	33c Tropical Flowers - Bird of Paradise,			
	Self-adhesive booklet stamp	.65	.20	☐☐☐☐☐
3311	33c Tropical Flowers - Royal Poinciana,			
	Self-adhesive booklet stamp	.65	.20	☐☐☐☐☐

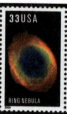

3384-3388

3389

3391

Library of Congress

3390

3393-3396

3397

3398

Scott No.	Description	Unused Value	Used Value	/ / / / / /
3312	33c Tropical Flowers - Gloriosa Lily, Self-adhesive booklet stamp.........	.65	.20	☐☐☐☐☐
3313	33c Tropical Flowers - Chinese Hibiscus, Self-adhesive booklet stamp.........	.65	.20	☐☐☐☐☐
a.	Block of 4, #3310-3313	2.60		☐☐☐☐☐
b.	Booklet pane of 20, 5 each #3310-3313	13.00		
3314	33c John & William Bartram, Self-Adhesive	.65	.20	☐☐☐☐☐
3315	33c Prostate Cancer Awareness, Self-Adhesive	.65	.20	☐☐☐☐☐
3316	33c California Gold Rush 150th Anniversary	.65	.20	☐☐☐☐☐
3317	33c Aquarium Fish, Self-Adhesive........	.65	.20	☐☐☐☐☐
3318	33c Aquarium Fish, Self-Adhesive........	.65	.20	☐☐☐☐☐
3319	33c Aquarium Fish, Self-Adhesive........	.65	.20	☐☐☐☐☐
3320	33c Aquarium Fish, Self-Adhesive........	.65	.20	☐☐☐☐☐
b.	Strip of 4, #3317-3320	2.60		☐☐☐☐☐
3321	33c Extreme Sports - Skateboarding, Self-Adhesive..............................	.65	.20	☐☐☐☐☐
3322	33c Extreme Sports - BMX Biking, Self-Adhesive..............................	.65	.20	☐☐☐☐☐
3323	33c Extreme Sports - Snowboarding, Self-Adhesive..............................	.65	.20	☐☐☐☐☐
3324	33c Extreme Sports - Inline Skating, Self-Adhesive..............................	.65	.20	☐☐☐☐☐
a.	Block or strip of 4, #3321-3324	2.60		☐☐☐☐☐
3325	33c American Glass - Free-Blown Glass	.65	.20	☐☐☐☐☐
3326	33c American Glass - Mold-Blown Glass	.65	.20	☐☐☐☐☐
3327	33c American Glass - Pressed Glass.	.65	.20	☐☐☐☐☐
3328	33c American Glass - Art Glass	.65	.20	☐☐☐☐☐
a.	Block of 4, #3325-3328	2.60		☐☐☐☐☐
3329	33c James Cagney - Legends of Hollywood	.65	.20	☐☐☐☐☐
3330	55c Gen. William "Billy" Mitchell........	1.10	.20	☐☐☐☐☐
3331	33c Honoring Those Who Served, Self-adhesive..............................	.65	.20	☐☐☐☐☐
1999, Lithographed, Perf. 11				
3332	45c Universal Postal Union	.90	.20	☐☐☐☐☐
3333	33c Famous Trains, Daylight	.65	.20	☐☐☐☐☐
3334	33c Famous Trains, Congressional	.65	.20	☐☐☐☐☐
3335	33c Famous Trains, 20th Century Limited	.65	.20	☐☐☐☐☐
3336	33c Famous Trains, Hiawatha	.65	.20	☐☐☐☐☐
3337	33c Famous Trains, Super Chief..........	.65	.20	☐☐☐☐☐
a.	Strip of 5, #3333-3337	3.25	—	☐☐☐☐☐
3338	33c Frederick Law Olmsted, Landscape Architect....................	.65	.20	☐☐☐☐☐
3339	33c Max Steiner	.65	.20	☐☐☐☐☐
3340	33c Dimitri Tiomkin............................	.65	.20	☐☐☐☐☐
3341	33c Bernard Herrmann	.65	.20	☐☐☐☐☐
3342	33c Franz Waxman..............................	.65	.20	☐☐☐☐☐
3343	33c Alfred Newman	.65	.20	☐☐☐☐☐
3344	33c Erich Wolfgang Korngold	.65	.20	☐☐☐☐☐

3399-3402

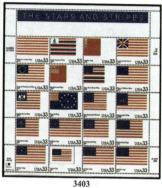

3403

2404-3407

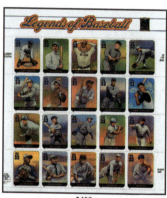

3408

3409

Scott No.	Description	Unused Value	Used Value	/ / / / / /
a.	Block of 6, #3339-3344	3.90	—	
3345	33c Ira & George Gershwin	.65	.20	
3346	33c Alan Jay Lerner & Frederick Loewe......................	.65	.20	
3347	33c Lorenz Hart	.65	.20	
3348	33c Richard Rodgers & Oscar Hammerstein II..................	.65	.20	
3349	33c Meredith Willson..........................	.65	.20	
3350	33c Frank Loesser	.65	.20	
a.	Block of 6, #3345-3350	3.90	—	
3351	Insects & Spiders, Pane of 20	13.00	—	
a.-t.	33c any single..................................	.65	.20	

Serpentine Die Cut 11, Self-Adhesive

3352	33c Hanukkah	.65	.20	

Coil Stamp Perf 9¾, Vertically

3353	22c Uncle Sam (3259).........................	.45	.20	

Perf.11¼

3354	33c Nato, 50th Anniv........................	.65	.20	

Serpentine Die Cut 11¼ on 2 or 3 sides, Self-Adhesive Booklet Stamp

3355	33c Madonna and Child, by Bartolomeo Vivarini	.65	.20	
a.	Booklet pane of 20	13.00		

Serpentine Die Cut 11¼

3356	33c Deer, gold & red	.65	.20	
3357	33c Deer, gold & blue	.65	.20	
3358	33c Deer, gold & purple......................	.65	.20	
3359	33c Deer, gold & green.......................	.65	.20	
a.	Block or strip of 4, #3356-3359....	2.60		

Booklet Stamps
Serpentine Die Cut 11¼ on 2, 3 or 4 sides

3360	33c Deer, gold & red (3356).............	.65	.20	
3361	33c Deer, gold & blue (3357)............	.65	.20	
3362	33c Deer, gold & purple (3358)...........	.65	.20	
3363	33c Deer, gold & green (3359)............	.65	.20	
a.	Booklet pane of 20, 5 each #3360-3363	13.00		

Size: 21x19mm
Serpentine Die Cut 11½ x11¼ on 2 or 3 sides

3364	33c Deer, gold & red (3356).............	.65	.20	
3365	33c Deer, gold & blue (3357)............	.65	.20	
3366	33c Deer, gold & purple (3358)...........	.65	.20	
3367	33c Deer, gold & green (3359)............	.65	.20	
a.	Booklet pane of 4, #3364-3367.....	2.60		
b.	Booklet pane of 5, #3364, 3366, 3367, 2 #3365 + label	3.25		
c.	Booklet pane of 6, #3365, 3367, 2 each #3364 & 3366.................	4.00		

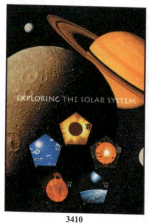

3410

3411

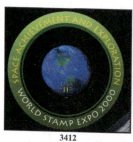

3412

3413

3414-3417

Scott No.	Description	Unused Value	Used Value	//////

Photogravure, Serpentine Die Cut 11, Self-Adhesive
3368 33c Kwanzaa (3175) .... .65 .20 ☐☐☐☐☐

Serpentine Die Cut 11¼, Self-Adhesive
3369 33c Year 2000, Baby New Year.......... .65 .20 ☐☐☐☐☐

2000, Lithographed, Perf. 11¼
3370 33c Chinese New Year,
Year of the Dragon .... .65 .20 ☐☐☐☐☐

Serpentine Die Cut 11½ x11¼, Self-Adhesive
3371 33c Patricia Roberts Harris .... .65 .20 ☐☐☐☐☐

Perf. 11
3372 33c Submarines, Los Angeles Class
with microprinted "USPS"
at base of sail .... .65 .20 ☐☐☐☐☐

Booklet Stamps
3373 22c Submarines, S Class .... .45 .20 ☐☐☐☐☐
3374 33c Submarines, Los Angeles Class,
no microprinting .... .65 .30 ☐☐☐☐☐
3375 55c Submarines, Ohio Class .... 1.10 .50 ☐☐☐☐☐
3376 60c Submarines, USS Holland .... 1.25 .55 ☐☐☐☐☐
3377 $3.20 Submarines, Gato Class .... 6.50 3.00 ☐☐☐☐☐
a. Booklet pane of 5, #3373-3377..... 10.00 — ☐☐☐☐☐

Serpentine Die Cut 11¼x11½, 11½ (horiz. stamps), Self-Adhesive
3378 Pacific Coast Rain Forest, Pane of 10 6.50 ☐☐☐☐☐
a.-j. 33c any single .... .65 .20 ☐☐☐☐☐

Perf. 11x11¼
3379 33c Louise Nevelson, Sculptor, Silent Music I .65 .20 ☐☐☐☐☐
3380 33c Louise Nevelson, Sculptor, Royal Tide I .65 .20 ☐☐☐☐☐
3381 33c Louise Nevelson, Sculptor, Black Chord .65 .20 ☐☐☐☐☐
3382 33c Louise Nevelson, Sculptor,
Nightsphere-Light....................... .65 .20 ☐☐☐☐☐
3383 33c Louise Nevelson, Sculptor,
Dawn's Wedding Chapel I........... .65 .20 ☐☐☐☐☐
a. Strip of 5, #3379-3383 .... 3.25 — ☐☐☐☐☐

Perf. 11
3384 33c Hubble Images, Eagle Nebula ..... .65 .20 ☐☐☐☐☐
3385 33c Hubble Images, Ring Nebula .... .65 .20 ☐☐☐☐☐
3386 33c Hubble Images, Lagoon Nebula .. .65 .20 ☐☐☐☐☐
3387 33c Hubble Images, Egg Nebula .... .65 .20 ☐☐☐☐☐
3388 33c Hubble Images, Galaxy NGC 1316 .65 .20 ☐☐☐☐☐
a. Strip of 5, #3384-3388................. 3.25 — ☐☐☐☐☐
b. As "a," imperf............................... 1,200. — ☐☐☐☐☐
3389 33c Samoan Double Canoe................. .65 .20 ☐☐☐☐☐
3390 33c Library Of Congress, ... .65 .20 ☐☐☐☐☐

Serpentine Die Cut 11, Self-Adhesive
3391 Road Runner & Wile E. Coyote,
Pane of 10 .... 6.50 ☐☐☐☐☐

3420

3426

3432

3438

3443

3444

3445

3446

3447

3448

3451

3457

3467

3468

3468A

Scott No.	Description	Unused Value	Used Value	/ / / / / /
a.	33c single	.65	.20	☐☐☐☐☐
b.	Booklet pane of 9 #3391a.............	5.85		☐☐☐☐☐
c.	Booklet pane of 1 #3391a.............	.65		☐☐☐☐☐
d.	All die cutting omitted, pane of 10	8,500.		☐☐☐☐☐
3392	Road Runner & Wile E. Coyote, Pane of 10 (3391)......................	6.50		☐☐☐☐☐
a.	33c single	.65		☐☐☐☐☐
b.	Booklet pane of 9 #3392a.............	—		☐☐☐☐☐
c.	Booklet pane of 1, imperf.	—		

Perf. 11

Scott No.	Description	Unused Value	Used Value	/ / / / / /
3393	33c Maj. Gen. John L. Hines.............	.65	.20	☐☐☐☐☐
3394	33c Gen. Omar N. Bradley	.65	.20	☐☐☐☐☐
3395	33c Sgt. Alvin C. York	.65	.20	☐☐☐☐☐
3396	33c Second Lt. Audie L. Murphy	.65	.20	☐☐☐☐☐
a.	Block or strip of 4, #3393-3396 ...	2.60	—	
3397	33c Summer Sports - Runners.............	.65	.20	☐☐☐☐☐

Serpentine Die Cut 11½, Self-Adhesive

Scott No.	Description	Unused Value	Used Value	/ / / / / /
3398	33c Adoption......................................	.65	.20	☐☐☐☐☐

Perf. 11

Scott No.	Description	Unused Value	Used Value	/ / / / / /
3399	33c Youth Team Sports, Basketball.....	.65	.20	☐☐☐☐☐
3400	33c Youth Team Sports, Football........	.65	.20	☐☐☐☐☐
3401	33c Youth Team Sports, Soccer..........	.65	.20	☐☐☐☐☐
3402	33c Youth Team Sports, Baseball........	.65	.20	☐☐☐☐☐
a.	Block or strip of 4, #3399-3402 ...	2.60	—	

Perf. 10½x11

Scott No.	Description	Unused Value	Used Value	/ / / / / /
3403	The Stars And Stripes, Pane of 20	13.00	—	☐☐☐☐☐
a.-t.	33c any single...................................	.65	.30	

Photogravure, Serpentine Die Cut 8½ Horiz., Self-Adhesive Coil Stamps

Scott No.	Description	Unused Value	Used Value	/ / / / / /
3404	33c Blueberries (3294).......................	.65	.20	☐☐☐☐☐
3405	33c Strawberries (3295)	.65	.20	☐☐☐☐☐
3406	33c Blackberries (3296)......................	.65	.20	☐☐☐☐☐
3407	33c Raspberries (3297)	.65	.20	☐☐☐☐☐
a.	Strip of 4, #3404-3407	2.60		

Serpentine Die Cut 11¼, Self-Adhesive

Scott No.	Description	Unused Value	Used Value	/ / / / / /
3408	Legends Of Baseball, Pane of 20 .	13.00		☐☐☐☐☐
a.-t.	33c any single...................................	.65	.20	

Souvenir Sheets

Scott No.	Description	Unused Value	Used Value	/ / / / / /
3409	Probing the Vastness of Space, Sheet of 6	7.50	—	☐☐☐☐☐
a.-f.	60c any single.....................................	1.25	.60	
3410	Exploring the Solar System, Sheet of 5 + label	10.00	—	☐☐☐☐☐

3471A 3472 3473

3475A 3484 3484A 3491

3495 3496 3499

3500 3501

Scott No.	Description	Unused Value	Used Value	/ / / / / /
a.-e.	$1 any single......................................	2.00	1.00	☐☐☐☐☐
f.	As No. 3410, imperf	—		☐☐☐☐☐

Untagged, Photogravure with Hologram Affixed,
3411	Escaping the Gravity of Earth, Sheet of 2	12.50	—	☐☐☐☐☐
a.-b.	$3.20 any single................................	6.25	3.00	☐☐☐☐☐
c.	Hologram omitted on right stamp .	—		
3412	$11.75 Space Achievement and Exploration.................................	22.50	11.50	☐☐☐☐☐
a.	$11.75 single	20.00	10.00	☐☐☐☐☐
b.	Hologram omitted	—		
3413	$11.75 Landing on the Moon	22.50	11.50	☐☐☐☐☐
a.	$11.75 single	20.00	10.00	☐☐☐☐☐

Stampin' The Future – Children's Stamp Design Contest Winners, Serpentine Die Cut 11¼, Self-Adhesive
3414	33c By Zachary Canter, Space Figures	.65	.20	☐☐☐☐☐
3415	33c By Sarah Lipsey, Heart	.65	.20	☐☐☐☐☐
3416	33c By Morgan Hill, "Mommy, Are We There Yet".............................	.65	.20	☐☐☐☐☐
3417	33c By Ashley Young, Space Dog	.65	.20	☐☐☐☐☐
a.	Horiz. strip of 4, #3414-3417	2.60		

Distinguished Americans Issue
3420	10c Joseph W. Stilwell	.20	.20	☐☐☐☐☐
3426	33c Claude Pepper, self-adhesive	.65	.20	☐☐☐☐☐
3431	76c Sen Hattie Caraway, self-adhesive, die cut 11	1.50	.20	☐☐☐☐☐
a.	Hattie Caraway, die cut 11.4x11 ...	—	—	☐☐☐☐☐
3432	83c Edna Ferber, self-adhesive	1.60	.30	☐☐☐☐☐

2000 Commemoratives
3438	33c California Statehood, 150th Anniv.	.65	.20	☐☐☐☐☐
3439	33c Deep Sea Creatures - Fanfin Anglerfish	.65	.20	☐☐☐☐☐
3440	33c Deep Sea Creatures - Sea Cucumber	.65	.20	☐☐☐☐☐
3441	33c Deep Sea Creatures - Fangtooth....	.65	.20	☐☐☐☐☐
3442	33c Deep Sea Creatures - Amphipod...	.65	.20	☐☐☐☐☐
3443	33c Deep Sea Creatures - Medusa.......	.65	.20	☐☐☐☐☐
a.	Vert. strip of 5, #3439-3443	3.25		
3444	33c Literary Arts - Thomas Wolfe, Novelist	.65	.20	☐☐☐☐☐
3445	33c White House, 200th Anniv.	.65	.20	☐☐☐☐☐
3446	33c Legends of Hollywood - Edward G. Robinson...................	.65	.20	☐☐☐☐☐

2001 Definitives
3447	(10c) New York Public Library Lion	.20	.20	☐☐☐☐☐
3448	(34c) Flag Over Farm, litho., perf 11 1/4	.65	.20	☐☐☐☐☐
3449	(34c) Flag Over Farm, litho. self-adhesive	.65	.20	☐☐☐☐☐

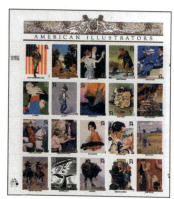

3502

3503

3505

3506

3504

3507

3508

3509

Scott No.	Description	Unused Value	Used Value	/ / / / / /
3450	(34c) Flag Over Farm, photo., self-adhesive booklet stamp	.65	.20	
3450a	Flag Over Farm, Booklet pane of 18	12.00		
3451	(34c) Statue of Liberty, self-adhesive booklet stamp	.65	.20	
a.	Statue of Liberty, booklet pane of 20	13.00		
b.	Statue of Liberty, Booklet pane of 4	2.60		
c.	Statue of Liberty, booklet pane of 6	3.90		
3452	(34c) Statue of Liberty, Coil stamp	.65	.20	
3453	(34c) Statue of Liberty self-adhesive coil	.65	.20	
3454	(34c) Flower, self-adhesive booklet stamp (purple bckgrnd)	.65	.20	
3455	(34c) Flower, self-adhesive booklet stamp (tan bckgrnd)	.65	.20	
3456	(34c) Flower, self-adhesive booklet stamp (green bckgrnd)	.65	.20	
3457	(34c) Flower, self-adhesive booklet stamp (red bckgrnd)	.65	.20	
a.	Flowers, Block of 4, #3454-3457	2.60		
b.	Flowers, Booklet pane of 4, #3454-3457	2.60		
c.	Flowers, Booklet pane of 6, #3456, 3457, 2 each #3454-3455	3.90		
d.	Flowers, Booklet pane of 6, #3454, 3455, 2 each #3456-3457	3.90		
e.	Flowers, Booklet pane of 20, 5 each #3454-3457 + label	13.00		
3458	(34c) Flower (purple bckgrnd), die cut 11.5x11.75"	.65	.20	
3459	(34c) Flower (tan bckgrnd), die cut 11.5x11.75	.65	.20	
3460	(34c) Flower (green bckgrnd), die cut 11.5x11.75	.65	.20	
3461	(34c) Flower (red bckgrnd), die cut 11.5x11.75	.65	.20	
a.	Block of 4, #3458-3461	2.60		
b.	Booklet pane of 20, 2 each #3461a, 3 each #3457a	25.00		
c.	Booklet pane of 20, 2 each #3457a, 3 each #3461a	30.00		
3462	(34c) Flower (purple bckgrnd), coil stamp	.65	.20	
3463	(34c) Flower (tan bckgrnd), coil stamp	.65	.20	
3464	(34c) Flower (green bckgrnd), coil stamp	.65	.20	
3465	(34c) Flower (red bckgrnd), coil stamp	.65	.20	
a.	Strip of 4, #3462-3465	2.60		
2001 Issues				
3466	34c Statue of Liberty, self-adhesive coil (rounded corners)	.65	.20	
3467	21c Buffalo, Self-Adhesive 11 1/4	.40	.20	

3511

3520

3521

3522

3523

3524

3528

3532

3533

3534-3535

Scott No.		Description	Unused Value	Used Value	/ / / / /
3468	21c	American Buffalo, self-adhesive perforated sheet stamp	.40	.20	☐☐☐☐☐
3468A	23c	George Washington, self-adhesive serpentine die cut 11¼x11¾.......	.45	.20	☐☐☐☐☐
3469	34c	Flag Over Farm, perf 11.25 sheet stamp	.65	.20	☐☐☐☐☐
3470		Flag Over Farm, self-adhesive sheet stamp	.65	.20	☐☐☐☐☐
3471A	57c	Eagle, self-adhesive, serpentine die cut 10¾.................................	1.10	.20	☐☐☐☐☐
3471	55c	Eagle, self-adhesive......................	1.10	.20	☐☐☐☐☐
3472	$3.50	Capitol Dome	7.00	3.50	☐☐☐☐☐
3473	$12.25	Washington Monument	22.50	10.00	☐☐☐☐☐
3475	21c	American Buffalo, self-adhesive coil stamp	.40	.20	☐☐☐☐☐
3475A	23c	George Washington, self-adhesive, coil stamp, serpentine die cut 8½ Vert.	.45	.20	☐☐☐☐☐
3476	34c	Statue of Liberty, perforated coil stamp	.65	.20	☐☐☐☐☐
3477	34c	Statue of Liberty, self-adhesive coil stamp (right angle corners)..................	.65	.20	☐☐☐☐☐
3478	34c	Flower, self-adhesive coil stamp, die cut 8.5 vert.	.65	.20	☐☐☐☐☐
3479	34c	Flower , self-adhesive coil stamp, die cut 8.5 vert.	.65	.20	☐☐☐☐☐
3480	34c	Flowers, self-adhesive coil stamp, die cut 8.5 vert.	.65	.20	☐☐☐☐☐
3481	34c	Flowers, self-adhesive coil stamp, die cut 8.5 vert.	.65	.20	☐☐☐☐☐
a.		Flowers, Strip of 4, #3478-3481, self-adhesive coil stamps	2.60		☐☐☐☐☐
3482	20c	George Washington, self-adhesive bklt stamp, die cut 11.25.............	.40	.20	☐☐☐☐☐
a.		Booklet pane of 10	4.00		☐☐☐☐☐
b.		Booklet pane of 4	1.60		☐☐☐☐☐
c.		Booklet pane of 6	2.40		☐☐☐☐☐
3483	20c	George Washington, self-adhesive bklt stamp, die cut 10.5x11.25....	.40	.20	☐☐☐☐☐
a.		Booklet pane of 4, 2 #3482 at L, 2 #3483 at R.............................	5.00		☐☐☐☐☐
b.		Booklet pane of 6, 3 #3482 at L, 3 #3483 at R.............................	8.00		☐☐☐☐☐
c.		Booklet pane of 10, 5 #3482 at L, 5 #3483 at R.............................	10.00		☐☐☐☐☐
d.		Booklet pane of 4, 2 #3483 at L, 2 #3482 at R.............................	5.00		☐☐☐☐☐
e.		Booklet pane of 6, 3 #3483 at L, 3 #3482 at R.............................	8.00		☐☐☐☐☐
f.		Booklet pane of 10, 5 #3483 at L, 5 #3482 at R.............................	10.00		☐☐☐☐☐

3536

3537

3538

3539

3540

3541

3542

3543

3544

3545

3546

3547

3548

3549

3549B

3550

3550A

3551

Scott No.	Description	Unused Value	Used Value	/ / / / / /
g.	Pair, #3482 at L, #3483 at R.........	2.00		☐☐☐☐☐
h.	Pair, #3483 at R, #3482 at L.........	2.00		☐☐☐☐☐
3484 21c	Buffalo (3467), self-adhesive, booklet stamp, serpentine die cut 11 1/4 on 3 Sides........................	.40	.20	☐☐☐☐☐
b.	Booklet pane of 4...........................	1.60		☐☐☐☐☐
c.	Booklet pane of 6...........................	2.40		☐☐☐☐☐
d.	Booklet pane of 10.........................	4.00		☐☐☐☐☐
3484A 21c	Buffalo, self-adhesive, booklet stamp serpentine die cut 10 1/2x 11 1/4	1.00	.30	☐☐☐☐☐
e.	Booklet pane of 4, 2 #3484 at L, 2 #3484A at R.............................	5.00		☐☐☐☐☐
f.	Booklet pane of 6, 3 #3484 at L, 3 #3484A at R, ...	8.00		☐☐☐☐☐
g.	Booklet pane of 10, 5 #3484 at L, 5 #3484A at R...........................	10.00		☐☐☐☐☐
h.	Booklet pane of 4, 2 #3484A at L, 2 #3484 at R.............................	5.00		☐☐☐☐☐
i.	Booklet pane of 6, 3 #3484A at L, 3 #3484 at R.............................	8.00		☐☐☐☐☐
j.	Booklet pane of 10, 5 #3484A at L, 5 #3484 at R...........................	10.00		☐☐☐☐☐
k.	Pair, #3484 at L, #3484A at R......	2.00		☐☐☐☐☐
l.	Pair, #3484A at L, #3484 at R......	2.00		☐☐☐☐☐
3485 34c	Statue of Liberty, self-adhesive booklet stamp...............................	.65	.20	☐☐☐☐☐
a.	Booklet pane of 10	6.50		☐☐☐☐☐
b.	Booklet pane of 20, ...	13.00		☐☐☐☐☐
c.	Booklet pane of 4...........................	2.60		☐☐☐☐☐
d.	Booklet pane of 6...........................	3.90		☐☐☐☐☐
e.	Imperf., pair...................................	—		☐☐☐☐☐
3487 34c	Flower, self-adhesive booklet stamp, die cut 10.25x10.75....................	.65	.20	☐☐☐☐☐
3488 34c	Flower, self-adhesive booklet stamp, die cut 10.25x10.75....................	.65	.20	☐☐☐☐☐
3489 34c	Flower, self-adhesive booklet stamp, die cut 10.25x10.75....................	.65	.20	☐☐☐☐☐
3490 34c	Flower, self-adhesive booklet stamp, die cut 10.25x10.75....................	.65	.20	☐☐☐☐☐
a.	Flowers, Block of 4, #3487-3490..	2.60		☐☐☐☐☐
b.	Flowers, Booklet pane of 4, #3487-3490	2.60		☐☐☐☐☐
c.	Flowers, Booklet pane of 6, #3489-3490, 2 each #3487-3488	3.90		☐☐☐☐☐
d.	Flowers, Booklet pane of 6, #3487-3488, 2 each #3489-3490.....................	3.90		☐☐☐☐☐
e.	Flowers, Booklet pane of 20, 5 each #3490a + label.............................	13.00		☐☐☐☐☐

3552   3553

3554   3555

3556   3557   3558

3559   3560

Scott No.	Description	Unused Value	Used Value	/ / / / / /
3491	34c Apple, self-Adhesive booklet stamp	.65	.20	
3492	34c Orange, self-Adhesive booklet stam	.65	.20	
a.	Orange, Apple, Pair, #3491-3492..	1.30		
b.	Orange, Apple, Booklet pane, 10 each #3491-3492	13.00		
c.	As "a," black ("34 USA") omitted	—		
d.	As "a," imperf.	—		
3493	34c Apple, self-adhesive Booklet stamp	.65	.20	
3494	34c Orange, self-adhesive Booklet stamp	.65	.20	
a.	Apple and Orange, Pair, #3493-3494	1.30		
b.	Apple and Orange, Booklet pane, 2 each #3493-3494	2.60		
c.	Apple and Orange, Booklet pane, 3 each #3493-3494, #3493 at UL..........	3.90		
d.	Apple and Orange, Booklet pane, 3 each #3493-3494, #3494 at UL..........	3.90		
3495	34c Flag Over Farm, self-adhesive, booklet stamp (3469), serpentine die cut 8 on 2, 3 or 4 sides".......	.65	.20	
a.	Booklet pane of 18	12.00		

2001 Commemoratives

Scott No.	Description	Unused Value	Used Value	/ / / / / /
3496	(34c) Love - Rose, Apr. 20, 1763 Love letter by John Adams.................................	.65	.20	
a.	Booklet pane of 20	13.00		
b.	Vert. pair, imperf. horiz...............	—		
3497	34c Love - Rose and Apr 20, 1763 Love Letter by John Adams, Self-Adhesive ...	.65	.20	
a.	Booklet pane of 20	13.00		
3498	34c Love - Rose and Apr 20, 1763 Love Letter by John Adams, 18x21mm	.65	.20	
a.	Booklet pane of 4	2.60		
b.	Booklet pane of 6	3.90		
3499	55c Rose, Aug. 11 1763 Love Letter by John Adams, self-adhesive booklet stamp	1.10	.20	
3500	34c Chinese New Year, Year of the Snake	.65	.20	
3501	34c Black Heritage, Roy Wilkins (1901-81), Civil Rights Leader	.65	.20	
3502	American Illustrators, Pane of 20 .	13.00		
3502a-t	American Illustrators, any single ..	.65	.20	
3503	34c Diabetes Awareness......................	.65	.20	
3504	34c Nobel Prize, Centenary	.65	.20	
3505	Pan-American Expo Invert Stamps, Cent., Pane	6.75		
a.	1c Pan-American Expo Invert Stamps, Cent. - Reproduction of Scott 294a	.20	.20	

3561

3562

3563

3564

3565

3566

3567

3568

3569

3570

Scott No.	Description	Unused Value	Used Value	/ / / / / /
b.	2c Pan-American Expo Invert Stamps, Cent. - Reproduction of Scott 295a	.20	.20	☐☐☐☐☐
c.	4c Pan-American Expo Invert Stamps, Cent. - Reproduction of Scott 296a	.20	.20	☐☐☐☐☐
d.	80c Pan-American Expo Invert Stamps, Cent. - Commemorative (cinderella) stamp depicting a buffalo............	1.60	.35	☐☐☐☐☐
3506	Great Plains Prairie, pane of 10....	7.00		☐☐☐☐☐
3506a-j34c	Great Plains Prairie, any single.....	.65	.20	☐☐☐☐☐
3507	34c Peanuts Comic Strip.....................	.65	.20	☐☐☐☐☐
3508	34c Honoring Veterans, self-adhesive..	.65	.20	☐☐☐☐☐
3509	34c Frida Kahlo (1907-54), Painter, Self-Portrait....................	.65	.20	☐☐☐☐☐
3510	34c Legendary Playing Fields, Ebbets Field, self-adhesive.....................	.65	.20	☐☐☐☐☐
3511	34c Legendary Playing Fields, Tiger Stadium, self-adhesive	.65	.20	☐☐☐☐☐
3512	34c Legendary Playing Fields, Crosley Field, self-adhesive..............................	.65	.20	☐☐☐☐☐
3513	34c Legendary Playing Fields, Yankee Stadium, self-adhesive....	.65	.20	☐☐☐☐☐
3514	34c Legendary Playing Fields, Polo Grounds, self-adhesive...............	.65	.20	☐☐☐☐☐
3515	34c Legendary Playing Fields, Forbes Field, self-adhesive..............................	.65	.20	☐☐☐☐☐
3516	34c Legendary Playing Fields, Fenway Park, self-adhesive..............................	.65	.20	☐☐☐☐☐
3517	34c Legendary Playing Fields, Comiskey Park, self-adhesive..............................	.65	.20	☐☐☐☐☐
3518	34c Legendary Playing Fields, Shibe Park, self-adhesive..............................	.65	.20	☐☐☐☐☐
3519	34c Legendary Playing fields, Wrigley Field, self-sdhesive..............................	.65	.20	☐☐☐☐☐
a.	Legendary Playing fields, Block of 10, #3510-3519	6.50		☐☐☐☐☐
3520	(10c) Atlas Statue, New York City, self-adhesive coil stamp..............	.20	.20	☐☐☐☐☐
3521	34c Leonard Bernstein (1918-90), Conductor	.65	.20	☐☐☐☐☐
3522	(15c) Woody Wagon, self-adhesive coil stamp	.30	.20	☐☐☐☐☐
3523	34c Legends of Hollywood - Lucille Ball (1911-89), self-adhesive..............	.65	.20	☐☐☐☐☐
3524	34c American Treasures Series, Amish Quilts - Diamond in the Square, c. 1920, self-adhesive..................	.65	.20	☐☐☐☐☐
3525	34c American Treasures Series, Amish Quilts - Lone Star, c. 1920, self-adhesive	.65	.20	☐☐☐☐☐

3571   3572

3573   3574

3575   3576

3577   3578

3579   3580

Scott No.	Description	Unused Value	Used Value	/ / / / / /
3526	34c American Treasures Series, Amish Quilts - Sunshine and Shadow, c. 1910, Self-Adhesive.............................	.65	.20	☐☐☐☐☐
3527	34c American Treasures Series, Amish Quilts - Double Ninepatch Variation, Self-Adhesive........................	.65	.20	☐☐☐☐☐
a.	Block or strip of 4, #3524-3527....	2.60		☐☐☐☐☐
3528	34c Carnivorous Plants - Venus Flytrap, self-adhesive...............................	.65	.20	☐☐☐☐☐
3529	34c Carnivorous Plants - Yellow Trumpet, self-adhesive...............................	.65	.20	☐☐☐☐☐
3530	34c Carnivorous Plants - Cobra Lily, self-adhesive...............................	.65	.20	☐☐☐☐☐
3531	34c Carnivorous Plants - English Sundew, self-adhesive...............................	.65	.20	☐☐☐☐☐
a.	Block or strip of 4, #3528-3531....	2.60		☐☐☐☐☐
3532	34c Eid - 'Eid Mubarak', self adhesive	.65	.20	☐☐☐☐☐
3533	34c Enrico Fermi, Physicist, self-adhesive	.65	.20	☐☐☐☐☐
3534	That's All Folks! Porky Pig at Mailbox, Pane of 10, self-adhesive...........	8.00		☐☐☐☐☐
a.	34c Single	.65	.20	☐☐☐☐☐
b.	Booklet pane of 9, #3534a............	5.85		☐☐☐☐☐
c.	Booklet pane of 1, #3534a............	.65		☐☐☐☐☐
3535	That's All Folks! Porky Pig at Mailbox, Pane of 10, self-adhesive, right stamp imperforate, ...	6.50		☐☐☐☐☐
a.	34c Single	.65		☐☐☐☐☐
b.	Booklet pane of 9, #3535a............	—		☐☐☐☐☐
c.	Booklet pane of 1, imperf.............	—		☐☐☐☐☐
3536	34c Virgin and Child, by Lorenzo Costa, self-adhesive, booklet stamp, ... serpentine die cut 11½ on 2, 3, or 4 Sides............................	.65	.20	☐☐☐☐☐
a.	Booklet pane of 20	13.00		☐☐☐☐☐
3537	34c Santa Claus, large date, self-adhesive serpentine die cut 10 3/4x11.......	.65	.20	☐☐☐☐☐
a.	Small date (from booklet pane), self-adhesive, serpentine die cut 10¾x11	.65	.20	☐☐☐☐☐
3538	34c Santa Claus, large date, self-adhesive, serpentine die cut 10¾x11...........	.65	.20	☐☐☐☐☐
a.	Small date (from booklet pane), self-adhesive, serpentine die cut 10¾x11	.65	.20	☐☐☐☐☐
3539	34c Santa Claus, large date, self-adhesive, serpentine die cut 10¾x11...........	.65	.20	☐☐☐☐☐

3581

3582

3583

3584

3585

3586

3587

3588

3589

3590

Scott No.	Description	Unused Value	Used Value	/ / / / / /
a.	Small date (from booklet pane), self-adhesive, serpentine die cut 10¾x11	.65	.20	☐☐☐☐☐
3540	34c Santa Claus, large date, self-adhesive, serpentine die cut 10¾x11	.65	.20	☐☐☐☐☐
a.	Small date (from booklet pane), self-adhesive, serpentine die cut 10¾x11	.65	.20	☐☐☐☐☐
b.	Santa Claus, Block of 4, #3537-3540	2.60		☐☐☐☐☐
c.	Santa Claus, Block of 4, small date, #3537a-3540a............................	2.60		☐☐☐☐☐
d.	Santa Claus, Booklet pane, 5 #3540c + label	13.00		☐☐☐☐☐
3541	34c Santa Claus, Green and Red denominations, self-adhesive, serpentine die cut 11	.65	.20	☐☐☐☐☐
3542	34c Santa Claus, Green and Red denominations, Self-Adhesive, serpentine die cut 11	.65	.20	☐☐☐☐☐
3543	34c Santa Claus, Green and Red denominations, self-adhesive, serpentine die cut 11	.65	.20	☐☐☐☐☐
3544	34c Santa Claus, Green and Red denominations, self-adhesive, serpentine die cut 11	.65	.20	☐☐☐☐☐
a.	Block of 4, #3541-3544 ....2.60			☐☐☐☐☐
b.	Booklet pane of 4, #3541-3544.....	2.60		☐☐☐☐☐
c.	Booklet pane of 6, #3543-3544, 2 #3541-3542	3.90		☐☐☐☐☐
d.	Booklet pane of 6, #3541-3542, 2 #3543-3544	3.90		☐☐☐☐☐
3545	34c James Madison (1751-1836), Montpelier, self-adhesive.............	.65	.20	☐☐☐☐☐
3546	34c Thanksgiving Cornicopia, self-adhesive	.65	.20	☐☐☐☐☐
3547	34c Hanukkah Type of 1996 (3118), self-adhesive	.65	.20	☐☐☐☐☐
3548	34c Kwanzaa Type of 1997 (3175), self-adhesive	.65	.20	☐☐☐☐☐
3549	34c United We Stand, self-adhesive, booklet stamp, serpentine die cut 11¼ on 2, 3, or 4 sides	.65	.20	☐☐☐☐☐
a.	Booklet pane of 20........................	13.00		☐☐☐☐☐
3549B	34c United We Stand (3549), self-adhesive, booklet stamp, serpentine die cut 10 1/2 x 10 3/4 on 2 or 3 Sides...........................	.65	.20	☐☐☐☐☐

3591

3592

3593

3594

3595

3596

3597

3598

3599

3600

Scott No.	Description	Unused Value	Used Value	//////
c.	Booklet pane of 4	2.60		☐☐☐☐☐
d.	Booklet pane of 6	3.90		☐☐☐☐☐
e.	Booklet pane of 20	13.00		☐☐☐☐☐
3550	34c United We Stand (3549), self-adhesive, coil stamp, square corners, ... serpentine die cut 9¾ Vert.	.65	.20	☐☐☐☐☐
3550A	34c United We Stand (3549), self-adhesive, coil stamp, round corners, spaced, serpentine die cut 9¾ Vert.	.65	.20	☐☐☐☐☐
3551	57c Love Letters (3496), self-adhesive, serpentine die cut 11 1/4.............	1.10	.20	☐☐☐☐☐

2002 Issues

Scott No.	Description	Unused Value	Used Value	//////
3552	34c Winter Olympics - Ski Jumping, self-adhesive	.65	.20	☐☐☐☐☐
3553	34c Winter Olympics - Snowboarding, self-adhesive	.65	.20	☐☐☐☐☐
3554	34c Winter Olympics - Ice Hockey, self-adhesive	.65	.20	☐☐☐☐☐
3555	34c Winter Olympics - Figure Skating, self-adhesive	.65	.20	☐☐☐☐☐
a.	Block or strip of 4, #3552-3555....	2.60		☐☐☐☐☐
3556	34c Child and Adult, self-adhesive	.65	.20	☐☐☐☐☐
3557	34c Langston Hughes, Writer, self-adhesive	.65	.20	☐☐☐☐☐
3558	34c Happy Birthday, self-adhesive.......	.65	.20	☐☐☐☐☐
3559	34c Year of the Horse, self-adhesive....	.65	.20	☐☐☐☐☐
3560	34c Military Academy Coat of Arms, self-adhesive	.65	.20	☐☐☐☐☐
3561	34c Greetings from Alabama, self-adhesive	.65	.20	☐☐☐☐☐
3562	34c Greetings from Alaska, self-adhesive	.65	.20	☐☐☐☐☐
3563	34c Greetings from Arizona, self-adhesive	.65	.20	☐☐☐☐☐
3564	34c Greetings from Arkansas, self-adhesive	.65	.20	☐☐☐☐☐
3565	34c Greetings from California, self-adhesive	.65	.20	☐☐☐☐☐
3566	34c Greetings from Colorado, self-adhesive	.65	.20	☐☐☐☐☐
3567	34c Greetings from Connecticut, self-adhesive	.65	.20	☐☐☐☐☐
3568	34c Greetings from Delaware, self-adhesive	.65	.20	☐☐☐☐☐
3569	34c Greetings from Florida, self-adhesive	.65	.20	☐☐☐☐☐
3570	34c Greetings from Georgia, self-adhesive	.65	.20	☐☐☐☐☐
3571	34c Greetings from Hawaii, self-adhesive	.65	.20	☐☐☐☐☐
3572	34c Greetings from Idaho, self-adhesive	.65	.20	☐☐☐☐☐
3573	34c Greetings from Illinois, self-adhesive	.65	.20	☐☐☐☐☐
3574	34c Greetings from Indiana, self-adhesive	.65	.20	☐☐☐☐☐
3575	34c Greetings from Iowa, self-adhesive	.65	.20	☐☐☐☐☐
3576	34c Greetings from Kansas, self-adhesive	.65	0.20	☐☐☐☐☐
3577	34c Greetings from Kentucky, self-adhesive	.65	.20	☐☐☐☐☐
3578	34c Greetings from Louisiana, self-adhesive	.65	.20	☐☐☐☐☐

3601

3602

3603

3604

3605

3606

3607

3608

3609

3610

Scott No.	Description	Unused Value	Used Value	/ / / / / /
3579	34c Greetings from Maine, self-adhesive	.65	.20	☐☐☐☐☐
3580	34c Greetings from Maryland, self-adhesive	.65	.20	☐☐☐☐☐
3581	34c Greetings from Massachusetts, self-adhesive	.65	.20	☐☐☐☐☐
3582	34c Greetings from Michigan, self-adhesive	.65	.20	☐☐☐☐☐
3583	34c Greetings from Minnesota, self-adhesive	.65	.20	☐☐☐☐☐
3584	34c Greetings from Mississippi, self-adhesive	.65	.20	☐☐☐☐☐
3585	34c Greetings from Missouri, self-adhesive	.65	.20	☐☐☐☐☐
3586	34c Greetings from Montana, self-adhesive	.65	.20	☐☐☐☐☐
3587	34c Greetings from Nebraska, self-adhesive	.65	.20	☐☐☐☐☐
3588	34c Greetings from Greetings from Nevada, self-adhesive	.65	.20	☐☐☐☐☐
3589	34c Greetings from New Hampshire, self-adhesive	.65	.20	☐☐☐☐☐
3590	34c Greetings from New Jersey, self-adhesive	.65	.20	☐☐☐☐☐
3591	34c Greetings from New Mexico, self-adhesive	.65	.20	☐☐☐☐☐
3592	34c Greetings from New York, self-adhesive	.65	.20	☐☐☐☐☐
3593	34c Greetings from North Carolina, self-adhesive	.65	.20	☐☐☐☐☐
3594	34c Greetings from North Dakota, self-adhesive	.65	.20	☐☐☐☐☐
3595	34c Greetings from Ohio, self-adhesive	.65	.20	☐☐☐☐☐
3596	34c Greetings from Oklahoma, self-adhesive	.65	.20	☐☐☐☐☐
3597	34c Greetings from Oregon, self-adhesive	.65	.20	☐☐☐☐☐
3598	34c Greetings from Pennsylvania, self-adhesive	.65	.20	☐☐☐☐☐
3599	34c Greetings from Rhode Island, self-adhesive	.65	.20	☐☐☐☐☐
3600	34c Greetings from South Carolina, self-adhesive	.65	.20	☐☐☐☐☐
3601	34c Greetings from South Dakota, self-adhesive	.65	.20	☐☐☐☐☐
3602	34c Greetings from Tennessee, self-adhesive	.65	.20	☐☐☐☐☐
3603	34c Greetings from Texas, self-adhesive	.65	.20	☐☐☐☐☐
3604	34c Greetings from Utah, self-adhesive	.65	.20	☐☐☐☐☐
3605	34c Greetings from Vermont, self-adhesive	.65	.20	☐☐☐☐☐
3606	34c Greetings from Virginia, self-adhesive	.65	.20	☐☐☐☐☐
3607	34c Greetings from Washington, self-adhesive	.65	.20	☐☐☐☐☐
3608	34c Greetings from West Virginia, self-adhesive	.65	.20	☐☐☐☐☐
3609	34c Greetings from Wisconsin, self-adhesive	.65	.20	☐☐☐☐☐
3610	34c Greetings from Wyoming, self-adhesive	.65	.20	☐☐☐☐☐

3611

3612

3613-3614

3616-3617

3618-3619

3620-3621

3622

3623

3624

3625

3626

3627

3628

3629

3630

3631-3633

3635

3636

Scott No.	Description	Unused Value	Used Value	/ / / / / /
a.	Greetings From America, Pane of 50, #3561-3610...............	32.50		☐☐☐☐☐
3611	Longleaf Pine Forest, Pane of 10, self-adhesive	7.00		☐☐☐☐☐
a.	34c Longleaf Pine Forest, Bachman's sparrow, ...	.65	.20	☐☐☐☐☐
b.	34c Longleaf Pine Forest, Northern bobwhite, yellow pitcher plants ..	.65	.20	☐☐☐☐☐
c.	34c Longleaf Pine Fores, Fox squirrel, red-bellied woodpecker...............	.65	.20	☐☐☐☐☐
d.	34c Longleaf Pine Forest, Brown-headed nuthatch........................	.65	.20	☐☐☐☐☐
e.	34c Longleaf Pine Forest, Broadhead skink, yellow pitcher plants, pipeworts .	.65	.20	☐☐☐☐☐
f.	34c Longleaf Pine Forest, Eastern towhee, yellow pitcher plants, Savannah meadow beauties, toothache grass	.65	.20	☐☐☐☐☐
g.	34c Longleaf Pine Forest, Gray fox, gopher tortoise..........................	.65	.20	☐☐☐☐☐
h.	34c Longleaf Pine Forest, Blind click beetle, sweetbay, pine woods treefrog	.65	.20	☐☐☐☐☐
i.	34c Longleaf Pine Forest, Rosebud orchid, pipeworts, southern toad, yellow pitcher plants..............................	.65	.20	☐☐☐☐☐
j.	34c Longleaf Pine Forest, Grass-pink orchid, yellow-sided skimmer, pipeworts, yellow pitcher plants	.65	.20	☐☐☐☐☐
3612	5c Toleware Coffeepot, Coil stamp, perf. 10 vert...................	.20	.20	☐☐☐☐☐
3613	3c Star, self-adhesive, serpentine die cut 11.....................................	.20	.20	☐☐☐☐☐
3614	3c Star (3613), self-adhesive, serpentine die cut 10	.20	.20	☐☐☐☐☐
3616	23c Washington (3468A) perf. 11¼	.45	.20	☐☐☐☐☐
3617	23c Washington (3468A), self-adhesive, Coil stamp" serpentine die cut 11¼	.45	.20	☐☐☐☐☐
3618	23c Washington (3468A), booklet stamp, self-adhesive, serpentine die cut 11¼	.45	.20	☐☐☐☐☐
a.	Booklet pane of 4.........................	1.80		☐☐☐☐☐
b.	Booklet pane of 6.........................	2.70		☐☐☐☐☐
3619	23c Washington (3468A), booklet stamp, self-adhesive serpentine die cut 11¼	.45	.20	☐☐☐☐☐
a.	Booklet pane of 4, 2 #3619 at L, 2 #3618 at R...............................	5.00		☐☐☐☐☐
b.	Booklet pane of 6, 3 #3619 at L, 3 #3618 at R...............................	8.00		☐☐☐☐☐

3649

3650   3651

Scott No.	Description	Unused Value	Used Value	/ / / / / /
g.	Pair, #3619 at L, #3618 at R	— .70	.20	
3620 (37c)	Flag perf.11¼ x11	.70	.20	
3621 (37c)	Flag (3620), self-adhesive, Serpentine die cut 11¼ x11	.70	.20	
3622 (37c)	Flag (3620), coil stamp, self-adhesive, serpentine die cut 10 Vert.	.70	.20	
3623 (37c)	Flag (3620), booklet stamps, self-adhesive, serpentine die cut 11¼	.70	.20	
a.	Booklet pane of 20	14.00		
3624 (37c)	Flag (3620), booklet stamp, self-adhesive, serpentine die cut 10 1/2 x10 3/4	.70	.20	
a.	Booklet pane of 4	2.80		
b.	Booklet pane of 6	4.20		
c.	Booklet pane of 20	14.00		
3625 (37c)	Flag (3620), booklet stamp, self-adhesive, serpentine die cut 8	.70	.20	
a.	Booklet pane of 18	13.00		
3626 (37c)	Toy Mail Wagon, self-adhesive, booklet stamp..............................	.70	.20	
3627 (37c)	Toy Locomotive, self-adhesive, booklet stamp..............................	.70	.20	
3628 (37c)	Toy Taxicab, self-adhesive, booklet stamp..............................	.70	.20	
3629 (37c)	Toy Fire Pumper, self-adhesive, booklet stamp..............................	.70	.20	
a.	Block of 4, #3626-3629	2.80		
b.	Booklet pane of 4, #3626-3629.....	2.80		
c.	Booklet pane of 6, #3627, 3629, 2 each #3626, 3628....................	4.20		
d.	Booklet pane of 6, #3626, 3628, 2 each #3627, 3629....................	4.20		
e.	Booklet pane of 20, 5 each #3626-3629	14.00		
3630	37c Flag, self-adhesive, serpentine die cut 11¼x11	.70	.20	
3631	37c Flag (3630), coil stamp, perf. 10 vert.	.70	.20	
3632	37c Flag (3630), self-adhesive, coil stamp, die cut 10 vert	.70	.20	
3633	37c Flag (3630), self-adhesive, coil stamp, serpentine die cut 8½ vert.	.70	.20	
3635	37c Flag (3630), self-adhesive, Booklet stamp, serpentine die cut 11¼.....	.70	.20	
a.	Booklet pane of 20......................	14.00		
3636	37c Flag (3630), self-adhesive, booklet			

Scott No.	Description	Unused Value	Used Value	/ / / / / /
	Stamp, serpentine die cut			
	10½ x 10¾....................................	.70	.20	☐☐☐☐☐
c	Booklet pane of 20	14.00		☐☐☐☐☐
3649	Masters of American Photography, Pane			
	of 20, self-adhesive....................	14.00		☐☐☐☐☐
a.	37c Portrait of Daniel Webster, by Albert			
	Sands...	.70	.30	☐☐☐☐☐
b.	37c Gen. Ulysses S. Grant and Officers,			
	by Timothy H. Olsullivan............	.70	.30	☐☐☐☐☐
c.	37c Cape Horn, Columbia River, by			
	Carleton E. Watkins	.70	.30	☐☐☐☐☐
d.	37c Blessed Art Thou Among Women, by			
	Gertrude Kasebier.......................	.70	.30	☐☐☐☐☐
e.	37c Looking for Lost Luggage, Ellis Island,			
	by Lewis W. Hine........................	.70	.30	☐☐☐☐☐
f.	37c The Octopus, by Alvin Langdon			
	Colburn	.70	0.30	☐☐☐☐☐
g.	37c Lotus, Mount Kisco, New York, by			
	Edward Steichen	.70	0.30	☐☐☐☐☐
h.	37c Hands and Thimble, by Alfred Stieglitz	.70	0.30	☐☐☐☐☐
i.	37c Rayograph, by Man Ray...............	.70	0.30	☐☐☐☐☐
j.	37c Two Shells, by Edward Weston.....	.70	.30	☐☐☐☐☐
k.	37c My Corsage, by James VanDerZee	.70	.30	☐☐☐☐☐
l.	37c Ditched, Stalled, and Stranded, San			
	Joaquin Valley, California, by			
	Dorothea Lange...........................	.70	.30	☐☐☐☐☐
m.	37c Washroom and Dining Area of Floyd			
	Burroughs' Home, Hale County,			
	Alabama, by Walker Evans	.70	.30	☐☐☐☐☐
n.	37c Frontline Soldier with Canteen,			
	Saipan, by W. Eugene Smith.......	.70	.30	☐☐☐☐☐
o.	37c Steeple, by Paul Strand	.70	.30	☐☐☐☐☐
p.	37c Sand Dunes, Sunrise, by Ansel Adams	.70	.30	☐☐☐☐☐
q.	37c Age and Its Symbols, by Imogen			
	Cunningham..............................	.70	.30	☐☐☐☐☐
r.	37c New York Cityscape, by Andre Kertesz	.70	.30	☐☐☐☐☐
s.	37c Photograph of pedestrians, by Garry			
	Winogrand.................................	.70	.30	☐☐☐☐☐
t.	37c Bristol, Vermont, by Minor White	.70	.30	☐☐☐☐☐
3650	37c Scarlet and Louisiana Tanagers,			
	self-adhesive..............................	.70	.20	☐☐☐☐☐
3651	37c Harry Houdini (1874-1926), Magician,			
	self-adhesive	.70	.20	☐☐☐☐☐

B1

SEMI-POSTAL STAMPS
1998, July 29
B1 (32c+8c) Breast Cancer Awareness,
self-adhesive..............................   .80   .25   □□□□□

2002, June 7
B2(34c+11c) Heroes of 2001, Firemen Atop World
Trade Center Rubble, self-adhesive   .90   .65   □□□□□

SCOTT
Stockbooks

Stockbooks are a safe convenient way to display and store your stamps. These German made stockbooks feature heavyweight archival quality paper with 9 pockets on each page. The 8 ½" 11 ⅝" pages are bound inside a sturdy leatherette grain cover and include glassine interleaving between the pages for added protection.

WHITE PAGE STOCKBOOKS GLASSINE POCKETS

Item	Description	Price
SW16BL	Blue 16 pgs.	$5.95
SW16GR	Green 16 pgs.	$5.95
SW16RD	Red 16 pgs.	$5.95

BLACK PAGE STOCKBOOKS ACETATE POCKETS

Item	Description	Price
ST16RD	Red 16 pgs.	$9.95
ST16GR	Green 16 pgs.	$9.95
ST16BL	Blue 16 pgs.	$9.95
ST16BK	Black 16 pgs.	$9.95
ST32RD	Red 32 pgs.	$14.95
ST32GR	Green 32 pgs.	$14.95
ST32BL	Blue 32 pgs.	$14.95
ST32BK	Black 32 pgs.	$14.95
ST64RD	Red 64 pgs.	$27.95
ST64GR	Green 64 pgs.	$27.95
ST64BL	Blue 64 pgs.	$27.95
ST64BK	Black 64 pgs.	$27.95

Available from your favorite stamp dealer or direct from:

1-800-572-6885
www.amosadvantage.com

328

329

Access to the entire Scott Publishing warehouse at the click of a mouse!

Shopping with Scott Publishing Co. has never been easier with our new, expanded web site. Now you have instant access the entire Scott warehouse 24 hours a day 7 days a week. Whether you're looking for an obscure supplement from years ago or the latest catalogue release, you'll find it all at the click of a mouse.

www.amosadvantage.com

SCOTT

P.O. Box 828 Sidney OH 45365-0828
1-800-572-6885

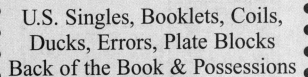

C1 C4 C5 C6

C7 C10

C11 C12

C13 C14

C15 C18

C20 C21 C23

Scott No.	Description	Unused Value	Used Value	/ / / / / /
AIR POST STAMPS				
1918				
C1	6c Curtiss Jenny, orange	65.00	30.00	
C2	16c Curtiss Jenny (C1), green	85.00	35.00	
C3	24c Curtiss Jenny (C1), car rose & blue	85.00	35.00	
a.	Center inverted	170,000.		
1923				
C4	8c Propeller	22.50	14.00	
C5	16c Air Service Emblem	85.00	30.00	
C6	24c Biplane	95.00	30.00	
1926-30				
C7	10c Map & Planes, dark blue	2.60	.35	
C8	15c Map & Planes (C7), olive brown	3.00	2.50	
C9	20c Map & Planes (C7), yellow green	8.00	2.00	
C10	10c "Spirit of St. Louis"	7.25	2.50	
a.	Booklet pane of 3	80.00	65.00	
C11	5c Beacon	5.00	.75	
a.	Vertical pair, imperf. btwn.	5,500.		
C12	5c Winged Globe, violet, perf. 11	10.50	.50	
a.	Horiz. pair, imperf. btwn.	4,500.		
1930				
C13	65c Zeppelin over Atlantic	250.00	160.00	
C14	$1.30 Zeppelin between Continents	475.00	375.00	
C15	$2.60 Zeppelin passing Globe	750.00	575.00	
1931-32, Perf. 10½x11				
C16	5c Winged Globe (C12), violet	5.25	.60	
C17	8c Winged Globe (C12), olive bister	2.40	.40	
1933				
C18	50c Century of Progress	70.00	65.00	
1934				
C19	6c Winged Globe (C12), dull orange	3.50	.25	
1935				
C20	25c Transpacific (dated 1935), blue	1.40	1.00	
1937				
C21	20c Transpacific (no date), green	11.00	1.75	
C22	50c Transpacific (C21), carmine	10.00	5.00	
1938				
C23	6c Eagle & Shield	.50	.20	
a.	Vert. pair, imperf. horiz.	350.00		
b.	Horiz. pair, imperf. vert.	12,500.		

C24

C25

C33

C32

C34

C35

C36

C40

C38

C42

C43

C44

C45

C46

C47

Scott No.	Description	Unused Value	Used Value	/ / / / / /
1939				
C24	30c Winged Globe (inscribed "Transatlantic"), dull blue	10.50	1.50	☐☐☐☐☐
1941-44				
C25	6c Airplane, carmine	.20	.20	☐☐☐☐☐
a.	Booklet pane of 3	5.00	*1.50*	☐☐☐☐☐
b.	Horiz. pair, imperf. btwn.	*2,250.*		☐☐☐☐☐
C26	8c Airplane (C25), olive green	.20	.20	☐☐☐☐☐
C27	10c Airplane (C25), violet	1.25	.20	☐☐☐☐☐
C28	15c Airplane (C25), brown carmine	2.25	.35	☐☐☐☐☐
C29	20c Airplane (C25), bright green	2.25	.30	☐☐☐☐☐
C30	30c Airplane (C25), blue	2.25	.35	☐☐☐☐☐
C31	50c Airplane (C25), orange	11.00	3.25	☐☐☐☐☐
1946				
C32	5c DC-4 Skymaster (entire plane)	.20	.20	☐☐☐☐☐
1947, Perf. 10½x11				
C33	5c DC-4 Skymaster	.20	.20	☐☐☐☐☐
C34	10c Pan American Union Building	.25	.20	☐☐☐☐☐
C35	15c Statue of Liberty	.35	.20	☐☐☐☐☐
a.	Horiz. pair, imperf. btwn.	*2,250.*		☐☐☐☐☐
C36	25c San Francisco-Oakland Bay Bridge	.85	.20	☐☐☐☐☐
1948, Coil Stamp, Perf. 10 Horizontally				
C37	5c DC-4 Skymaster (C33)	1.00	.80	☐☐☐☐☐
1948				
C38	5c New York City	.20	.20	☐☐☐☐☐
1949, Perf. 10½x11				
C39	6c DC-4 Skymaster (C33)	.20	.20	☐☐☐☐☐
a.	Booklet pane of 6	10.00	*5.00*	☐☐☐☐☐
1949				
C40	6c Alexandria Bicentennial	.20	.20	☐☐☐☐☐
Coil Stamp, Perf. 10 Horizontally				
C41	6c DC-4 Skymaster (C33)	3.00	.20	☐☐☐☐☐
1949				
C42	10c Universal Postal Union	.20	.20	☐☐☐☐☐
C43	15c Universal Postal Union	.30	.25	☐☐☐☐☐
C44	25c Universal Postal Union	.50	.40	☐☐☐☐☐
C45	6c Wright Brothers	.20	.20	☐☐☐☐☐
1952-58				
C46	80c Diamond Head, Hawaii	5.00	1.25	☐☐☐☐☐

C48

C49

C51

C53

C55

C57

C58

C59

C63-Redrawn

C54

C56

C68

C70

C64

C66

C67

C69

Scott No.	Description	Unused Value	Used Value	//////
C47	6c Powered Flight	.20	.20	
C48	4c Eagle, bright blue	.20	.20	
C49	6c Air Force	.20	.20	
C50	5c Eagle (C48), red	.20	.20	

Perf. 10½x11

C51	7c Jet, blue	.20	.20	
a.	Booklet pane of 6	13.00	7.00	

Coil Stamp, Perf. 10 Horizontally

C52	7c Jet (C51), blue	2.00	.20	

1959

C53	7c Alaska Statehood	.20	.20	
C54	7c Balloon Jupiter	.20	.20	
C55	7c Hawaii Statehood	.20	.20	
C56	10c Pan American Games	.25	.25	

1959-66

C57	10c Liberty Bell, black & green	1.10	.70	
C58	15c Statue of Liberty, black & orange	.35	.20	
C59	25c Abraham Lincoln, black & maroon	.50	.20	
a.	Tagged	.60	.30	

Perf. 10½x11

C60	7c Jet (C51), carmine	.20	.20	
a.	Booklet pane of 6	16.00	8.00	
b.	Vert. pair, imperf. btwn. (from booklet pane)	5,500.	—	

Coil Stamp, Perf. 10 Horizontally

C61	7c Jet (C51), carmine	4.00	.25	

1961-67

C62	13c Liberty Bell (C57), black & red	.40	.20	
a.	Tagged	.75	.50	
C63	15c Statue of Liberty (redrawn), blk & org	.30	.20	
a.	Tagged	.35	.20	
b.	As "a.," horiz. pair, imperf. vert.	15,000.		

Perf. 10½x11

C64	8c Jet & Capitol	.20	.20	
a.	Tagged	.20	.20	
b.	Booklet pane 5 + label	7.00	3.00	
c.	As "b.," tagged	2.00	.75	

Coil Stamp, Perf. 10 Horizontally

C65	8c Jet & Capitol (C64)	.40	.20	
a.	Tagged	.35	.20	

C72

C77

C78

C79

C71

C76

C84

C74

C75

C80

C85

C86

C87

C88

C89

C90

C97

Scott No.	Description	Unused Value	Used Value	/ / / / / /
1963-67				
C66	15c Montgomery Blair	.60	.55	
C67	6c Eagle	.20	.20	
a.	Tagged	4.00	3.00	
C68	8c Amelia Earhart	.20	.20	
C69	8c Robert H. Goddard	.40	.20	
C70	8c Alaska Purchase	.25	.20	
C71	20c Columbia Jays by Audubon	.80	.20	
a.	Tagging omitted	10.00		
1968, Perf. 11x10½				
C72	10c Star Runway	.20	.20	
b.	Booklet pane of 8	2.00	.75	
c.	Booklet pane of 5 + label	3.75	.75	
d.	Vert. pair, imperf. btwn. (from booklet pane)	8,000	—	
Coil Stamp, Perf. 10 Vertically				
C73	10c Star Runway (C72)	.30	.20	
a.	Imperf., pair	600.00		
1968				
C74	10c 50th Anniversary of Air Mail	.25	.20	
C75	20c "USA" & Jet, red, blue & black	.35	.20	
1969				
C76	10c Moon Landing	.25	.20	
a.	Rose red (litho.) omitted	500.00	—	
1971-73				
C77	9c Delta Wing Plane	.20	.20	
C78	11c Jet	.20	.20	
a.	Booklet pane of 4 + 2 labels	1.25	.75	
b.	Untagged (Bureau precanceled)		.30	
C79	13c Winged Envelope	.25	.20	
a.	Booklet pane of 5 + label	1.50	.75	
b.	Untagged (Bureau precanceled)		.30	
C80	17c Statue of Liberty	.35	.20	
C81	21c "USA" & Jet (C75), red, blue & black	.40	.20	
b.	Black (engr.) omitted	—		
Coil Stamps, Perf. 10 Vertically				
C82	11c Jet (C78)	.25	.20	
a.	Imperf., pair	275.00		
C83	13c Winged Envelope (C79)	.30	.20	
a.	Imperf., pair	75.00		
1972-74				
C84	11c City of Refuge	.20	.20	
a.	Blue & green (litho.) omitted	800.00		

C91-C92   C93-C94   C95-C96

C99   C98   C100

C108   C113   C114

C115   C116   C117

C118   C119

Scott No.	Description	Unused Value	Used Value	/ / / / / /
C85	11c Olympics - Skiing............................	.20	.20	
C86	11c Progress in Electronics	.20	.20	
a.	Vermilion & olive (litho.) omitted	1,100.		
c.	Olive omitted	—		
C87	18c Statue of Liberty..............................	.35	.30	
C88	26c Mt. Rushmore..................................	.50	.20	
1976				
C89	25c Plane & Globes................................	.50	.20	
C90	31c Plane, Globes & Flag	.60	.20	
1978				
C91	31c Wright Brothers - Portraits at top	.65	.30	
C92	31c Wright Brothers - Plane at top	.65	.30	
a.	Vertical pair, #C91-C92....................	1.30	1.20	
b.	As "a.," ultra & black (engr.) omitted	750.00		
c.	As "a.," black (engr.) omitted............	—		
d.	As "a.," black, yel, mag, blue & brown (litho.) omitted..................................	2,250.		
1979				
C93	21c Octave Chanute - Portrait at top........	.70	.35	
C94	21c Octave Chanute - Plane at top...........	.70	.35	
a.	Vertical pair, #C93-C94....................	1.40	1.20	
b.	As "a.," ultra & black (engr.) omitted	4,500.		
C95	25c Wiley Post - Portrait at top	1.10	.45	
C96	25c Wiley Post - Plane at top	1.10	.45	
a.	Vertical pair, #C95-C96....................	2.25	1.50	
C97	31c Olympics - High Jump	.70	.30	
1980				
C98	40c Philip Mazzei, perf. 11	.80	.20	
b.	Imperf., pair	2,750.		
C98A	40c Philip Mazzei, perf. 10½ x 11¼ ('82) (C98)..	7.50	1.50	
c.	Horiz. pair, imperf. vert.....................	—		
C99	28c Blanche Stuart Scott........................	.60	.20	
C100	35c Glenn Curtiss	.65	.20	
1983				
C101	28c Olympics - Women's Gymnastics.	1.00	.30	
C102	28c Olympics - Hurdles	1.00	.30	
C103	28c Olympics - Women's Basketball	1.00	.30	
C104	28c Olympics - Soccer	1.00	.30	
a.	Block of 4, #C101-C104.....................	4.50	2.50	
b.	As "a.," imperf. vert.	—		
C105	40c Olympics - Shot put, Perf. 11 bullseye.	.90	.40	
a.	Perf. 11 line..	1.00	.45	

C120

C121

C122-C125

C127

C128

C130

C131

C132

C133

C134

C135

C136

C137

C138

Scott No.	Description	Unused Value	Used Value	/ / / / / /
C106	40c Olympics - Gymnast, Perf. 11 bullseye	.90	.40	
a.	Perf. 11 line	1.00	.45	
C107	40c Olympics - Swimmer, Perf. 11 bullseye	.90	.40	
a.	Perf. 11 line	1.00	.45	
C108	40c Olympics - Weightlifting, perf. 11 bullseye	.90	.40	
a.	Perf. 11 line	1.00	.45	
b.	Block of 4, #C105-C108	4.25	3.00	
c.	Block of 4, #C105a-C108a	5.00	4.00	
d.	Block of 4, imperf.	1,250.		
C109	35c Olympics - Women's fencing	.90	.55	
C110	35c Olympics - Cycling	.90	.55	
C111	35c Olympics - Women's volleyball	.90	.55	
C112	35c Olympics - Pole vaulting	.90	.55	
a.	Block of 4, #C109-C112	4.00	3.25	

1985

Scott No.	Description	Unused Value	Used Value	/ / / / / /
C113	33c Alfred V. Verville	.65	.20	
a.	Imperf., pair	850.00		
C114	39c Lawrence & Elmer Sperry	.80	.25	
a.	Imperf., pair	1,500.		
C115	44c Transpacific Airmail	.85	.25	
a.	Imperf., pair	850.00		
C116	44c Father Junipero Serra	1.00	.35	
a.	Imperf., pair	1,500.		

1988

Scott No.	Description	Unused Value	Used Value	/ / / / / /
C117	44c Settling of New Sweden	1.00	.25	
C118	45c Samuel P. Langley	.90	.20	
C119	36c Igor Sikorsky	.70	.25	

1989

Scott No.	Description	Unused Value	Used Value	/ / / / / /
C120	45c French Revolution	.95	.20	
C121	45c Carved Figure	.90	.20	
C122	45c Futuristic Space Craft	1.00	.50	
C123	45c Futuristic Hover Car	1.00	.50	
C124	45c Futuristic Moon Rover	1.00	.50	
C125	45c Space Shuttle	1.00	.50	
a.	Block of 4, #C122-C125	4.25	3.25	
b.	As "a.," light blue (engr.) omitted	800.00		
C126	UPU Congress, sheet of 4, imperf.	4.75	3.75	
a.	45c Futuristic Space Craft (C122)	1.00	.50	
b.	45c Futuristic Hover Car (C123)	1.00	.50	
c.	45c Futuristic Moon Rover (C124)	1.00	.50	
d.	45c Space Shuttle (C125)	1.00	.50	

1990

Scott No.	Description	Unused Value	Used Value	/ / / / / /
C127	45c Tropical Coast	.90	.20	

Scott No.	Description	Unused Value	Used Value	/ / / / /
1991, Perf. 11				
C128	50c Harriet Quimby, perf 11	1.10	.25	
a.	Vert pair, imperf. horiz.	1,900.		
b.	Perf. 11.2..	1.10	.25	
C129	40c William T. Piper (C132), hair does not touch top edge	.80	.20	
C130	50c Antarctic Treaty	1.00	.35	
C131	50c Bering Land Bridge...........................	1.00	.35	
1993, Perf. 11.2				
C132	40c Piper, hair touches top edge	1.20	.35	
C133	48c Niagara Falls, self-adhesive...............	.95	.20	
C134	40c Rio Grande, self-adhesive	.80	.60	
2000-01				
C135	60c Grand Canyon, self-adhesive	1.25	.25	
a.	Imperf, pair	—		
C136	70c Nine-Mile Prairie, Nebraska, self-adhesive	1.40	.30	
C137	80c Mt. McKinley, self-adhesive	1.60	.35	
C138	60c Arcadia National Park, self-adhesive	1.25	.25	

CE1

E1

E3

E4

E6

E12

E7

E14

E20

E22

HOW TO USE THIS BOOK

In cases where two or more Scott numbers share a common design, the illustration shows the first Scott number that bears that design. Subsequent Scott numbers showing the same design will have the first Scott number in parentheses following the description to guide the user to the correct design.

Scott No.	Description	Unused Value	Used Value	/ / / / / /

AIR POST SPECIAL DELIVERY STAMPS
1934, Perf. 11

CE1	16c Great Seal, dark blue	.60	.70	☐☐☐☐☐

1936

CE2	16c Great Seal (CE1), red & blue............	.40	.25	☐☐☐☐☐
a.	Horiz. pair, imperf. vert....................	4,000.		☐☐☐☐☐

SPECIAL DELIVERY STAMPS
1885-93

E1	10c Messenger Running, blue.................	350.00	45.00	☐☐☐☐☐
E2	10c Messenger Running, "Post Office" Curved (E3), blue..............	350.00	17.50	☐☐☐☐☐
E3	10c Messenger Running, orange.............	225.00	22.50	☐☐☐☐☐

1894, Line under "TEN CENTS"

E4	10c Messenger Running, blue..................	800.00	30.00	☐☐☐☐☐

1895, Watermark 191

E5	10c Messenger Running (E4), blue	175.00	3.25	☐☐☐☐☐
b.	Printed on both sides	—		☐☐☐☐☐

1902

E6	10c Bicycle Messenger, ultramarine.......	135.00	3.25	☐☐☐☐☐

1908

E7	10c Helmet of Mercury............................	60.00	40.00	☐☐☐☐☐

1911, Watermark 190, Perf. 12

E8	10c Bicycle Messenger (E6), ultramarine	100.00	5.25	☐☐☐☐☐
b.	10c violet blue	100.00	5.25	☐☐☐☐☐

1914, Perf. 10

E9	10c Bicycle Messenger (E6), ultramarine	180.00	6.50	☐☐☐☐☐
a.	10c blue..	210.00	6.50	☐☐☐☐☐

1916, Perf. 10, Unwatermarked

E10	10c Bicycle Messenger (E6), pale ultra...	290.00	27.50	☐☐☐☐☐
a.	10c blue..	325.00	27.50	☐☐☐☐☐

1917-25, Perf. 11

E11	10c Bicycle Messenger (E6), ultramarine	22.50	.50	☐☐☐☐☐
b.	10c gray violet.......................................	22.50	.50	☐☐☐☐☐
c.	10c blue..	60.00	2.50	☐☐☐☐☐
E12	10c Motorcycle Delivery, gray violet......	35.00	.50	☐☐☐☐☐
a.	10c deep ultramarine	42.50	.60	☐☐☐☐☐
E13	15c Motorcycle Delivery (E12), dp orange	24.00	1.00	☐☐☐☐☐
E14	20c Post Office Truck............................	1.75	1.00	☐☐☐☐☐

Scott No.	Description	Unused Value	Used Value	/ / / / /
1927-51, Perf. 11x10½				
E15	10c Motorcycle Delivery (E12), gray violet	.60	.20	
a.	10c red lilac...	.60	.20	
b.	10c gray lilac...	.60	.20	
c.	Horiz. pair, imperf. btwn.	300.00		
E16	15c Motorcycle Delivery (E12), orange .	.70	.20	
E17	13c Motorcycle Delivery (E12), blue......	.60	.20	
E18	17c Motorcycle Delivery (E12), yellow..	2.75	1.75	
E19	20c Post Office Truck.............................	1.25	.20	
1954-57				
E20	20c Hands & Letter, deep blue...............	.40	.20	
E21	30c Hands & Letter (E20), lake	.50	.20	
1969-71				
E22	45c Arrows, carmine & violet blue.........	1.25	.25	
E23	60c Arrows (E22), violet blue & carmine	1.25	.20	

F1

FA1

Scott No.	Description	Unused Value	Used Value	/ / / / / /

REGISTRATION STAMP
1911

| F1 | 10c Eagle | 75.00 | 7.50 | ☐☐☐☐☐ |

CERTIFIED MAIL STAMP
1955

| FA1 | 15c Mailman | .45 | .30 | ☐☐☐☐☐ |

J1

J29

J69

J87

J88

Scott No.	Description	Unused Value	Used Value	/ / / / / /

POSTAGE DUE STAMPS
1879, Perf. 12

J1	1c Numeral, brown	65.00	10.00	
J2	2c Numeral (J1), brown	400.00	9.00	
J3	3c Numeral (J1), brown	62.50	5.00	
J4	5c Numeral (J1), brown	650.00	50.00	
J5	10c Numeral (J1), brown	750.00	50.00	
a.	Imperf., pair	*2,000.*		
J6	30c Numeral (J1), brown	350.00	55.00	
J7	50c Numeral (J1), brown	550.00	75.00	

1879, Special Printing

J8	1c Numeral (J1), deep brown	*13,000.*		
J9	2c Numeral (J1), deep brown	*9,000.*		
J10	3c Numeral (J1), deep brown	*13,000.*		
J11	5c Numeral (J1), deep brown	*8,500.*		
J12	10c Numeral (J1), deep brown	*4,000.*		
J13	30c Numeral (J1), deep brown	*4,000.*		
J14	50c Numeral (J1), deep brown	*4,000.*		

1884-89

J15	1c Numeral (J1), red brown	65.00	6.00	
J16	2c Numeral (J1), red brown	75.00	5.00	
J17	2c Numeral (J1), red brown	1,100.	200.00	
J18	5c Numeral (J1), red brown	550.00	30.00	
J19	10c Numeral (J1), red brown	550.00	25.00	
J20	30c Numeral (J1), red brown	175.00	55.00	
J21	50c Numeral (J1), red brown	1,750.	200.00	

1891-93

J22	1c Numeral (J1), bright claret	30.00	1.00	

Scott No.	Description	Unused Value	Used Value	/ / / / / /
J23	2c Numeral (J1), bright claret	35.00	1.00	
J24	3c Numeral (J1), bright claret	70.00	10.00	
J25	5c Numeral (J1), bright claret	85.00	10.00	
J26	10c Numeral (J1), bright claret	140.00	20.00	
J27	30c Numeral (J1), bright claret	550.00	175.00	
J28	50c Numeral (J1), bright claret	575.00	175.00	

1894

J29	1c Numeral, vermilion	2,000.	500.00	
J30	2c Numeral (J29), vermilion	800.00	175.00	
J31	1c Numeral (J29), deep claret	55.00	6.00	
b.	Vert. pair, imperf. horiz.	—		
J32	2c Numeral (J29), deep claret	50.00	4.00	
J33	3c Numeral (J29), deep claret	200.00	30.00	
J34	5c Numeral (J29), deep claret	300.00	35.00	
J35	10c Numeral (J29), deep clare	300.00	25.00	
J36	30c Numeral (J29), deep claret	500.00	150.00	
a.	30c carmine	500.00	150.00	
b.	30c pale rose	400.00	110.00	
J37	50c Numeral (J29), deep claret	1,700.	500.00	
a.	50c pale rose	1,500.	450.00	

1895, Watermark 191

J38	1c Numeral (J29), deep claret	10.00	.75	
J39	2c Numeral (J29), deep claret	10.00	.70	
J40	3c Numeral (J29), deep claret	70.00	1.75	
J41	5c Numeral (J29), deep claret	75.00	1.75	
J42	10c Numeral (J29), deep claret	75.00	3.50	
J43	30c Numeral (J29), deep claret	600.00	50.00	
J44	50c Numeral (J29), deep claret	400.00	37.50	

1910-12, Watermark 190

J45	1c Numeral (J29), deep claret	35.00	3.00	
a.	1c rose carmine	32.50	3.00	
J46	2c Numeral (J29), deep claret	37.50	1.00	
a.	2c rose carmine	35.00	1.00	
J47	3c Numeral (J29), deep claret	600.00	30.00	
J48	5c Numeral (J29), deep claret	110.00	6.50	
a.	5c rose carmine	105.00	6.50	
J49	10c Numeral (J29), deep claret	125.00	12.50	
a.	10c rose carmine	120.00	12.50	
J50	50c Numeral (J29), deep claret	1,100.	120.00	

1914-15, Perf. 10

J52	1c Numeral (J29), carmine lake	60.00	11.00	
a.	1c dull rose	70.00	11.00	
J53	2c Numeral (J29), carmine lake	47.50	.40	
a.	2c dull rose	52.50	.50	
b.	2c vermilion	52.50	.50	

Scott No.	Description	Unused Value	Used Value	/ / / / / /
J54	3c Numeral (J29), carmine lake	950.00	50.00	☐☐☐☐☐
a.	3c dull rose	950.00	50.00	☐☐☐☐☐
J55	5c Numeral (J29), carmine lake	37.50	2.50	☐☐☐☐☐
a.	5c dull rose	37.50	2.50	☐☐☐☐☐
J56	10c Numeral (J29), carmine lake	57.50	2.00	☐☐☐☐☐
a.	10c dull rose	70.00	3.00	☐☐☐☐☐
J57	30c Numeral (J29), carmine lake	240.00	17.50	☐☐☐☐☐
J58	50c Numeral (J29), carmine lake	*12,500.*	*1,000.*	☐☐☐☐☐

1916, Perf. 10, Unwatermarked

Scott No.	Description	Unused Value	Used Value	/ / / / / /
J59	1c Numeral (J29), rose	4,000.	500.00	☐☐☐☐☐
J60	2c Numeral (J29), rose	200.00	35.00	☐☐☐☐☐

1917, Perf. 11

Scott No.	Description	Unused Value	Used Value	/ / / / / /
J61	1c Numeral (J29), carmine rose	2.75	.25	☐☐☐☐☐
a.	1c rose red	2.75	.25	☐☐☐☐☐
b.	1c deep claret	2.75	.25	☐☐☐☐☐
J62	2c Numeral (J29), carmine rose	2.50	.25	☐☐☐☐☐
a.	2c rose red	2.50	.25	☐☐☐☐☐
b.	2c deep claret	2.50	.25	☐☐☐☐☐
J63	3c Numeral (J29), carmine rose	19.00	.25	☐☐☐☐☐
a.	3c rose red	11.00	.25	☐☐☐☐☐
b.	3c deep claret	11.00	.35	☐☐☐☐☐
J64	5c Numeral (J29), carmine	11.00	.25	☐☐☐☐☐
a.	5c rose red	11.00	.25	☐☐☐☐☐
b.	5c deep claret	11.00	.25	☐☐☐☐☐
J65	10c Numeral (J29), carmine rose	17.00	.30	☐☐☐☐☐
a.	10c rose red	17.00	.25	☐☐☐☐☐
b.	10c deep claret	17.00	.25	☐☐☐☐☐
J66	30c Numeral (J29), carmine rose	87.50	.75	☐☐☐☐☐
a.	30c deep claret	87.50	.75	☐☐☐☐☐
J67	50c Numeral (J29), carmine rose	110.00	.30	☐☐☐☐☐
a.	50c rose red	110.00	.30	☐☐☐☐☐
b.	50c deep claret	110.00	.30	☐☐☐☐☐

1925

Scott No.	Description	Unused Value	Used Value	/ / / / / /
J68	½ c Numeral (J29), dull red	1.00	.25	☐☐☐☐☐

1930-31, Perf. 11

Scott No.	Description	Unused Value	Used Value	/ / / / / /
J69	½ c Numeral, carmine	4.50	1.40	☐☐☐☐☐
J70	1c Numeral (J69), carmine	3.00	.25	☐☐☐☐☐
J71	2c Numeral (J69), carmine	4.00	.25	☐☐☐☐☐
J72	3c Numeral (J69), carmine	21.00	1.75	☐☐☐☐☐
J73	5c Numeral (J69), carmine	19.00	2.50	☐☐☐☐☐
J74	10c Numeral (J69), carmine	40.00	1.00	☐☐☐☐☐
J75	30c Numeral (J69), carmine	125.00	2.00	☐☐☐☐☐
J76	50c Numeral (J69), carmine	175.00	.75	☐☐☐☐☐
J77	$1 Numeral, carmine	30.00	.25	☐☐☐☐☐
a.	$1 scarlet	25.00	.25	☐☐☐☐☐
J78	$5 Numeral (J77), carmine	37.50	.25	☐☐☐☐☐

Scott No.	Description	Unused Value	Used Value	/ / / / / /
a.	$5 scarlet	32.50	.25	

1931-56, Perf. 11x10½, 10½x11

Scott No.	Description	Unused Value	Used Value	/ / / / / /
J79	½ c Numeral (J69), dull carmine	.90	.20	
a.	½ c scarlet	.90	.20	
J80	1c Numeral (J69), dull carmine	.20	.20	
a.	1c scarlet	.20	.20	
J81	2c Numeral (J69), dull carmine	.20	.20	
a.	2c scarlet	.20	.20	
J82	3c Numeral (J69), dull carmine	.25	.20	
a.	3c scarlet	.25	.20	
J83	5c Numeral (J69), dull carmine	.40	.20	
a.	5c scarlet	.40	.20	
J84	10c Numeral (J69), dull carmine	1.10	.20	
a.	10c scarlet	1.10	.20	
J85	30c Numeral (J69), dull carmine	7.50	.25	
a.	30c scarlet	7.50	.25	
J86	50c Numeral (J69), dull carmine	10.00	.25	
a.	50c scarlet	10.00	.25	
J87	$1 Numeral (J77), scarlet	32.50	.25	

1959, Black numerals

Scott No.	Description	Unused Value	Used Value	/ / / / / /
J88	½ c Numeral, carmine rose	1.50	1.10	
J89	1c Numeral (J88), carmine rose	.20	.20	
a.	"1 CENT" omitted	300.00		
b.	Pair, one without "1 CENT"	525.00		
J90	2c Numeral (J88), carmine rose	.20	.20	
J91	3c Numeral (J88), carmine rose	.20	.20	
a.	Pair, one without "3 CENTS"	725.00		
J92	4c Numeral (J88), carmine rose	.20	.20	
J93	5c Numeral (J88), carmine rose	.20	.20	
a.	Pair, one without "5 CENTS"	1,250.		
J94	6c Numeral (J88), carmine rose	.20	.20	
a.	Pair, one without "6 CENTS"	850.00		
J95	7c Numeral (J88), carmine rose	.20	.20	
J96	8c Numeral (J88), carmine rose	.20	.20	
a.	Pair, one without "8 CENTS"	850.00		
J97	10c Numeral (J88), carmine rose	.20	.20	
J98	30c Numeral (J88), carmine rose	.75	.20	
J99	50c Numeral (J88), carmine rose	1.10	.20	
J100	$1 Numeral (J88), carmine rose	2.00	.20	
J101	$5 Numeral (J88), carmine rose	9.00	.20	

1978

Scott No.	Description	Unused Value	Used Value	/ / / / / /
J102	11c Numeral (J88), carmine rose	.25	.20	
J103	13c Numeral (J88), carmine rose	.25	.20	

1985

Scott No.	Description	Unused Value	Used Value	/ / / / / /
J104	17c Numeral (J88), carmine rose	.40	.35	

United States Stamps
of 1917-19
Surcharged

SHANGHAI

2¢

CHINA

Scott No.	Description	Unused Value	Used Value	/ / / / / /

U.S. OFFICES IN CHINA
1919

Scott No.	Description	Unused Value	Used Value	
K1	2c on 1c Washington, green...................	25.00	*32.50*	☐☐☐☐☐
K2	4c on 2c Washington, rose, type I..........	25.00	*32.50*	☐☐☐☐☐
K3	6c on 3c Washington, violet, type II......	52.50	*75.00*	☐☐☐☐☐
K4	8c on 4c Washington, brown..................	57.50	*75.00*	☐☐☐☐☐
K5	10c on 5c Washington, blue	65.00	*75.00*	☐☐☐☐☐
K6	12c on 6c Washington, red orange...........	85.00	*110.00*	☐☐☐☐☐
K7	14c on 7c Washington, black	87.50	*125.00*	☐☐☐☐☐
K8	16c on 8c Washington, olive bister	65.00	*80.00*	☐☐☐☐☐
a.	16c on 8c olive green	60.00	*60.00*	☐☐☐☐☐
K9	18c on 9c Franklin, salmon red..............	65.00	*85.00*	☐☐☐☐☐
K10	20c on 10c Franklin, orange yellow........	60.00	*70.00*	☐☐☐☐☐
K11	24c on 12c Franklin, brown carmine	70.00	*80.00*	☐☐☐☐☐
a.	24c on 12c claret brown	92.50	*125.00*	☐☐☐☐☐
K12	30c on 15c Franklin, gray	87.50	*140.00*	☐☐☐☐☐
K13	40c on 20c Franklin, deep ultramarine	140.00	*225.00*	☐☐☐☐☐
K14	60c on 30c Franklin, orange red	120.00	*175.00*	☐☐☐☐☐
K15	$1 on 50c Franklin, light violet............	575.00	*650.00*	☐☐☐☐☐
K16	$2 on $1 Franklin, violet brown.............	450.00	*550.00*	☐☐☐☐☐
a.	Double surcharge...............................	*5,000.*	*6,000.*	☐☐☐☐☐

Nos. 498 and 528B
Surcharged

SHANGHAI

2 Cts.

CHINA

1922, Surcharged locally

Scott No.	Description	Unused Value	Used Value	
K17	2c on 1c Washington, green	110.00	125.00	☐☐☐☐☐
K18	4c on 2c Washington, carmine, type VII.	100.00	*110.00*	☐☐☐☐☐

O1

O68

O47

O121

O127

O138A

O144

Scott No.	Description	Unused Value	Used Value	/ / / / / /

OFFICIAL STAMPS
AGRICULTURE DEPT.
Continental Bank Note Printings, Thin Hard Paper

O1	1c Franklin, yellow	170.00	160.00	
O2	2c Jackson (O1), yellow	135.00	65.00	
O3	3c Washington (O1), yellow....................	120.00	13.00	
O4	6c Lincoln (O1), yellow.........................	135.00	52.50	
O5	10c Jefferson (O1), yellow	270.00	180.00	
O6	12c Clay (O1), yellow............................	360.00	240.00	
O7	15c Webster (O1), yellow........................	300.00	210.00	
O8	24c Scott (O1), yellow............................	300.00	190.00	
O9	30c Hamilton (O1), yellow......................	390.00	250.00	

EXECUTIVE DEPT.

O10	1c Franklin (O1), carmine	650.00	425.00	
O11	2c Jackson (O1), carmine.......................	425.00	210.00	
O12	3c Washington (O1), carmine	475.00	170.00	
a.	3c violet rose...	475.00	170.00	
O13	6c Lincoln (O1), carmine	725.00	500.00	
O14	10c Jefferson (O1), carmine	700.00	575.00	

INTERIOR DEPT.

O15	1c Franklin (O1), vermilion	37.50	8.50	
O16	2c Jackson (O1), vermilion......................	32.50	9.50	
O17	3c Washington (O1), vermilion..............	50.00	5.25	
O18	6c Lincoln (O1), vermilion	37.50	5.25	
O19	10c Jefferson (O1), vermilion	37.50	16.00	
O20	12c Clay (O1), vermilion	52.50	8.00	

Scott No.	Description	Unused Value	Used Value	/ / / / / /
O21	15c Webster (O1), vermilion	90.00	18.00	
O22	24c Scott (O1), vermilion	65.00	15.00	
a.	Double impression		—	
O23	30c Hamilton (O1), vermilion	90.00	15.00	
O24	90c Perry (O1), vermilion	200.00	40.00	

JUSTICE DEPT.

O25	1c Franklin (O1), purple	120.00	90.00	
O26	2c Jackson (O1), purple	210.00	90.00	
O27	3c Washington (O1), purple	210.00	22.50	
O28	6c Lincoln (O1), purple	190.00	32.50	
O29	10c Jefferson (O1), purple	225.00	75.00	
O30	12c Clay (O1), purple	170.00	50.00	
O31	15c Webster (O1), purple	325.00	160.00	
O32	24c Scott (O1), purple	875.00	350.00	
O33	30c Hamilton (O1), purple	850.00	275.00	
O34	90c Perry (O1), purple	1,250.	525.00	

NAVY DEPT.

O35	1c Franklin (O1), ultramarine	80.00	42.50	
a.	1c dull blue	85.00	45.00	
O36	2c Jackson (O1), ultramarine	65.00	18.00	
a.	2c dull blue	70.00	16.00	
O37	3c Washington (O1), ultramarine	62.00	10.00	
a.	3c dull blue	67.50	11.00	
O38	6c Lincoln (O1), ultramarine	62.50	15.00	
a.	6c dull blue	67.50	15.00	
O39	7c Stanton (O1), ultramarine	425.00	190.00	
a.	7c dull blue	425.00	190.00	
O40	10c Jefferson (O1), ultramarine	85.00	32.50	
a.	10c dull blue	85.00	32.50	
O41	12c Clay (O1), ultramarine	100.00	32.50	
O42	15c Webster (O1), ultramarine	180.00	60.00	
O43	24c Scott (O1), ultramarine	200.00	70.00	
a.	24c dull blue	200.00	—	
O44	30c Hamilton (O1), ultramarine	150.00	37.50	
O45	90c Perry (O1), ultramarine	725.00	240.00	
a.	Double impression		3,750.	

POST OFFICE DEPT.

O47	1c Numeral, black	14.00	8.00	
O48	2c Numeral (O47), black	17.50	7.50	
a.	Double impression	325.00	300.00	
O49	3c Numeral (O47), black	5.50	1.10	
a.	Printed on both sides		3,000.	
O50	6c Numeral (O47), black	16.00	6.50	
a.	Diagonal half used as 3c on cover		3,000.	
O51	10c Numeral (O47), black	75.00	42.50	
O52	12c Numeral (O47), black	37.50	8.75	

Scott No.	Description	Unused Value	Used Value	/ / / / / /
O53	15c Numeral (O47), black	50.00	15.00	
O54	24c Numeral (O47), black	65.00	18.00	
O55	30c Numeral (O47), black	65.00	18.00	
O56	90c Numeral (O47), black	95.00	15.00	

STATE DEPT.

Scott No.	Description	Unused Value	Used Value	/ / / / / /
O57	1c Franklin (O1), bright green	120.00	57.50	
O58	2c Jackson (O1), dark green	225.00	80.00	
O59	3c Washington (O1), bright green	90.00	18.00	
O60	6c Lincoln (O1), bright green	85.00	24.00	
O61	7c Stanton (O1), dark green	170.00	55.00	
O62	10c Jefferson (O1), dark green	130.00	42.50	
O63	12c Clay (O1), dark green	210.00	100.00	
O64	15c Webster (O1), dark green	220.00	70.00	
O65	24c Scott (O1), dark green	450.00	190.00	
O66	30c Hamilton (O1), dark green	425.00	150.00	
O67	90c Perry (O1), dark green	800.00	300.00	
O68	$2 Seward, green & black	1,000.	800.00	
O69	$5 Seward (O68), green & black	6,000.	3,750.	
O70	$10 Seward (O68), green & black	4,500.	2,600.	
O71	$20 Seward (O68), green & black	3,500.	1,900.	

TREASURY DEPT.

Scott No.	Description	Unused Value	Used Value	/ / / / / /
O72	1c Franklin (O1), brown	40.00	5.50	
O73	2c Jackson (O1), brown	50.00	5.50	
O74	3c Washington (O1), brown	35.00	1.40	
a.	Double impression		—	
O75	6c Lincoln (O1), brown	45.00	2.60	
O76	7c Stanton (O1), brown	95.00	26.00	
O77	10c Jefferson (O1), brown	95.00	8.25	
O78	12c Clay (O1), brown	95.00	6.50	
O79	15c Webster (O1), brown	90.00	8.25	
O80	24c Scott (O1), brown	450.00	75.00	
O81	30c Hamilton (O1), brown	150.00	9.50	
O82	90c Perry (O1), brown	160.00	10.50	

WAR DEPT.

Scott No.	Description	Unused Value	Used Value	/ / / / / /
O83	1c Franklin (O1), rose	145.00	9.00	
O84	2c Jackson (O1), rose	130.00	10.00	
O85	3c Washington (O1), rose	135.00	3.00	
O86	6c Lincoln (O1), rose	450.00	6.50	
O87	7c Stanton (O1), rose	130.00	77.50	
O88	10c Jefferson (O1), rose	45.00	16.00	
O89	12c Clay (O1), rose	170.00	10.50	
O90	15c Webster (O1), rose	40.00	12.00	
O91	24c Scott (O1), rose	40.00	7.25	
O92	30c Hamilton (O1), rose	42.50	7.25	
O93	90c Perry (O1), rose	95.00	42.50	

AGRICULTURE DEPT.
1879, American Bank Note Co. Printings, Soft Porous Paper

Scott No.	Description	Unused Value	Used Value	/ / / / / /
O94	1c Franklin (O1), yellow, no gum	3,750.		
O95	3c Washington (O1), yellow	375.00	70.00	

INTERIOR DEPT.

Scott No.	Description	Unused Value	Used Value	/ / / / / /
O96	1c Franklin (O1), vermilion	250.00	230.00	
O97	2c Jackson (O1), vermilion	6.00	1.40	
O98	3c Washington (O1), vermilion	5.50	1.10	
O99	6c Lincoln (O1), vermilion	8.00	6.00	
O100	10c Jefferson (O1), vermilion	85.00	65.00	
O101	12c Clay (O1), vermilion	160.00	100.00	
O102	15c Webster (O1), vermilion	325.00	240.00	
O103	24c Scott (O1), vermilion	3,500.	—	

JUSTICE DEPT.

Scott No.	Description	Unused Value	Used Value	/ / / / / /
O106	3c Washington (O1), bluish purple	100.00	70.00	
O107	6c Lincoln (O1), bluish purple	250.00	190.00	

POST OFFICE DEPT.

Scott No.	Description	Unused Value	Used Value	/ / / / / /
O108	3c Numeral (O47), black	20.00	5.50	

TREASURY DEPT.

Scott No.	Description	Unused Value	Used Value	/ / / / / /
O109	3c Washington (O1), brown	60.00	7.25	
O110	6c Lincoln (O1), brown	100.00	37.50	
O111	10c Jefferson (O1), brown	175.00	55.00	
O112	30c Hamilton (O1), brown	1,500.	300.00	
O113	90c Perry (O1), brown	2,400.	300.00	

WAR DEPT.

Scott No.	Description	Unused Value	Used Value	/ / / / / /
O114	1c Franklin (O1), rose red	3.75	3.00	
O115	2c Jackson (O1), rose red	7.00	3.50	
O116	3c Washington (O1), rose red	7.00	1.30	
a.	Imperf., pair	900.00		
b.	Double impression	750.00		
O117	6c Lincoln (O1), rose red	7.00	1.10	
O118	10c Jefferson (O1), rose red	40.00	37.50	
O119	12c Clay (O1), rose red	35.00	11.00	
O120	30c Hamilton (O1), rose red	110.00	75.00	

1875, SPECIAL PRINTINGS, Ovptd. "SPECIMEN" (Type D)
Thin hard white paper
AGRICULTURE DEPT., Carmine Overprint

Scott No.	Description	Unused Value	Used Value	/ / / / / /
O1S	1c Franklin (O1), yellow	15.00		
a.	"Sepcimen" error	1,000.		
b.	Small dotted "i" in "Specimen"	425.00		
c.	Horiz. Ribbed paper	20.00		
O2S	2c Jackson (O1), yellow	27.50		
a.	"Sepcimen" error	1,000.		

Scott No.	Description	Unused Value	Used Value	/ / / / / /
O3S	3c Washington (O1), yellow..................	75.00		
a.	"Sepcimen" error..............................	4,000.		
O4S	6c Lincoln (O1), yellow......................	130.00		
a.	"Sepcimen" error..............................	5,500.		
O5S	10c Jefferson (O1), yellow	130.00		
a.	"Sepcimen" error..............................	4,000.		
O6S	12c Clay (O1), yellow..........................	125.00		
a.	"Sepcimen" error..............................	4,000.		
O7S	15c Webster (O1), yellow	125.00		
a.	"Sepcimen" error..............................	4,000.		
O8S	24c Scott (O1), yellow........................	125.00		
a.	"Sepcimen" error..............................	4,000.		
O9S	30c Hamilton (O1), yellow	125.00		
a.	"Sepcimen" error..............................	4,000.		

EXECUTIVE DEPT., Blue Overprint

Scott No.	Description	Unused Value	Used Value	/ / / / / /
O10S	1c Franklin (O1), carmine	15.00		
a.	Small dotted "i" in "Specimen"	325.00		
b.	Horiz. Ribbed paper........................	20.00		
O11S	2c Jackson (O1), carmine......................	30.00		
O12S	3c Washington (O1), carmine	30.00		
O13S	6c Lincoln (O1), carmine......................	30.00		
O14S	10c Jefferson (O1), carmine	30.00		

INTERIOR DEPT., Blue Overprint

Scott No.	Description	Unused Value	Used Value	/ / / / / /
O15S	1c Franklin (O1), vermilion	30.00		
O16S	2c Jackson (O1), vermilion	37.50		
a.	"Sepcimen" error..............................	3,750.		
O17S	3c Washington (O1), vermilion............	500.00		
O18S	6c Lincoln (O1), vermilion..................	500.00		
O19S	10c Jefferson (O1), vermilion	500.00		
O20S	12c Clay (O1), vermilion......................	500.00		
O21S	15c Webster (O1), vermilion	500.00		
O22S	24c Scott (O1), vermilion......................	500.00		
O23S	30c Hamilton (O1), vermilion...............	475.00		
O24S	90c Perry (O1), vermilion	475.00		

JUSTICE DEPT., Blue Overprint

Scott No.	Description	Unused Value	Used Value	/ / / / / /
O25S	1c Franklin (O1), purple........................	15.00		
a.	"Sepcimen" error..............................	675.00		
b.	Small dotted "i" in "Specimen"........	275.00		
c.	Horiz. Ribbed paper	20.00		
O26S	2c Jackson (O1), purple	30.00		
a.	"Sepcimen" error..............................	1,200.		
O27S	3c Washington (O1), purple..................	300.00		
a.	"Sepcimen" error..............................	3,750.		
O28S	6c Lincoln (O1), purple.........................	300.00		
O29S	10c Jefferson (O1), purple	300.00		

Scott No.	Description	Unused Value	Used Value	/ / / / / /
O30S	12c Clay (O1), purple	300.00		
a.	"Sepcimen" error	*4,000.*		
O31S	15c Webster (O1), purple	325.00		
a.	"Sepcimen" error	*4,000.*		
O32S	24c Scott (O1), purple	350.00		
a.	"Sepcimen" error	*4,000.*		
O33S	30c Hamilton (O1), purple	350.00		
a.	"Sepcimen" error	*4,000.*		
O34S	90c Perry (O1), purple	350.00		

NAVY DEPT., Carmine Overprint

Scott No.	Description	Unused Value	Used Value	/ / / / / /
O35S	1c Franklin (O1), ultramarine	20.00		
a.	"Sepcimen" error	750.00		
O36S	2c Jackson (O1), ultramarine	35.00		
a.	"Sepcimen" error	1,000.		
O37S	3c Washington (O1), ultramarine	300.00		
O38S	6c Lincoln (O1), ultramarine	350.00		
O39S	7c Stanton (O1), ultramarine	150.00		
a.	"Sepcimen" error	3,000.		
O40S	10c Jefferson (O1), ultramarine	350.00		
a.	"Sepcimen" error	*4,250.*		
O41S	12c Clay (O1), ultramarine	300.00		
a.	"Sepcimen" error	*4,000.*		
O42S	15c Webster (O1), ultramarine	300.00		
a.	"Sepcimen" error	*7,500.*		
O43S	24c Scott (O1), ultramarine	300.00		
a.	"Sepcimen" error	*4,000.*		
O44S	30c Hamilton (O1), ultramarine	300.00		
a.	"Sepcimen" error	*4,500.*		
O45S	90c Perry (O1), ultramarine	300.00		

POST OFFICE DEPT., Carmine Overprint

Scott No.	Description	Unused Value	Used Value	/ / / / / /
O47S	1c Numeral (O47), black	25.00		
a.	"Sepcimen" error	900.00		
b.	Inverted overprint	*1,000.*		
O48S	2c Numeral (O47), black	65.00		
a.	"Sepcimen" error	1,750.		
O49S	3c Numeral (O47), black	450.00		
a.	"Sepcimen" error	—		
O50S	6c Numeral (O47), black	425.00		
O51S	10c Numeral (O47), black	275.00		
a.	"Sepcimen" error	*4,250.*		
O52S	12c Numeral (O47), black	400.00		
O53S	15c Numeral (O47), black	475.00		
a.	"Sepcimen" error	*4,250.*		
O54S	24c Numeral (O47), black	425.00		
a.	"Sepcimen" error	*4,250.*		
O55S	30c Numeral (O47), black	425.00		

Scott No.	Description	Unused Value	Used Value	/ / / / / /
O56S	90c Numeral (O47), black	425.00		
a.	"Sepcimen" error	*8,000.*		

STATE DEPT., Carmine Overprint

Scott No.	Description	Unused Value	Used Value	/ / / / / /
O57S	1c Franklin (O1), bluish green	15.00		
a.	"Sepcimen" error	400.00		
b.	Small dotted "i" in "Specimen"	400.00		
c.	Horiz. Ribbed paper	20.00		
d.	Double overprint	—		
O58S	2c Jackson (O1), dark green	30.00		
a.	"Sepcimen" error	750.00		
O59S	3c Washington (O1), bright green	45.00		
a.	"Sepcimen" error	*2,500.*		
O60S	6c Lincoln (O1), bright green	95.00		
a.	"Sepcimen" error	*3,250.*		
O61S	7c Stanton (O1), dark green	47.50		
a.	"Sepcimen" error	*2,500.*		
O62S	10c Jefferson (O1), dark green	180.00		
a.	"Sepcimen" error	*7,500.*		
O63S	12c Clay (O1), dark green	190.00		
a.	"Sepcimen" error	*3,500.*		
O64S	15c Webster (O1), dark green	180.00		
O65S	24c Scott (O1), dark green	180.00		
a.	"Sepcimen" error	*3,500.*		
O66S	30c Hamilton (O1), dark green	180.00		
a.	"Sepcimen" error	*3,750.*		
O67S	90c Perry (O1), dark green	180.00		
a.	"Sepcimen" error	*3,750.*		
O68S	$2 Seward (O68), green & black	*7,500.*		
O69S	$5 Seward (O68), green & black	*15,000.*		
O70S	$10 Seward (O68), green & black	*20,000.*		
O71S	$20 Seward (O68), green & black	*25,000.*		

TREASURY DEPT., Blue Overprint

Scott No.	Description	Unused Value	Used Value	/ / / / / /
O72S	1c Franklin (O1), brown	27.50		
O73S	2c Jackson (O1), brown	130.00		
O74S	3c Washington (O1), brown	475.00		
O75S	6c Lincoln (O1), brown	425.00		
O76S	7c Stanton (O1), brown	275.00		
O77S	10c Jefferson (O1), brown	450.00		
O78S	12c Clay (O1), brown	475.00		
O79S	15c Webster (O1), brown	475.00		
O80S	24c Scott (O1), brown	375.00		
O81S	30c Hamilton (O1), brown	500.00		
O82S	90c Perry (O1), brown	500.00		

WAR DEPT., Blue Overprint

Scott No.	Description	Unused Value	Used Value	/ / / / / /
O83S	1c Franklin (O1), deep rose	17.50		
a.	"Sepcimen" error	550.00		

Scott No.	Description	Unused Value	Used Value	//////
O84S	2c Jackson (O1), deep rose	35.00		
a.	"Sepcimen" error	1,000.		
O85S	3c Washington (O1), deep rose	350.00		
a.	"Sepcimen" error	*4,000.*		
O86S	6c Lincoln (O1), deep rose	350.00		
a.	"Sepcimen" error	*4,250.*		
O87S	7c Stanton (O1), deep rose	72.50		
a.	"Sepcimen" error	1,900.		
O88S	10c Jefferson (O1), deep rose	325.00		
a.	"Sepcimen" error	*4,250.*		
O89S	12c Clay (O1), deep rose	375.00		
a.	"Sepcimen" error	*4,250.*		
O90S	15c Webster (O1), deep rose	375.00		
a.	"Sepcimen" error	*4,250.*		
O91S	24c Scott (O1), deep rose	375.00		
a.	"Sepcimen" error	*4,250.*		
O92S	30c Hamilton (O1), deep rose	375.00		
a.	"Sepcimen" error	*4,250.*		
O93S	90c Perry (O1), deep rose	375.00		
a.	"Sepcimen" error	*4,750.*		

Soft, porous paper
EXECUTIVE DEPT., Blue Overprint

O10xS	1c Franklin (O1), violet rose	45.00		

NAVY DEPT., Carmine Overprint

O35xS	1c Franklin (O1), gray blue	50.00		
a.	Double overprint	850.00		

STATE DEPT., Carmine Overprint

O57xS	1c Franklin (O1), yellow green	200.00		

OFFICIAL POSTAL SAVINGS MAIL

1911, Watermark 191

O121	2c Text, black	15.00	1.50	
O122	50c Text (O121), dark green	145.00	40.00	
O123	$1 Text (O121), ultramarine	135.00	11.00	

Watermark 190

O124	1c Text (O121), dark violet	8.00	1.50	
O125	2c Text (O121), black	47.50	5.50	
O126	10c Text (O121), carmine	18.00	1.60	

1983-85

O127	1c Great Seal	.20	.20	
O128	4c Great Seal (O127)	.20	.25	
O129	13c Great Seal (O127)	.45	.75	
O129A	14c Great Seal (O127)	.45	.50	
O130	17c Great Seal (O127)	.60	.40	
O132	$1 Great Seal (O127)	2.00	1.00	

Scott No.	Description	Unused Value	Used Value	/ / / / / /
O133	$5 Great Seal (O127)	9.00	9.00	☐☐☐☐☐

Coil Stamps, Perf 10 Vertically

O135	20c Great Seal (O127)	1.75	2.00	☐☐☐☐☐
a.	Imperf., pair	2,000.		☐☐☐☐☐
O136	22c Great Seal (O127)	.80	2.00	☐☐☐☐☐

1985

O138	(14c) Great Seal (O127), inscribed "Postal Card Rate D"	5.25	5.00	☐☐☐☐☐

1985-88, Coil Stamps, Perf. 10 Vertically

O138A	15c Great Seal, frame line completely around design	.45	.50	☐☐☐☐☐
O138B	20c Great Seal (O138A)	.40	.30	☐☐☐☐☐
O139	(22c) Great Seal (O127), inscribed "Domestic Letter Rate D"	5.25	3.00	☐☐☐☐☐
O140	(25c) Great Seal (O138A), inscribed "Domestic Letter Rate E"	.75	2.00	☐☐☐☐☐
O141	25c Great Seal (O138A)	.65	.50	☐☐☐☐☐
a.	Imperf., pair	1,750.	—	☐☐☐☐☐

1989

O143	1c Great Seal (O138A)	.20	.20	☐☐☐☐☐

1991, Coil Stamps, Perf. 10 Vertically

O144	(29c) Great Seal	.75	.50	☐☐☐☐☐
O145	29c Great Seal (O138A)	.65	.30	☐☐☐☐☐

1991-93

O146	4c Great Seal (O138A)	.20	.30	☐☐☐☐☐
O146A	10c Great Seal (O138A)	.25	.30	☐☐☐☐☐
O147	19c Great Seal (O138A)	.40	.50	☐☐☐☐☐
O148	23c Great Seal (O138A)	.45	.30	☐☐☐☐☐
a.	Imperf., pair	100.00		☐☐☐☐☐
O151	$1 Great Seal (O138A)	2.00	.75	☐☐☐☐☐

Coil Stamps, Perf. 10 Vertically

O152	(32c) Great Seal (O144), inscribed "G"	.65	—	☐☐☐☐☐
O153	32c Great Seal (O138A), with micro text	.65	.30	☐☐☐☐☐

1995

O154	1c Great Seal (O138A), with micro text	.20	.20	☐☐☐☐☐
O155	20c Great Seal (O138A), with micro text	.45	.30	☐☐☐☐☐
O156	23c Great Seal (O138A), with micro text	.50	.30	☐☐☐☐☐

1999, Oct. 8 Perf. 9¾ Vertically Coil Stamp

O157	33c Great Seal (O138A), with micro text	.65	—	☐☐☐☐☐
O158	34c Eagle, Type of 1985, coil	.65	.30	☐☐☐☐☐

PR1   PR2   PR3

PR9   PR16   PR24   PR25

PR26   PR27   PR28   PR29

PR30   PR31   PR32

PR102 PR106

PR108 PR109 PR110

PR111 PR112 PR113

HOW TO USE THIS BOOK

In cases where two or more Scott numbers share a common design, the illustration shows the first Scott number that bears that design. Subsequent Scott numbers showing the same design will have the first Scott number in parentheses following the description to guide the user to the correct design.

364

Scott No.	Description	Unused Value	Used Value	/ / / / / /
NEWSPAPER STAMPS				
1865, Thin Hard Paper, No Gum				
PR1	5c Washington, dark blue	475.00	—	
a.	5c light blue	500.00	—	
PR2	10c Franklin, blue green	175.00	—	
a.	10c green	175.00	—	
b.	Pelure paper	200.00	—	
PR3	25c Lincoln, orange red	240.00	—	
a.	25c carmine red	275.00	—	
b.	Pelure paper	240.00	—	
White Border, Yellowish Paper				
PR4	5c Washington (PR1), light blue	125.00	—	
a.	5c dark blue	125.00	—	
b.	Pelure paper	125.00	—	
1875, Reprints, Hard White Paper, No Gum				
PR5	5c Washington (PR1), dull blue	130.00		
a.	Printed on both sides	—		
PR6	10c Franklin (PR2), dark bluish green	140.00		
a.	Printed on both sides	*2,000.*		
PR7	25c Lincoln (PR3), dark carmine	175.00		
1881, Reprint, Soft Porous Paper, White Border				
PR8	5c Washington (PR1), dark blue	350.00		
1875, Thin Hard Paper				
PR9	2c Statue of Freedom, black	65.00	22.50	
PR10	3c Statue of Freedom (PR9), black	70.00	25.00	
PR11	4c Statue of Freedom (PR9), black	70.00	22.50	
PR12	6c Statue of Freedom (PR9), black	90.00	25.00	
PR13	8c Statue of Freedom (PR9), black	105.00	35.00	
PR14	9c Statue of Freedom (PR9), black	225.00	80.00	
PR15	10c Statue of Freedom (PR9), black	120.00	30.00	
PR16	12c "Justice" (PR16), rose	300.00	75.00	
PR17	24c "Justice" (PR16), rose	350.00	90.00	
PR18	36c "Justice" (PR16), rose	400.00	100.00	
PR19	48c "Justice" (PR16), rose	675.00	160.00	
PR20	60c "Justice" (PR16), rose	500.00	90.00	
PR21	72c "Justice" (PR16), rose	800.00	210.00	
PR22	84c "Justice" (PR16), rose	1,100.	300.00	
PR23	96c "Justice" (PR16), rose	800.00	200.00	
PR24	$1.92 Ceres, dark brown	875.00	275.00	
PR25	$3 "Victory," vermilion	1,250.	290.00	
PR26	$6 Clio, ultramarine	2,000.	425.00	
PR27	$9 Minerva, yellow orange	2,600.	475.00	
PR28	$12 Vesta, blue green	3,250.	600.00	
PR29	$24 "Peace," dark gray violet	3,250.	600.00	

Scott No.	Description	Unused Value	Used Value	/ / / / / /
PR30	$36 "Commerce," brown rose	3,250.	750.00	
PR31	$48 Hebe, red rose	4,250.	900.00	
PR32	$60 Indian Maiden, violet	5,000.	900.00	

1875, Special Printing, Hard White Paper, No Gum

Scott No.	Description	Unused Value	Used Value	/ / / / / /
PR33	2c Statue of Freedom (PR9), gray black	450.00		
a.	Horiz. ribbed paper	450.00		
PR34	3c Statue of Freedom (PR9), gray black	475.00		
a.	Horiz. ribbed paper	525.00		
PR35	4c Statue of Freedom (PR9), gray black	575.00		
a.	Horiz. ribbed paper	625.00		
PR36	6c Statue of Freedom (PR9), gray black	625.00		
PR37	8c Statue of Freedom (PR9), gray black	700.00		
PR38	9c Statue of Freedom (PR9), gray black	850.00		
PR39	10c Statue of Freedom (PR9), gray black	1,050.		
a.	Horiz. ribbed paper	—		
PR40	12c "Justice" (PR16), pale rose	1,250.		
PR41	24c "Justice" (PR16), pale rose	1,800.		
PR42	36c "Justice" (PR16), pale rose	2,400.		
PR43	48c "Justice" (PR16), pale rose	2,800.		
PR44	60c "Justice" (PR16), pale rose	3,250.		
PR45	72c "Justice" (PR16), pale rose	3,750.		
PR46	84c "Justice" (PR16), pale rose	4,000.		
PR47	96c "Justice" (PR16), pale rose	6,250.		
PR48	$1.92 Ceres (PR24), dark brown	15,000.		
PR49	$3 "Victory" (PR25), vermilion	27,500.		
PR50	$6 Clio (PR26), ultramarine	35,000.		
PR51	$9 Minerva (PR27), yellow orange	—		
PR52	$12 Vesta (PR28), blue green	50,000.		
PR53	$24 "Peace" (PR29), dark gray violet	—		
PR54	$36 "Commerce" (PR30), brown rose	—		
PR55	$48 Hebe (PR31), red brown	—		
PR56	$60 Indian Maiden (PR32), violet	—		

1879, Soft Porous Paper

Scott No.	Description	Unused Value	Used Value	/ / / / / /
PR57	2c Statue of Freedom (PR9), black	27.50	5.50	
PR58	3c Statue of Freedom (PR9), black	32.50	7.00	
PR59	4c Statue of Freedom (PR9), black	32.50	7.00	
PR60	6c Statue of Freedom (PR9), black	65.00	15.00	
PR61	8c Statue of Freedom (PR9), black	65.00	15.00	
PR62	10c Statue of Freedom (PR9), black	65.00	15.00	
PR63	12c "Justice" (PR16), red	325.00	60.00	
PR64	24c "Justice" (PR16), red	325.00	60.00	
PR65	36c "Justice" (PR16), red	700.00	175.00	
PR66	48c "Justice" (PR16), red	650.00	130.00	
PR67	60c "Justice" (PR16), red	525.00	110.00	
a.	Imperf., pair	3,250.		
PR68	72c "Justice" (PR16), red	1,000.	210.00	
PR69	84c "Justice" (PR16), red	925.00	160.00	

Scott No.	Description	Unused Value	Used Value	/ / / / / /
PR70	96c "Justice" (PR16), red	600.00	110.00	
PR71	$1.92 Ceres (PR24), pale brown	450.00	105.00	
PR72	$3 "Victory" (PR25), red vermilion	450.00	105.00	
PR73	$6 Clio (PR26), blue	850.00	160.00	
PR74	$9 Minerva (PR27), orange	550.00	110.00	
PR75	$12 Vesta (PR28), yellow green	700.00	150.00	
PR76	$24 "Peace" (PR29), dark violet	650.00	180.00	
PR77	$36 "Commerce" (PR30), Indian red	800.00	200.00	
PR78	$48 Hebe (PR31), yellow brown	850.00	275.00	
PR79	$60 Indian Maiden (PR32), purple	825.00	275.00	

1883, Special Printing

PR80	2c Statue of Freedom (PR9), intense black	800.00		

1885

PR81	1c Statue of Freedom (PR9), black	45.00	7.50	
PR82	12c "Justice" (PR16), carmine	120.00	17.50	
PR83	24c "Justice" (PR16), carmine	120.00	20.00	
PR84	36c "Justice" (PR16), carmine	160.00	30.00	
PR85	48c "Justice" (PR16), carmine	225.00	45.00	
PR86	60c "Justice" (PR16), carmine	300.00	65.00	
PR87	72c "Justice" (PR16), carmine	300.00	70.00	
PR88	84c "Justice" (PR16), carmine	600.00	160.00	
PR89	96c "Justice" (PR16), carmine	500.00	120.00	

1894

PR90	1c Statue of Freedom (PR9), intense black	275.00		
PR91	2c Statue of Freedom (PR9), intense black	275.00		
PR92	4c Statue of Freedom (PR9), intense black	300.00		
PR93	6c Statue of Freedom (PR9), intense black	4,000.		
PR94	10c Statue of Freedom (PR9), intense black	650.00		
PR95	12c "Justice" (PR16), pink	1,900.	—	
PR96	24c "Justice" (PR16), pink	2,250.		
PR97	36c "Justice" (PR16), pink	20,000.		
PR98	60c "Justice" (PR16), pink	25,000.	—	
PR99	96c "Justice" (PR16), pink	35,000.		
PR100	$3 "Victory" (PR25), scarlet	30,000.		
PR101	$6 Clio (PR26), pale blue	60,000.	—	

1895

PR102	1c Statue of Freedom, black	120.00	12.50	
PR103	2c Statue of Freedom (PR102), black	120.00	12.50	
PR104	5c Statue of Freedom (PR102), black	175.00	20.00	

Scott No.	Description	Unused Value	Used Value	/ / / / / /
PR105	10c Statue of Freedom (PR102), black....	350.00	52.50	
PR106	25c "Justice," carmine	475.00	55.00	
PR107	50c "Justice" (PR106), carmine..............	1,100.	150.00	
PR108	$2 "Victory"..	1,250.	110.00	
PR109	$5 Clio, ultramarine	1,600.	225.00	
PR110	$10 Vesta	1,750.	250.00	
PR111	$20 "Peace"..	2,350.	450.00	
PR112	$50 "Commerce"	2,450.	450.00	
PR113	$100 Indian Maiden	2,800.	525.00	

1895-97, Watermark 191

Scott No.	Description	Unused Value	Used Value	/ / / / / /
PR114	1c Statue of Freedom (PR102), black....	6.00	5.00	
PR115	2c Statue of Freedom (PR102), black....	6.50	5.00	
PR116	5c Statue of Freedom (PR102), black....	10.00	7.50	
PR117	10c Statue of Freedom (PR102), black....	6.50	5.00	
PR118	25c "Justice" (PR106), carmine..............	12.50	12.50	
PR119	50c "Justice" (PR106), carmine..............	15.00	15.00	
PR120	$2 "Victory" (PR108)..............................	20.00	22.50	
PR121	$5 Clio (PR109), dark blue	35.00	35.00	
a.	$5 light blue	175.00	70.00	
PR122	$10 Vesta (PR110)....................................	35.00	35.00	
PR123	$20 "Peace" (PR111)................................	37.50	37.50	
PR124	$50 "Commerce" (PR112).......................	50.00	42.50	
PR125	$100 Indian Maiden (PR113)...................	55.00	47.50	

ScottMounts

Protect your stamps from the harmful effects of dust and moisture. Available in clear or black backs.

Pre-Cut Single Mounts

Size	Description	# Mounts	Item	Price
40 x 25	U.S. Stand. Com.-Hor.	40	901	$2.99
25 x 40	U.S. Stand. Com.-Vert.	40	902	2.99
25 x 22	U.S. Reg Issue-Hor.	40	903	2.99
22 x 25	U.S. Reg. Issue-Vert.	40	904	2.99
41 x 31	U.S. Semi-Jumbo-Hor.	40	905	2.99
31 x 41	U.S. Semi-Jumbo-Vert.	40	906	2.99
50 x 31	U.S. Jumbo-Hor.	40	907	2.99
31 x 50	U.S. Jumbo-Vert.	40	908	2.99
25 x 27	U.S. Famous Americans	40	909	2.99
33 x 27	United Nations	40	910	2.99
40 x 27	United Nations	40	911	2.99
67 x 25	PNC, Strips of Three	40	976	5.29
67 x 34	Pacific '97 Triangle	10	984	2.99
111 x 25	PNC, Strips of Five	25	985	5.29
51 x 36	U.S. Hunting Permit/Express Mail	40	986	2.99

Pre-Cut Plate Block, FDC & Postal Card Mounts

Size	Description	# Mounts	Item	Price
57 x 55	Reg Issue Plate Block	25	912	$5.29
73 x 63	Champions of Liberty	25	913	5.29
106 x 55	Rotary Press Stand. Com.	20	914	5.29
105 x 57	Giori Press Stand. Com.	20	915	5.29
165 x 94	First Day Cover	10	917	5.29
140 x 90	Postal Card Size	10	918	5.29

Strips 215mm Long

Size	Description	# Mounts	Item	Price
20	U.S. 19th Century/Hor. Coil	22	919	$ 6.99
22	U.S. Early Air Mail	22	920	6.99
24	U.S., Canada, Great Britain	22	921	6.99
25	U.S. Comm. and Regular	22	922	6.99
27	U.S. Famous Americans	22	923	6.99
28	U.S. 19th Century	22	924	6.99
30	U.S. 19th Century	22	925	6.99
31	U.S. Jumbo and Semi-Jumbo	22	926	6.99
33	United Nations	22	927	6.99
36	U.S. Hunting Permit, Canada	15	928	6.99
39	U.S. Early 20th Century	15	929	6.99
41	U.S. Semi-Jumbo	15	930	6.99
	Multiple Assortment: one strip of each size 22-41 (Two 25mm strips)	12	931	6.99
44	U.S. Vertical Coil Pair	15	932	6.99
48	U.S. Farley, Gutter Pair	15	933	6.99
50	U.S. Jumbo	15	934	6.99
52	U.S. Standard Comm. Block	15	935	6.99
55	U.S. Century of Progress	15	936	6.99
57	U.S. Famous Americans Block	15	937	6.99
61	U.S. Blocks, Israel Tab	15	938	6.99

Strips 240mm Long

Size	Description	# Mounts	Item	Price
63	U.S. Jumbo Com.-Hor.Block	10	939	$7.99
66	Israel Tab Block	10	940	7.99
68	U.S. Farley, Gutter Pair			

Available from your favorite stamp dealer or direct from:

SCOTT

1-800-572-6885

Strips 265mm Long

	Description		Item	Price
	& Souvenir Sheets	10	941	6.75
74	U.S. TIPEX Souvenir Sheet	10	942	6.75
80	U.S. Stand. Com.-Vert. Block	10	943	6.75
82	U.S. Blocks of 4	10	944	6.75
84	Israel Tab Block	10	945	6.75
89	U.S. Postal Card Size	10	946	6.75
100	U.N. Margin Inscribed Block	7	947	6.75
120	Souvenir Sheets and Blocks	7	948	6.75

			Item	Price
40	Standard Comm. Vertical	10	949	$7.99
55	U.S. Reg. Plate Block Strip 20	10	950	7.99
59	U.S. Double Issue Strip	10	951	7.99
70	U.S. Jumbo Com. Plate Block	10	952	10.99
91	Great Britain Souvenir Sheet	10	953	10.99
105	U.S. Stand. Plate No. Strip	10	954	10.99
107	Same as above-Wide Margin	10	955	10.99
111	U.S. Gravure-Intaglio Plate No. Strip	10	956	12.99
127	U.S. Jumbo Comm. Plate No. Strip	10	957	14.99
137	Great Britain Coronation	10	958	14.99
158	U.S. Apollo-Soyuz Plate No. Strip	10	959	15.99
231	U.S. Full Post Office Pane Regular and Comm.	5	961	15.99

Souvenir Sheets/Small Panes

			Item	Price
111 x 25	PNC, Strips of Five	25	985	$5.29
204 x 153	U.S. Bicent. New Year 2000	4	962	7.99
187 x 144	U.N. Flag Sheet	10	963	13.49
160 x 200	New U.N., Israel Sheet	10	964	13.49
120 x 207	AMERIPEX President Sht.	4	965	5.29
229 x 131	World War II Com. Sheet	5	968	7.49
111 x 91	Columbian Souv. Sheet	6	970	3.99
148 x 196	Apollo Moon Landing	4	972	6.99
129 x 122	U.S. Definitive Mini-Sheet	9	989	8.99
189 x 151	Chinese New Year	5	990	8.99
150 x 185	Dr. Davis/World Cup	5	991	8.99
198 x 151	Cherokee	5	992	8.99
198 x 187	Postal Museum	4	994	8.99
156 x 187	Sign Lang., Statehood	5	995	8.99
188 x 197	Country-Western	4	996	8.99
151 x 192	Olympic	5	997	8.99
174 x 185	Buffalo Soldiers	5	998	8.99
130 x 198	Silent Screen Stars	5	999	8.99
190 x 199	Leg. West, Civil, Comic	4	1000	8.99
178 x 181	Cranes	4	1001	8.99
183 x 212	Wonders of the Sea	3	1002	8.99
156 x 264	$14 Eagle	4	1003	8.99
159 x 270	$9.95 Moon Landing	4	1004	8.99
159 x 259	Priority/Express Mail	5	1005	8.99
223 x 187	Marilyn Monroe	3	1006	8.99
185 x 181	Challenger Shuttle	4	1007	8.99
152 x 228	Indian Dances/Antique Autos	5	1008	8.99
165 x 150	River Boat/Hanukkah	6	1009	8.99
275 x 200	Large Gutter Blocks	2	1010	8.99
161 x 160	Pacific '97 Sheet	6	1011	8.99
174 x 150	Bugs Bunny	6	1012	8.99
196 x 158	Football Coaches	4	1013	8.99
184 x 184	American Dolls	4	1014	8.99
186 x 230	Classic Movie Monsters	3	1015	8.99
187 x 160	Trans-Mississippi Sheet	4	1016	8.99
192 x 230	Celebrate The Century	3	1017	8.99
156 x 204	Space Discovery	5	1018	8.99
182 x 209	American Ballet	4	1019	8.99
139 x 151	Christmas Wreaths	5	1020	8.99
129 x 126	Justin Morrill, Henry Luce	8	1021	8.99
184 x 165	Bright Eyes	4	1022	8.99
185 x 172	Shuttle Landing	4	1023	8.99
172 x 153	Sonoran Desert	5	1024	8.99
150 x 166	Prostate Cancer	5	1025	8.99
201 x 176	Famous Fishins	4	1026	8.99
176 x 124	Canada Historic Vehicles	5	1027	8.99
245 x 114	Canada Provincial Leaders	5	1028	8.99
177 x 133	Canada Year of Family	5	1029	8.99
181 x 213	Arctic Animals	3	1034	8.99
179 x 242	Louise Nevelson	3	1037	8.99
179 x 217	Library Of Congress	3	1038	8.99
182 x 232	Youth Team Sports	3	1039	8.99

Q1

Q2

Q3

Q4

Q5

Q6

Q7

Q8

Q9

Q10

Q11

Q12

QE1

HOW TO USE THIS BOOK

In cases where two or more Scott numbers share a common design, the
illustration shows the first Scott number that bears that design. Subsequent
Scott numbers showing the same design will have the first Scott number in
parentheses following the description to guide the user to the correct design.

JQ1

Scott No.	Description	Unused Value	Used Value	/ / / / / /

PARCEL POST STAMPS
1913

Q1	1c Post Office Clerk	5.75	1.50	☐☐☐☐☐
Q2	2c City Carrier	9.50	1.25	☐☐☐☐☐
Q3	3c Railway Postal Clerk	13.50	5.75	☐☐☐☐☐
Q4	4c Rural Carrier	37.50	3.00	☐☐☐☐☐
Q5	5c Mail Train	32.50	2.25	☐☐☐☐☐
Q6	10c Steamship & Mail Tender	52.50	3.00	☐☐☐☐☐
Q7	15c Automobile Service	67.50	12.00	☐☐☐☐☐
Q8	20c Airplane Carrying Mail	140.00	25.00	☐☐☐☐☐
Q9	25c Manufacturing	67.50	6.75	☐☐☐☐☐
Q10	50c Dairying	280.00	40.00	☐☐☐☐☐
Q11	75c Harvesting	95.00	35.00	☐☐☐☐☐
Q12	$1 Fruit Growing	350.00	35.00	☐☐☐☐☐

PARCEL POST POSTAGE DUE STAMPS
1912

JQ1	1c Numeral, dark green	11.00	4.50	☐☐☐☐☐
JQ2	2c Numeral (JQ1), dark green	85.00	17.50	☐☐☐☐☐
JQ3	5c Numeral (JQ1), dark green	15.00	5.50	☐☐☐☐☐
JQ4	10c Numeral (JQ1), dark green	175.00	45.00	☐☐☐☐☐
JQ5	25c Numeral (JQ1), dark green	105.00	5.00	☐☐☐☐☐

SPECIAL HANDLING STAMPS
1925-28

QE1	10c Numeral, yellow green	1.60	1.00	☐☐☐☐☐
QE2	15c Numeral (QE1), yellow green	1.75	.90	☐☐☐☐☐
QE3	20c Numeral (QE1), yellow green	2.75	1.50	☐☐☐☐☐
QE4	25c Numeral (QE1), yellow green	22.50	7.50	☐☐☐☐☐
a.	25c deep green	32.50	5.50	☐☐☐☐☐

1

3

31   32

Scott No.	Description	Unused Value	Used Value	/ / / / / /
COMPUTER VENDED POSTAGE				
1989, Aug. 23, Washington, D.C., Machine 82				
CVP1	25c USA, 1st Class	6.00	—	
a.	1st day dated, serial #12501-15500.	4.50	—	
b.	1st day dated, serial #00001-12500.	4.50	—	
c.	1st day dated, serial over #27500	—	—	
CVP2	$1 USA (1), 3rd Class	—	—	
a.	1st day dated, serial #24501-27500.	—	—	
b.	1st day dated, serial over #27500	—	—	
CVP3	$1.69 Bar code, Parcel Post	—	—	
a.	1st day dated, serial #21501-24500.	—	—	
b.	1st day dated, serial over #27500	—	—	
CVP4	$2.40 USA (1), Priority Mail	—	—	
a.	1st day dated, serial #18501-21500.	—	—	
b.	Priority Mail ($2.74), with bar code	*100.00*	—	
c.	1st day dated, serial over #27500	—	—	
CVP5	$8.75 USA (1), Express Mail	—	—	
a.	1st day dated, serial #15501-18500.	—	—	
b.	1st day dated, serial over #27500	—	—	
	Nos. 1a-5a	82.50	—	
Washington, D.C., Machine 83				
CVP6	25c USA (1), 1st Class	6.00	—	
a.	1st day dated, serial #12501-15500..	4.50	—	
b.	1st day dated, serial #00001-12500.	4.50	—	
c.	1st day dated, serial over #27500	—	—	
CVP7	$1 USA (1), 3rd Class	—	—	
a.	1st day dated, serial #24501-27500	—	—	
b.	1st day dated, serial over #27500 ...	—	—	

Scott No.	Description	Unused Value	Used Value	/ / / / / /
CVP8 $1.69	Bar Code (3), Parcel Post	—	—	
a.	1st day dated, serial #21501-24500	—	—	
b.	1st day dated, serial over #27500 ...	—	—	
CVP9 $2.40	USA (1), Priority Mail...................	—	—	
a.	1st day dated, serial #18501-21500	—	—	
b.	1st day dated, serial over #27500 ...	—	—	
c.	Priority Mail ($2.74), with bar code	100.00	—	
CVP10 $8.75	USA (1), Express Mail...................	—	—	
a.	1st day dated, serial #15501-18500	—	—	
b.	1st day dated, serial over #27500 ...	—	—	
	Nos. 6a-10a	57.50	—	

1989, Sept. 1, Kensington, MD, Machine 82

CVP11 25c	USA (1), 1st Class	6.00	—	
a.	1st day dated, serial #12501-15500	4.50	—	
b.	1st day dated, serial #00001-12500	4.50	—	
c.	1st day dated, serial over #27500 ...	—	—	
CVP12 $1	USA (1), 3rd Class........................	—	—	
a.	1st day dated, serial #24501-27500	—	—	
b.	1st day dated, serial over #27500 ...	—	—	
CVP13 $1.69	Bar Code (3), Parcel Post...............	—	—	
a.	1st day dated, serial #21501-24500	—	—	
b.	1st day dated, serial over #27500 ...	—	—	
CVP14 $2.40	USA (1), Priority Mail	—	—	
a.	1st day dated, serial #18501-21500	—	—	
b.	1st day dated, serial over #27500 ...	—	—	
c.	Priority Mail ($2.74), with bar code	100.00	—	
CVP15 $8.75	USA (1), Express Mail...................	—	—	
a.	1st day dated, serial #15501-18500	—	—	
b.	1st day dated, serial over #27500 ...	—	—	
	Nos. 11a-15a	57.50	—	
	Nos. 1b-11b.....................................	9.00	—	

Kensington, MD, Machine 83

CVP16 25c	USA (1), 1st Class	6.00	—	
a.	1st day dated, serial #12501-15500	4.50	—	
b.	1st day dated, serial #00001-12500	4.50	—	
c.	1st day dated, serial over #27500 ...	—	—	
CVP17 $1	USA (1), 3rd Class........................	—	—	
a.	1st day dated, serial #24501-27500	—	—	
b.	1st day dated, serial over #27500...	—	—	
CVP18 $1.69	Bar Code (3), Parcel Post.............	—	—	
a.	1st day dated, serial #21501-24500	—	—	
b.	1st day dated, serial over #27500...	—	—	
CVP19 $2.40	USA (1), Priority Mail	—	—	
a.	1st day dated, serial #18501-21500	—	—	
b.	1st day dated, serial over #27500...	—	—	
c.	Priority Mail ($2.74), with bar code	100.00	—	

Scott No.	Description	Unused Value	Used Value	//////
CVP20 $8.75	USA (1), Express Mail..............	—	—	☐☐☐☐☐
a.	1st day dated, serial #15501-18500	—	—	☐☐☐☐☐
b.	1st day dated, serial over #27500..	—	—	☐☐☐☐☐
	Nos. 16a-20a...............................	57.50	—	☐☐☐☐☐
	Nos. 6b, 16b	9.00	—	☐☐☐☐☐

1989, Nov., Washington, D.C., Machine 11

Scott No.	Description	Unused Value	Used Value	//////
CVP21 25c	USA (1), 1st Class	*150.00*		☐☐☐☐☐
a.	1st Class, with bar code	—		☐☐☐☐☐
CVP22 $1	USA (1), 3rd Class........................	*500.00*		☐☐☐☐☐
CVP23 $1.69	Bar Code (3), Parcel Post.............	*500.00*		☐☐☐☐☐
CVP24 $2.40	USA (1), Priority Mail	*500.00*		☐☐☐☐☐
a.	Priority Mail ($2.74), with bar code	—		☐☐☐☐☐
CVP25 $8.75	USA (1), Express Mail..................	*500.00*		☐☐☐☐☐

Washington, D.C., Machine 12

Scott No.	Description	Unused Value	Used Value	//////
CVP26 25c	USA (1), 1st Class	*150.00*		☐☐☐☐☐
CVP27 $1	USA (1), 3rd Class........................	—		☐☐☐☐☐
CVP28 $1.69	Bar Code (3), Parcel Post.............	—		☐☐☐☐☐
CVP29 $2.40	USA (1), Priority Mail	—		☐☐☐☐☐
a.	Priority Mail ($2.74), with bar code	—		☐☐☐☐☐
CVP30 $8.75	USA (1), Express Mail..................	—		☐☐☐☐☐

1992, Coil Stamp

Scott No.	Description	Unused Value	Used Value	//////
CVP31 29c	Shield, red & blue, Type I............	.60	.25	☐☐☐☐☐
b.	Type II	.90	.40	☐☐☐☐☐

Type I has small serifed numerals preceded by an asterisk 1 1/2 mm across. Type II has large sans-serif numerals preceded by an asterisk 2 mm across.

1994, Coil Stamp

Scott No.	Description	Unused Value	Used Value	//////
CVP32 29c	Shield, red & blue	.60	.25	☐☐☐☐☐

1996, Coil Stamp

Scott No.	Description	Unused Value	Used Value	//////
CVP33 32c	Shield (32), bright red & blue dated "1996"..............................	.60	.25	☐☐☐☐☐

Stockbooks

Stockbooks are a safe convenient way to display and store your stamps. These German made stockbooks feature heavyweight archival quality paper with 9 pockets on each page. The 8 ½" 11 ⅝" pages are bound inside a sturdy leatherette grain cover and include glassine interleaving between the pages for added protection.

WHITE PAGE STOCKBOOKS GLASSINE POCKETS

Item	Description	Price
SW16BL	Blue 16 pgs.	$5.95
SW16GR	Green 16 pgs.	$5.95
SW16RD	Red 16 pgs.	$5.95

BLACK PAGE STOCKBOOKS ACETATE POCKETS

Item	Description	Price
ST16RD	Red 16 pgs.	$9.95
ST16GR	Green 16 pgs.	$9.95
ST16BL	Blue 16 pgs.	$9.95
ST16BK	Black 16 pgs.	$9.95
ST32RD	Red 32 pgs.	$14.95
ST32GR	Green 32 pgs.	$14.95
ST32BL	Blue 32 pgs.	$14.95
ST32BK	Black 32 pgs.	$14.95
ST64RD	Red 64 pgs.	$27.95
ST64GR	Green 64 pgs.	$27.95
ST64BL	Blue 64 pgs.	$27.95
ST64BK	Black 64 pgs.	$27.95

Available from your favorite stamp dealer or direct from:

1-800-572-6885
www.amosadvantage.com

LO1

LO2

1LB1

1LB6

1LB8

3LB1

3LB2

4LB1

4LB3

4LB5

4LB8

4LB1

4LB3

4LB14

4LB15

4LB16

4LB18

4LB19

9LB1

10LB1

10LB2

376

Scott No.	Description	Unused Value	Used Value	/ / / / /
CARRIER'S STAMPS				
OFFICIAL ISSUES				
1851				
LO1	(1c) Franklin, dull blue on *rose*...............	5,000.	5,000.	
LO2	1c Eagle, blue, imperf...........................	25.00	50.00	
1875 REPRINTS, No gum				
LO3	(1c) Franklin (LO1), blue on *rose*, imperf.	50.00		
LO4	(1c) Franklin (LO1), blue, perf. 12	16,000.		
LO5	1c Eagle (LO2), blue, imperf.	25.00		
LO6	1c Eagle (LO2), blue, perf. 12...............	160.00		
SEMI-OFFICIAL ISSUES				
1850-55, Imperf.				
1LB1	1c Post Office Despatch, red on *bluish*..	180.00	160.00	
1LB2	1c Post Office Despatch, blue on *bluish*	200.00	150.00	
a.	Bluish laid paper...............................	—	—	
1LB3	1c Post Office Despatch, blue	160.00	100.00	
a.	Laid paper	200.00	150.00	
b.	Block of 14 containing three tete-beche pairs	5,500.		
1LB4	1c Post Office Despatch, green..............	—	850.00	
1LB5	1c Post Office Despatch, red.................	2,250.	1,750.	
1856				
1LB6	1c Carriers Dispatch, blue	130.00	90.00	
1LB7	1c Carriers Dispatch (1LB6) , red..........	130.00	90.00	
1857				
1LB8	1c Horse & Rider, black	65.00	50.00	
a.	SENT...	100.00	75.00	
b.	Short rays...	100.00	75.00	
1LB9	1c Horse & Rider (1LB8), red	100.00	90.00	
a.	SENT...	140.00	110.00	
b.	Short rays...	140.00	110.00	
c.	As "b," double impression................	—		
1849-50				
3LB1	1c "Penny Post.," blue...........................	375.00	180.00	
a.	Wrong ornament at left, on cover (not tied)...		400.00	
1851				
3LB2	1c "Penny Post. Paid," blue (shades) on *slate*...	190.00	100.00	
1849				
4LB1	2c Honour's City Express, black on *brown rose*	10,000.		
4LB2	2c Honour's City Express (4LB1),			

5LB1   5LB2   6LB1

6LB2   6LB7

6LB9   7LB1   7LB6

7LB11   7LB14   7LB18   C3(8LB1

Actual Size
8LB2

HOW TO USE THIS BOOK

The number in the first column is its Scott number or identifying number.
Following that is the denomination of the stamp and its color. Finally, the value,
unused and used is shown.

Scott No.	Description	Unused Value	Used Value	/ / / / /
	black on *yellow*, cut to shape...........	—		☐☐☐☐☐

1854

4LB3	2c City Post, black		1,500.	☐☐☐☐☐

1849-50

4LB5	2c Honour's City Post, black on *bluish*, pelure paper	750.00	500.00	☐☐☐☐☐
a.	"Ceuts"..	5,750.		☐☐☐☐☐
4LB7	2c Honour's City Post (4LB5) , black on *yellow*	750.00	1,000.	☐☐☐☐☐
a.	"Ccnts"...		14,500.	☐☐☐☐☐

1851-58

4LB8	2c Paid, Honour's City Post, black on *bluish*...............................	350.00	175.00	☐☐☐☐☐
a.	Period after Paid................................	500.00	250.00	☐☐☐☐☐
b.	Cens..	700.00	900.00	☐☐☐☐☐
c.	Conours and Bents.............................		—	☐☐☐☐☐
4LB9	2c Paid, Honour's City Post (4LB8), black on *bluish*, pelure paper	850.00	950.00	☐☐☐☐☐
4LB11	(2c) Honour's Penny Post Paid, black on *bluish*...............................	—	375.00	☐☐☐☐☐
4LB12	(2c) Honour's Penny Post Paid (4LB11), black on *bluish*, pelure paper	—	—	☐☐☐☐☐
4LB13	(2c) Honour's City Post Paid, black on *bluish*...............................	750.00	400.00	☐☐☐☐☐
a.	Comma after PAID	1,100.		☐☐☐☐☐
b.	No period after Post...........................	1,400.		☐☐☐☐☐

1851(?)-58(?)

4LB14	2c Kingsman's City Post Paid, black on *bluish*...............................	1,400.	900.00	☐☐☐☐☐
a.	"Kingman's" erased	—	5,000.	☐☐☐☐☐
4LB15	2c Paid, Kingsman's City Post, black on *bluish*...............................	800.00	800.00	☐☐☐☐☐
a.	"Kingman's" erased on cover with 3c #11, tied by pen cancel (unique)	—	5,000.	☐☐☐☐☐

1858

4LB16	2c Martin's City Post, black on *bluish* ...	8,000.		☐☐☐☐☐

1860

4LB17	2c Beckman's City Post (4LB18), black		—	☐☐☐☐☐

1859

4LB18	2c Circle Frame, Steinmeyer's, black on *bluish*...............................	21,000.		☐☐☐☐☐
4LB19	2c Steinmeyer's, Rods & Circles Frame, black on *bluish*...............................	4,500.	—	☐☐☐☐☐

Scott No.		Description	Unused Value	Used Value	/ / / / / /
4LB20	2c	Steinmeyer's, Rods & Circles (4LB19), black on *pink*	200.00	—	☐☐☐☐☐
4LB21	2c	Steinmeyer's, Rods & Circles (4LB19), black on *yellow*	200.00		☐☐☐☐☐

1854

9LB1	2c	Williams' City Post, brown	—	3,000.	☐☐☐☐☐

1854

10LB1		Bishop's, nondenominated, blue	5,000.	2,000.	☐☐☐☐☐
10LB2	2c	Bishop's, black on *bluish*	7,000.	3,750.	☐☐☐☐☐

1857

5LB1	(2c)	Wharton's, bluish green	125.00		☐☐☐☐☐

1858

5LB2	(2c)	Brown & McGill's, blue	250.00	750.00	☐☐☐☐☐
5LB3	(2c)	Brown & McGill's (5LB2), black	4,500.	15,000.	☐☐☐☐☐

1842

6LB1	3c	City Despatch Post, black on *grayish*		1,750.	☐☐☐☐☐

1842-45

6LB2	3c	United States City Despatch Post black on *rosy buff*	2,500.		☐☐☐☐☐
6LB3	3c	United States City Despatch Post (6LB2) black on *light blue*	550.00	500.00	☐☐☐☐☐
6LB4	3c	United States City Despatch Post (6LB2) black on *green*	11,500.		☐☐☐☐☐
6LB5	3c	United States City Despatch Post (6LB2) black on *blue green (shades)*	200.00	175.00	☐☐☐☐☐
a.		Double impression		1,500.	☐☐☐☐☐
b.	3c	black on *blue*	650.00	250.00	☐☐☐☐☐
c.		As "b.," double impression		850.00	☐☐☐☐☐
d.	3c	black on *green*	1,000.	900.00	☐☐☐☐☐
e.		As "d.," double impression	—		☐☐☐☐☐
6LB6	3c	black on *pink*	14,500.		☐☐☐☐☐

1846

6LB7		No. 6LB5 surcharged "2" in red		55,000.	☐☐☐☐☐

1849

6LB9	1c	U.S. Mail, black on *rose*	90.00	90.00	☐☐☐☐☐

1849-50

6LB10	1c	U.S. Mail (6LB9), black on *yellow*	90.00	90.00	☐☐☐☐☐
6LB11	1c	U.S. Mail (6LB9), black on *buff*	90.00	90.00	☐☐☐☐☐
a.		Pair, one stamp sideways	2,250.		☐☐☐☐☐

Scott No.	Description	Unused Value	Used Value	/ / / / / /
1849-50				
7LB1	1c U.S.P.O., black on *rose* (with letters L.P.)	450.00		☐☐☐☐☐
7LB2	1c U.S.P.O. (7LB1), black on *rose* (with letter S)	3,000.		☐☐☐☐☐
7LB3	1c U.S.P.O. (7LB1), black on *rose* (with letter H)	275.00		☐☐☐☐☐
7LB4	1c U.S.P.O. (7LB1), black on *rose* (with letters L.S.)	400.00	500.00	☐☐☐☐☐
7LB5	1c U.S.P.O. (7LB1), black on *rose* (with letters J.J.)	7,500.		☐☐☐☐☐
7LB6	1c U.S.P.O. , no letters, black on *rose*	300.00	250.00	☐☐☐☐☐
7LB7	1c U.S.P.O. (7LB6), black on *blue*, glazed	1,000.		☐☐☐☐☐
7LB8	1c U.S.P.O. (7LB6), black on *vermilion*, glazed	700.00		☐☐☐☐☐
7LB9	1c U.S.P.O. (7LB6), black on *yellow*, glazed	2,750.	2,250.	☐☐☐☐☐
1850-52				
7LB11	1c U.S.P.O., fancy frame, gold on *black*, glazed	175.00	110.00	☐☐☐☐☐
7LB12	1c U.S.P.O. (7LB11), fancy frame, blue.	400.00	275.00	☐☐☐☐☐
7LB13	1c U.S.P.O. (7LB11), fancy frame, black	750.00	550.00	☐☐☐☐☐
7LB14	1c Eagle above oval, blue on *buff*	3,000.		☐☐☐☐☐
1855(?)				
7LB16	1c Eagle above oval (7LB14), black		5,000.	☐☐☐☐☐
1856(?)				
7LB18	1c Oval, black	1,250.	2,000.	☐☐☐☐☐
1849				
8LB1	2c U.S. Penny Post, Numeral, black, type 1	7,000.	—	☐☐☐☐☐
8LB2	2c U.S. Penny Post, Numeral, black, type 2	5,500.	—	☐☐☐☐☐
1857				
8LB3	2c U.S. Penny Post, Star, blue		22,500.	☐☐☐☐☐
				☐☐☐☐☐
				☐☐☐☐☐
				☐☐☐☐☐
				☐☐☐☐☐
				☐☐☐☐☐
				☐☐☐☐☐
				☐☐☐☐☐
				☐☐☐☐☐

RW1

RW6

RW16

RW26

RW27

RW36

RW45

RW58

RW64

RW65

RW67

Scott No.	Description	Unused Value	Used Value	/ / / / / /

HUNTING PERMIT STAMPS

1934
RW1 $1 *Mallards Alighting* .... 750.00   125.00 ☐☐☐☐☐ ☐☐☐☐☐
a.   Imperf., pair .... —
b.   Vert. pair, imperf. horiz. .... —

1935
RW2 $1 *Canvasback Ducks Taking to Flight*.. 675.00   140.00 ☐☐☐☐☐

1936
RW3 $1 *Canada Geese in Flight*................... 325.00   75.00 ☐☐☐☐☐

1937
RW4 $1 *Scaup Ducks Taking to Flight*........... 275.00   57.50 ☐☐☐☐☐

1938
RW5 $1 *Pintail Drake and Duck Alighting*..... 400.00   57.50 ☐☐☐☐☐

1939
RW6 $1 *Green-Winged Teal*........................... 250.00   45.00 ☐☐☐☐☐

1940
RW7 $1 *Black Mallards*................................. 225.00   45.00 ☐☐☐☐☐

1941
RW8 $1 *Family of Ruddy Ducks*..................... 225.00   45.00 ☐☐☐☐☐

1942
RW9 $1 *Baldpates*... 225.00   45.00 ☐☐☐☐☐

1943
RW10 $1 *Wood Ducks*...................................... 75.00   32.50 ☐☐☐☐☐

1944
RW11 $1 *White-fronted Geese* .... 87.50   25.00 ☐☐☐☐☐

1945
RW12 $1 *Shoveller Ducks in Flight* .... 60.00   25.00 ☐☐☐☐☐

1946
RW13 $1 *Redhead Ducks*, red brown.............. 45.00   16.00 ☐☐☐☐☐ ☐☐☐☐☐
a. $1 bright rose pink................................. —

1947
RW14 $1 *Snow Geese* .... 45.00   16.00 ☐☐☐☐☐

1948
RW15 $1 *Bufflehead Ducks in Flight*............... 50.00   15.00 ☐☐☐☐☐

1949
RW16 $2 *Greeneye Ducks* .... 65.00   14.00 ☐☐☐☐☐

1950
RW17 $2 *Trumpeter Swans in Flight* .... 75.00   11.00 ☐☐☐☐☐

1951
RW18 $2 *Gadwall Ducks*.................................. 75.00   11.00 ☐☐☐☐☐

Scott No.	Description	Unused Value	Used Value	/ / / / /
1952				
RW19	$2 *Harlequin Ducks*	75.00	11.00	☐☐☐☐☐
1953				
RW20	$2 *Blue-winged Teal*	75.00	11.00	☐☐☐☐☐
1954				
RW21	$2 *Ring-necked Ducks*	75.00	10.50	☐☐☐☐☐
1955				
RW22	$2 *Blue Geese*	75.00	10.50	☐☐☐☐☐
a.	Back inscription inverted	—		☐☐☐☐☐
1956				
RW23	$2 *American Merganser*	75.00	10.50	☐☐☐☐☐
1957				
RW24	$2 *American Eider*	75.00	10.50	☐☐☐☐☐
1958				
RW25	$2 *Canada Geese*	75.00	10.50	☐☐☐☐☐
1959				
RW26	$3 *Labrador Retriever carrying Mallard Drake*	100.00	11.00	☐☐☐☐☐
a.	Back inscription inverted	—		☐☐☐☐☐
1960				
RW27	$3 *Redhead Ducks*	85.00	10.50	☐☐☐☐☐
1961				
RW28	$3 *Mallard Hen and Ducklings*	85.00	10.50	☐☐☐☐☐
1962				
RW29	$3 *Pintail Drakes Landing*	100.00	10.50	☐☐☐☐☐
a.	Back inscription omitted	—		☐☐☐☐☐
1963				
RW30	$3 *Pair of Brant Landing*	100.00	10.50	☐☐☐☐☐
1964				
RW31	$3 *Hawaiian Nene Geese*	100.00	10.50	☐☐☐☐☐
1965				
RW32	$3 *Three Canvasback Drakes*	100.00	10.50	☐☐☐☐☐
1966				
RW33	$3 *Whistling Swans*	100.00	10.50	☐☐☐☐☐
1967				
RW34	$3 *Old Squaw Ducks*	125.00	10.00	☐☐☐☐☐
1968				
RW35	$3 *Hooded Mergansers*	65.00	10.00	☐☐☐☐☐
1969				
RW36	$3 *White-winged Scoters*	65.00	7.00	☐☐☐☐☐

Scott No.	Description	Unused Value	Used Value	/ / / / / /
1970 RW37	$3 Ross's Geese	65.00	7.00	☐☐☐☐☐
1971 RW38	$3 *Three Cinnamon Teal*	42.50	7.75	☐☐☐☐☐
1972 RW39	$5 *Emperor Geese*	25.00	7.00	☐☐☐☐☐
1973 RW40	$5 *Stellers Eiders*	18.00	7.00	☐☐☐☐☐
1974 RW41	$5 *Wood Ducks*	18.00	6.00	☐☐☐☐☐
1975 RW42	$5 *Canvasback Decoy and three flying Canvasbacks*	15.00	6.00	☐☐☐☐☐
1976 RW43	$5 *Family of Canada Geese*	15.00	6.00	☐☐☐☐☐
1977 RW44	$5 *Pair of Ross's Geese*	15.00	6.00	☐☐☐☐☐
1978 RW45	$5 *Hooded Merganser Drake*	12.50	6.00	☐☐☐☐☐
1979 RW46	$7.50 *Green-winged teal*	14.00	7.00	☐☐☐☐☐
1980 RW47	$7.50 *Mallards*	14.00	7.00	☐☐☐☐☐
1981 RW48	$7.50 *Ruddy Ducks*	14.00	7.00	☐☐☐☐☐
1982 RW49	$7.50 *Canvasbacks*	15.00	7.00	☐☐☐☐☐
1983 RW50	$7.50 *Pintails*	15.00	7.00	☐☐☐☐☐
1984 RW51	$7.50 *Widgeon*	15.00	7.00	☐☐☐☐☐
1985 RW52	$7.50 *Cinnamon Teal*	15.00	7.00	☐☐☐☐☐
1986 RW53	$7.50 *Fulvous Whistling Duck*	15.00	7.00	☐☐☐☐☐
a.	Black omitted	3,750.		☐☐☐☐☐
1987 RW54	$10 *Redheads*	17.50	9.50	☐☐☐☐☐

Scott No.	Description	Unused Value	Used Value	//////
1988				
RW55	$10 *Snow Goose*	15.00	10.00	☐☐☐☐☐
1989				
RW56	$12.50 *Lesser Scaups*	19.00	10.00	☐☐☐☐☐
1990				
RW57	$12.50 *Black Bellied Whistling Duck*	19.00	10.00	☐☐☐☐☐☐☐☐☐☐
a.	Back inscription omitted	425.00		
1991				
RW58	$15 *King Eiders*	22.50	11.00	☐☐☐☐☐☐☐☐☐☐
a.	Black (engr.) omitted	8,500.		
1992				
RW59	$15 *Spectacled Eider*	24.00	12.50	☐☐☐☐☐
1993				
RW60	$15 *Canvasbacks*	22.50	11.00	☐☐☐☐☐☐☐☐☐☐
a.	Black (engr.) omitted	3,250.		
1994				
RW61	$15 *Red-breasted Mergansers*	24.00	11.00	☐☐☐☐☐
1995				
RW62	$15 *Mallards*	24.00	11.00	☐☐☐☐☐
1996				
RW63	$15 *Surf Scoters*	24.00	11.00	☐☐☐☐☐
1997				
RW64	$15 *Canada Goose*	22.50	11.00	☐☐☐☐☐
1998				
RW65	$15 *Barrow's Goldeneye*	22.50	11.00	☐☐☐☐☐
RW65A	$15 *Barrow's Goldeneye* Self-adhesive (RW65)	22.50	12.50	☐☐☐☐☐
1999				
RW66	$15 Greater Scaup	22.50	11.00	☐☐☐☐☐
RW66A	$15 Greater Scaup, Self-adhesive (RW66)	22.50	11.00	☐☐☐☐☐
2000				
RW67	$15 Mottled Duck	22.50	11.00	☐☐☐☐☐☐☐☐☐☐
RW67A	$15 Mottled Duck, Self-adhesive (RW67)	22.50	12.50	
2001				
RW68	$15 Northern Pintail, Inscribed Void after June 30, 2002	22.50	11.00	☐☐☐☐☐☐☐☐☐☐
RW68A	$15. Northern Pintail, Self-adhesive (RW68)	22.50	12.50	
RW69	$15. Black Scoters	22.50	11.00	
RW69A	$15."Black Scoters, Self-Adhesive (RW69)"	22.50	11.00	☐☐☐☐☐

Scott No.	Description	Unused Value	Used Value	/ / / / / /
				☐☐☐☐☐
				☐☐☐☐☐
				☐☐☐☐☐
				☐☐☐☐☐
				☐☐☐☐☐
				☐☐☐☐☐
				☐☐☐☐☐
				☐☐☐☐☐
				☐☐☐☐☐
				☐☐☐☐☐
				☐☐☐☐☐
				☐☐☐☐☐
				☐☐☐☐☐
				☐☐☐☐☐
				☐☐☐☐☐
				☐☐☐☐☐
				☐☐☐☐☐
				☐☐☐☐☐
				☐☐☐☐☐
				☐☐☐☐☐
				☐☐☐☐☐
				☐☐☐☐☐
				☐☐☐☐☐
				☐☐☐☐☐
				☐☐☐☐☐
				☐☐☐☐☐
				☐☐☐☐☐
				☐☐☐☐☐
				☐☐☐☐☐
				☐☐☐☐☐
				☐☐☐☐☐
				☐☐☐☐☐
				☐☐☐☐☐
				☐☐☐☐☐
				☐☐☐☐☐
				☐☐☐☐☐
				☐☐☐☐☐
				☐☐☐☐☐
				☐☐☐☐☐
				☐☐☐☐☐
				☐☐☐☐☐
				☐☐☐☐☐
				☐☐☐☐☐

INDEX TO ADVERTISERS

★ ★ ★ ★ ★ ★ ★ ★ ★ ★ ★ ★ ★

Scott Advertising Opportunities

To receive information about advertising in next year's Scott U.S. Pocket Catalogue or any other Scott product, contact Scott Publishing Co., P.O. Box 828, Sidney, OH 45365-0828 USA. Phone 937-498-0832, FAX 937-498-0814.

ScottMounts

Protect your stamps from the harmful effects of dust and moisture. Available in clear or black backs.

Pre-Cut Single Mounts

Size	Description	# Mounts	Item	Price
40 x 25	U.S. Stand. Com.–Hor.	40	901	$2.99
25 x 40	U.S. Stand. Com.–Vert.	40	902	2.99
25 x 22	U.S. Reg Issue–Hor.	40	903	2.99
22 x 25	U.S. Reg. Issue–Vert.	40	904	2.99
41 x 31	U.S. Semi-Jumbo–Hor.	40	905	2.99
31 x 41	U.S. Semi-Jumbo–Vert.	40	906	2.99
50 x 31	U.S. Jumbo–Hor.	40	907	2.99
31 x 50	U.S. Jumbo–Vert.	40	908	2.99
25 x 27	U.S. Famous Americans	40	909	2.99
33 x 27	United Nations	40	910	2.99
40 x 27	United Nations	40	911	2.99
67 x 25	PNC, Strips of Three	40	976	5.29
67 x 34	Pacific '97 Triangle	10	984	2.99
111 x 25	PNC, Strips of Five	25	985	5.29
51 x 36	U.S. Hunting Permit/ Express Mail	40	986	5.29

Pre-Cut Plate Block, FDC & Postal Card Mounts

57 x 55	Reg Issue Plate Block	25	912	$5.29
73 x 63	Champions of Liberty	25	913	5.29
106 x 55	Rotary Press Stand. Com.	20	914	5.29
105 x 57	Giori Press Stand. Com.	20	915	5.29
165 x 94	First Day Cover	10	917	5.29
140 x 90	Postal Card Size	10	918	5.29

Strips 215mm Long

20	U.S. 19th Century/Hor. Coil	22	919	$ 6.99
22	U.S. Early Air Mail	22	920	6.99
24	U.S., Canada, Great Britain	22	921	6.99
25	U.S. Comm. and Regular	22	922	6.99
27	U.S. Famous Americans	22	923	6.99
28	U.S. 19th Century	22	924	6.99
30	U.S. 19th Century	22	925	6.99
31	U.S. Jumbo and Semi-Jumbo	22	926	6.99
33	United Nations	22	927	6.99
36	U.S. Hunting Permit, Canada	15	928	6.99
39	U.S. Early 20th Century	15	929	6.99
41	U.S. Semi-Jumbo	15	930	6.99
Multiple Assortment: one strip of each size 22-41 (Two 25mm strips)		12	931	6.99
44	U.S. Vertical Coil Pair	15	932	6.99
48	U.S. Farley, Gutter Pair	15	933	6.99
50	U.S. Jumbo	15	934	6.99
52	U.S. Standard Comm. Block	15	935	6.99
55	U.S. Century of Progress	15	936	6.99
57	U.S. Famous Americans Block	15	937	6.99
61	U.S. Blocks, Israel Tab	15	938	6.99

Strips 240mm Long

Size	Description	# Mounts	Item	Price
63	U.S. Jumbo Com.–Hor.Block	10	939	$7.99
66	Israel Tab Block	10	940	7.99
68	U.S. Farley, Gutter Pair			

Available from your favorite stamp dealer or direct from:

SCOTT
1-800-572-6885

	& Souvenir Sheets	10	941	6.75
74	U.S. TIPEX Souvenir Sheet	10	942	6.75
80	U.S. Stand. Com.–Vert. Block	10	943	6.75
82	U.S. Blocks of 4	10	944	6.75
84	Israel Tab Block	10	945	6.75
89	U.S. Postal Card Size	10	946	6.75
100	U.N. Margin Inscribed Block	7	947	6.75
120	Souvenir Sheets and Blocks	7	948	6.75

Strips 265mm Long

40	Standard Comm. Vertical	10	949	$7.99
55	U.S. Reg. Plate Block Strip 20	10	950	7.99
59	U.S. Double Issue Strip	10	951	7.99
70	U.S. Jumbo Com. Plate Block	10	952	10.99
91	Great Britain Souvenir Sheet	10	953	10.99
105	U.S. Stand. Plate No. Strip	10	954	10.99
107	Same as above–Wide Margin	10	955	10.99
111	U.S. Gravure-Intaglio Plate No. Strip	10	956	12.99
127	U.S. Jumbo Comm. Plate No. Strip	10	957	14.99
137	Great Britain Coronation	10	958	14.99
158	U.S. Apollo-Soyuz Plate No. Strip	10	959	15.99
231	U.S. Full Post Office Pane Regular and Comm.	5	961	15.99

Souvenir Sheets/Small Panes

111 x 25	PNC, Strips of Five	25	985	$5.29
204 x 153	U.S. Bicent. New Year 2000	4	962	7.99
187 x 144	U.N. Flag Sheet	10	963	13.49
160 x 200	New U.N., Israel Sheet	10	964	13.49
120 x 207	AMERIPEX President Sht.	4	965	5.29
229 x 131	World War II Com. Share	5	968	7.49
111 x 91	Columbian Souv. Sheet	6	970	3.99
148 x 196	Apollo Moon Landing	4	972	6.99
129 x 122	*U.S. Definitive Mini-Sheet*	9	989	8.99
189 x 151	Chinese New Year	5	990	8.99
150 x 185	*Dr. Davis–World Cup*	5	991	8.99
198 x 151	Cherokee	5	992	8.99
198 x 187	Postal Museum	4	994	8.99
156 x 187	Sign Lang., Statehood	5	995	8.99
188 x 197	Country–Western	4	996	8.99
151 x 192	Olympic	5	997	8.99
174 x 185	Buffalo Soldiers	5	998	8.99
130 x 198	Silent Screen Stars	5	999	8.99
190 x 199	Leg. West, Civil, Comic	4	1000	8.99
178 x 181	Cranes	4	1001	8.99
183 x 212	Wonders of the Sea	3	1002	8.99
156 x 264	$14 Eagle	4	1003	8.99
159 x 270	$9.95 Moon Landing	4	1004	8.99
159 x 259	Priority/Express Mail	4	1005	8.99
223 x 187	Marilyn Monroe	3	1006	8.99
185 x 181	Challenger Shuttle	4	1007	8.99
152 x 228	Indian Dances/Antique Autos	5	1008	8.99
165 x 150	River Boat/Hanukkah	6	1009	8.99
275 x 200	Large Gutter Blocks	2	1010	8.99
161 x 160	Pacific '97 Sheet	6	1011	8.99
174 x 130	Bugs Bunny	6	1012	8.99
196 x 158	Football Coaches	4	1013	8.99
184 x 184	American Dolls	4	1014	8.99
186 x 230	Classic Movie Monsters	3	1015	8.99
187 x 160	Trans-Mississippi Sheet	4	1016	8.99
192 x 230	Celebrate The Century	3	1017	8.99
156 x 204	Space Discovery	5	1018	8.99
182 x 209	American Ballet	5	1019	8.99
139 x 151	Christmas Wreaths	5	1020	8.99
129 x 126	Justin Morrill, Henry Luce	8	1021	8.99
184 x 165	Bright Eyes	4	1022	8.99
185 x 172	Shuttle Landing	4	1023	8.99
172 x 323	Sonoran Desert	5	1024	8.99
150 x 166	Prostate Cancer	5	1025	8.99
201 x 176	Famous Trains	4	1026	8.99
176 x 124	Canada Historic Vehicles	5	1027	8.99
245 x 114	Canada Provincial Leaders	5	1028	8.99
177 x 133	Canada Year of Family	5	1029	8.99
181 x 213	Arctic Animals	3	1034	8.99
179 x 242	Louise Nevelson	3	1037	8.99
179 x 217	Library Of Congress	3	1038	8.99
182 x 232	Youth Team Sports	3	1039	8.99